D0198513

THE ANATOMY OF REVOLUTION

THE ANATOMY
OF
REVOLUTION

CRANE BRINTON

Revised and Expanded Edition

VINTAGE BOOKS

A DIVISION OF RANDOM HOUSE

New York

To Alden and Helen Hoag
who listened to it all

PREFACE

I have gone carefully over the original text of this book, making many changes throughout, and bringing the bibliographical suggestions up to date. Naturally the Russian Revolution has given me my greatest difficulties. I have tried to take account of the recrudescence of Terror in 1936-39 as well as the continued abnormal isolation of Russia in a new section of Chapter Eight, section V, "Russia: Permanent Revolution?" I still incline to the belief that the great Russian Revolution is over—as far as such great social movements can ever be said to be over. Chapter One I have also in part rewritten, attempting to make as clear as possible what I mean by the "clinical" character of the social sciences. No doubt in the last fifteen years what must be called "anti-scientism" has increased, at least on the surface of our Western thought. But I suspect that only the very exalted new man of feeling—or the very careless reader—will hold that I am defending old-fashioned views of science as a form, as indeed the form, of absolute truth. Science no doubt has its own metaphysics—but like decent underclothing, its metaphysics is not normally visible. I have in my brief expository attempt in Chapter One carefully observed the decencies.

In addition to those whom I have thanked for aid in my preface to the first edition, I should like to thank especially Mrs. Bernard Barber, Mr. Franklin Ford, and Mr. Henry Vyverberg, three of my students, whose researches have enriched my knowledge of eighteenth-century France and the "prodromal symptoms" of the great Revolution; and Miss Elizabeth F. Hoxie, whose discerning care is responsible for the many corrections in the original text this revised edition has made possible.

CRANE BRINTON

PREFACE TO THE VINTAGE EDITION

A book of this sort must constantly tempt its author to afterthoughts. Five years after my revision of 1952 I should like now to make three brief comments. First, though I still hold that the "desertion [or alienation] of the intellectuals" is a real uniformity in the societies herein studied, I am more than ever convinced that a certain alienation among intellectuals is normal in the modern West—normal in the sociological sense developed by Durkheim and his school. The whole subject of the role of the intellectual classes in human societies is worth all the attention it can get. Colin Wilson's recent *The Outsider* (Boston, 1956) is pertinent here.

Second, events in Russia since the death of Stalin surely reinforce the commonplace that the great Russian Revolution is quite over, finished. What is going on now is a working out of what went on from 1917 to 1924, the years of what may be called the Russian Revolution proper. That working out must be very different from the working out of the "principles of 1776 and 1789."

Third, although I am convinced that the Russian Revolution belongs, as a "popular" revolution, a revolution of the Left, along with the English, American, and French revolutions, I do not think its relation to these earlier revolutions is by any means a simple one of affiliation, let alone repetition. Indeed, I have perhaps not sufficiently underlined in this book some of the major differences that set the Russian off from those revolutions with which it is here compared. I should like to call the reader's attention to a suggestive essay by T. H. von Laue of the University of California at Riverside, *"Die Revolution von aussen als erste Phase der russischen Revolution 1917,"* in *Jahrbücher für Geschichte Osteuropas,* Vol. IV, no. 2 (Munich, 1956). Von Laue puts the Russian Revolution in a "new category of modern revolutions," the "revolution of backward countries" (*Revolution der rückständigen Länder*); and he further emphasizes the extent to which the guiding ideas and impulses of the Revolution of 1917 came from outside Russia, from a West more advanced economically, socially, politically. Obviously in contrast, England in the early seventeenth century, with its background of Elizabethan greatness, France in 1789, still *"la grande nation,"* were quite the opposite of "backward"; and, although they both drew, as did the Americans of 1776, on a reservoir of Western culture by no means limited to any one nation, theirs were nonetheless in no sense revolutions imported from the outside by a native minority.

I should like to add two other suggestive recent works in German: Karl Griewank, *Der neuzeitliche Revolutions-begriff* (Weimar, 1955), and Willy Andreas, *Das Zeitalter Napoleons und die Erhebung der Völker* (Heidelberg, 1955).

CRANE BRINTON

Cambridge, November 1956

ACKNOWLEDGMENTS

I wish to thank the following authors and publishers for permission to quote from copyrighted works:

F. Beck and W. Godin, *Russian Purge and the Extraction of Confession*. The Viking Press, New York, 1951.

W. H. Chamberlin, *The Russian Revolution, 1917-1921*. The Macmillan Company, New York, 1935.

Waldemar Gurian, editor, *The Soviet Union: Background, Ideology, Reality*. University of Notre Dame Press, Notre Dame, Indiana, 1951.

Eric Hoffer, *The True Believer*. Harper & Row, Publishers, Inc. New York, 1951.

A. M. Schlesinger, *The Colonial Merchants and the American Revolution*. Columbia University Press, New York, 1918.

CONTENTS

Chapter

1

INTRODUCTION

---

1. *The Field of Study*

Revolution is one of the looser words. The great French Revolution, the American Revolution, the Industrial Revolution, a revolution in Haiti, a social revolution, the American Negro revolution, a revolution in our thinking, or in the ladies' garment trade, or in the automotive industry—the list could be almost endless. Indeed, at one end of its spectrum of meanings revolution has come in common usage to be hardly more than an emphatic synonym for "change," perhaps with a suggestion of sudden or striking change. Even such emphasis is not always implied. The editors of *Fortune* in their *U.S.A.: The Permanent Revolution,* though they have borrowed their title from Leon Trotsky, obviously mean no more than "permanent change of a good kind," or "progress," or "development." They do not even mean what Jefferson meant when he said in his letter to Samuel Kercheval in 1816 that a "revision" every nineteen years or so would be desirable. Jefferson was clearly thinking of a wholesale change in the governing personnel of a nation, in the political and to some extent the social, economic, cultural complex of habits and institutions a people lived under. He may have been thinking of the great French Revolution, or of nothing more violent than his own succession to power in the election of 1800.

For though we use the noun "revolution," and still more perhaps its adjective "revolutionary," to indicate a most varied set of changes, we keep in the corners of our mind a much more definite meaning, a kind of central tough core not eroded out into looser strata of meaning. We think of the great overturns in previously stable political societies in the past—the English Revolution of the 1640's and its sequel in 1688, the American Revolution, the French Revolution and its nineteenth-century sequels, the Russian Revolution of 1917 and its twentieth-century sequels; or we think of nationalist revolutions like the twentieth-century revolutions in Ireland and Algeria. We may also think of violence and terror, purges and guillotines. But our focus is on drastic, sudden substitution of one group in charge of the running of a territorial political entity by another group hitherto not running that government. There is one further implication: the revolutionary substitution of one group for another, if not made by actual violent uprising, is made by *coup d'état, Putsch,* or some other kind of skullduggery. If the change is made without violence in a free election, as in the British election of 1945 which gave socialism power (to most of us Americans a revolutionary thing), then the strongest expression the commentators can allow themselves is the "British revolution by consent." But is a revolution by consent really a revolution?

The term "revolution" troubles the semanticist not only because of its wide range in popular usage, but also because it is one of those words charged with emotional content. Indeed, any complete sociology of revolution in our Western world would have to take into account the way different groups in different times and places were moved by the complex associations of "revolution" and "revolutionary." The Daughters of the American Revolution find joy and elevation in the thought of what went on here in 1776, but not in what has gone on in Russia since November, 1917, or in China. The old French upper classes have never quite recovered from the shock of the Reign of Terror; nothing—not its association with the

Right, or integral nationalism, or even with *Nous, Philippe Pétain*—can make a French aristocrat feel comfortable about a revolution. In Russia the word is still enshrined as a holy word. In China and Cuba revolution seems rather more than a word.

At any rate, revolution in its stricter as in its looser sense is once more in this mid-twentieth century fully topical. The nineteenth century, which thought it was about to abolish foreign wars, thought also that it was about to abolish the kind of internal or civil war we associate with revolution, and indeed would make revolution unnecessary. Change was still to be the characteristic of our culture, but it was to be orderly, peaceful, gradual change. Our grandfathers' catch phrase, "evolution, not revolution," now has a faraway sound. We live in the midst of the alarums of war and revolution, of what can be not unfairly called world-wide revolution. We live, indeed, in a world where in actual fact the government, the constitution, the whole moral, juridical, political structure of the United States is just about the oldest, the most continuously functioning, of the great states of our world. The paradox is unavoidable: this new country is in some senses one of the oldest—older than socialist Britain, older than the Fifth French Republic, older than any soviet republic, older, incredibly, than the governments of those immemorial lands of the East, India and China.

We Americans, then, seem in many ways to be a stable society in the midst of societies undergoing revolutionary change. We are a little afraid of revolutions—the wrong kind of revolutions, the Communist or the Fascist kind. Indeed, some of our critics hold that we are essentially reactionary, essentially out of touch with the kind of hopes and aspirations in other peoples which in ourselves a century and more ago spurred us on to revolution. Arnold Toynbee keeps telling us we have deserted our own revolution, that we fail to realize that the echoes of that shot fired at Concord are still heard round the world. These critics are no doubt unfair. But we *are* a stable society, as Western societies go, and cling in spite of all that has happened since to the hopeful nineteenth-century "evolution, not revolution." Perhaps we cannot do much as yet to control the processes of social change. Perhaps what goes on in human group relations must be for a long time to us as uncontrollable as the weather. Revolutions may be as "inevitable" as thunderstorms—and often as useful as a storm in a parched countryside.

But we understand thunderstorms—or so we must believe unless we give up two thousand years of Western scientific study—better than did the earlier peoples who saw in them Thor or Jupiter at work; we can take certain steps to protect ourselves against them. We can at least try to understand a revolution, whether we want one or not. Yet we shall not go far toward understanding one unless we can maintain toward it, if not indifference, at least detachment.

This last word, one may hope, is not just a favorable way of saying what "indifference" says unfavorably. A physician may feel far from indifferent toward his patient, but he will not be a good physician unless he is detached in his observation and treatment of his patient's malady. We may dodge here a whole lurking set of philosophical difficulties, and say simply that what we commonly call modern science has as one of its basic elements the detachment of the scientist. The scientist, *as a private person*, may love and hate, hope and fear; *as a scientist*, he must try to leave all this behind when he enters his laboratory, his clinic, or his study.

To attempt to maintain in the analysis of human affairs the detachment of the physicist or the chemist is very difficult, and to a great many upright and intelligent people seems unprofitable, even treasonous. You should, they feel, hate Mao or Castro all the time, before, while, and after you start explaining him; otherwise your explanation may edge into extenuation.

But to understand all is by no means to pardon all. At any rate, the scientific understanding of the place of the mosquito in yellow fever has not led us to tolerance of that particular type of mosquito. Quite the contrary. We cannot, of course, expect such immediate and apparently spectacular results as were obtained with yellow fever from the study of man in society, from what are a bit optimistically called the social sciences—anthropology, economics, political science, history, sociology, and the like. But we may well consider the possibility of approaching the study of revolutions in something of the spirit the natural scientist carries to his work.

Our aim in the following study is the modest one of attempting to establish, as the scientist might, certain first approximations of uniformities to be noted in the course of four successful revolutions in modern states: the English Revolution of the 1640's, the American Revolution, the great French Revolution, and the recent—or present—revolution in Russia. Were we attempting to find an ideal type for revolution, were we seeking a kind of Platonic idea of revolution, we might be fairly reproached with picking four nice neat revolutions which made almost too good a case, too perfect a pattern. But we are making no such attempt. It should be very clear that not all revolutions, past, present, and future, will conform to the pattern here drawn. Our four revolutions are not necessarily even "typical" in the sense the word "typical" has for literary critics or moralists. They are simply four important revolutions with which we have chosen to begin a work of systematization still in its infancy.

At this point it may be objected that since the social sciences have been aping the natural sciences for several centuries, and got no further forward, that they ought therefore to try and stand on their own feet, that they ought to work out their own methods without bothering about what has been done in the natural sciences. There is a kernel of truth in this objection. Certainly writers like Fourier or Herbert Spencer, who have proclaimed themselves literally the Newtons or the Darwins of social science, appear to have gone wrong from the start. A prophetic soul drawing upon philosophy and the arts—a Spengler, a Toynbee, for instance—will probably make at least as much sense out of the study of men in society as will the social scientist who tries to take over *unaltered* the methods and materials of physics or biology. Yet one hesitates to turn the study of men in society wholly over to the Spenglers or even to the Toynbees; and one hesitates equally to accept the radical separation Dilthey and his followers make between *Naturwissenschaften* (the natural sciences) and *Geisteswissenschaften* (the historical or social sciences). The long tradition of what may be called scientific rationalism has in our society made conquests not to be lightly abandoned even in this postwar world. That tradition makes it imperative for us to attempt to continue, and extend, the kind of work we call scientific.

There has, indeed, been a great deal of nonsense written under the protecting name of science. It is easy to sympathize with Mr. Max Lerner's outburst:

> I am frankly skeptical when people working on the study of societies begin arming themselves with scalpels, slide-rules and test-tubes. For they are promising more than they can possibly fulfill. The protestations of complete objectivity that we have been hearing from students of society in the past quarter century take on a religious note: it is as if they were washing themselves in the blood of the scientific lamb.

Some of Mr Lerner's objections to the appeal to science and to scientific detachment are probably those of the liberal reformer, but some are those of the skeptic and critic. These last objections can be shown to rest in good part on a misunderstanding of scientific method not by any means limited to Mr. Lerner. So common is the misunderstanding that we must attempt here to put the matter as clearly as possible in a very few words.

II. *The Bare Elements of Scientific Methods*

First, not even the "exact" sciences like astronomy or physics are exact in the sense of "absolute" or "infallible." Their firmest laws or uniformities are to be regarded as tentative. They may be upset at any time by further work. But at any given moment they are not to be tampered with unless they prove unreliable *in relation to observed facts*. In the contemporary revolution in physics, Newton's laws have not been "disproved"; nor has the principle of indeterminacy been so firmly established as to make all men equal before the game of poker. What has happened in modern physics, as far as a layman can judge, is that the physicist has been sharply reminded that even his neatest uniformities are not absolutes, but are subject to correction, that he is safer in regarding these uniformities as based on observations rather than on the will of God, or the nature of things, or on reality. Or more radically, he should regard these uniformities as his *invention* rather than his *discovery*.

This brings us easily to the second point. Science makes no attempt to study or describe reality—certainly not ultimate reality. Science is not even concerned with truth, in the sense that word has for theologians, for most philosophers, for a good many other people, and perhaps for common sense. The desire to find a final cause, an unmoved mover, a *Ding an sich*, seems to be so common in men that we have no grounds for believing that this search is not, in one form or another, a fairly constant and in fact essential element in human society. Only, scientists *as scientists* can have no part in such a search. Eddington, Jeans, even Whitehead, ceased to practice science while they were pursuing theology. Science is based, not on faith, but on skepticism, on a skepticism that will not even worry itself over its status in the universe. And so the scientist works on serenely, undisturbed by the philosopher's final thrust: that to be constantly skeptical is to believe in doubt, which is after all a form of faith.

Third, the scientist by no means confines himself to "the facts and nothing but the facts." Dangerous epistemological depths yawn at this point, but we shall have to try and go ahead in spite of them. The popularization of Baconian ideas on induction is probably the chief source of the erroneous notion that the scientist does nothing to the facts he laboriously and virtuously digs up, except to let them fall neatly into a place they make for themselves. Facts themselves are not just "out there" and we should be willing to accept L. J. Henderson's definition of "fact" as an empirically verifiable *statement* (italics mine) about phenomena in terms of a conceptual scheme. Actually the scientist cannot work without a conceptual scheme; and though the relation between facts and conceptual schemes is not by any means clear, it is at least clear that a conceptual scheme involves something besides facts, involves, indeed, a working mind.

Let no one be frightened of the term "conceptual scheme." The meaning is really very simple: thunder and lightning impinge on our senses of hearing and sight—probably the mere differentiating of this sound and this flash from other sounds and flashes means that we are employing a conceptual scheme. Certainly when we think of Jupiter with his bolts, Thor with his hammer, or the electrical discharge of modern physics, we have clearly arranged our sense-perceptions in accordance with definite conceptual schemes. We possess, indeed, the basic elements of three different theories of thunder and lightning, three differently stated uniformities in these phenomena. But the crucial reason why we should prefer our electrical discharge to Jupiter or Thor *as a conceptual scheme* is that it is more useful, and that we can by using it get on better also with other conceptual schemes we use for similar purposes. But in the sense which the word *true* has for the theologian, and most moralists and philosophers, our electrical discharge is not a bit *truer* than the old notions about Jupiter and Thor.

We may even use two contradictory conceptual schemes, choosing one or the other of convenience, or from habit. We are all of us educated out of the old Ptolemaic conceptual scheme, which saw the sun moving about a stationary earth, into the Copernican conceptual scheme, which sees the earth moving about a stationary sun. Einstein, of course, used a conceptual scheme somewhat different from both of these, but most of us are not yet up to Einstein; in daily life we all, however, contentedly say "the sun rises," and should be very pedantic indeed if we insisted on saying in Copernican terms "the earth has revolved into sight of the sun."

The scientist, then, goes to work roughly in some such fashion as this. He starts with a conceptual scheme of some sort, and with questions, or even hypotheses, which he frames in terms of that scheme. He then hunts for a suitable supply of facts. These facts he seeks to arrange in uniformities or theories which will answer his questions, and perhaps suggest other questions. He then immerses himself again in the hunt for facts, and emerges with new or modified uniformities. The scientist is not interested in where his conceptual scheme came from, or whether it preceded or followed on facts, or whether it is "subjective" and the facts "objective." These questions he leaves to the philosophers, who have not settled them yet after two thousand years of debate. But the scientist does, by his recognition that a conceptual scheme is as essential to his activity as are observed facts, emancipate himself completely from self-styled "scientific" materialists, positivists, empiricists, who naïvely assert that our sense-perceptions filtered through a "mind" are somehow in themselves an orderly and sole reality, or a "reflection" of such a reality. For, note particularly, the facts with which the scientist deals are not phenomena, sense-perceptions, the "external world," those dear absolutes of innocent positivists, but merely *statements about* phenomena. A properly verifiable statement about Cromwell or Lenin is then as much a fact as the reading of a thermometer in a laboratory. We cannot here go into the thorny problem of what satisfactory verification is; the practicing scientist, the practicing historian, the practicing judge (and, one hopes, jury) have their own well-tried craft-methods of verification.

Fourth, though the scientist is very careful indeed about matters of definition, and is as disdainful of sloppiness as any historian and of bad thinking as any logician, he distrusts rigidity and attempts at perfection. He is interested less in beauty and neatness of definition than in having his definitions fit not his sentiments and aspirations, but the facts. Above all, he does not dispute over words. He is less interested in the accurate theoretical distinction between a mountain and a hill than he is in making sure that he is dealing with concrete elevations on this earth. He does not expect class terms to be perfect, mutually exclusive; when he distinguishes between a plant and an animal, he is not at all offended if you call his attention to a living thing that seems to belong to both his classifications at once. He sets to work studying the living thing and will, if necessary, modify his class terms. But he is quite willing also, if it proves more convenient, to set up a new class term of borderline plant-animals. This simple willingness to be guided by convenience is of course one of the amazing things about the scientist and one of the most difficult for us who have not had a scientific training to adapt ourselves to. Most of us are early trained to prefer our opinions to our convenience.

Fifth, perfectly respectable scientific work can be and is constantly done in fields where the kind of controlled experimentation classically associated for instance with physics and chemistry is not possible. We may call this sort of scientific work, based indeed on experimental work auxiliary to it, but not in itself a series of *controlled* experiments, *clinical*. The clinician is best known in the medical sciences, where he appears very early in fifth-century Greece with Hippocrates. The clinician works through the case method. His data are amassed, not through experiments he can control, but through a series of cases which he observes and compares. The clinician, again, is not sloppy; but he can rarely be rigorously exact. He is helped greatly when he can draw on experimental sciences—organic chemistry, for example. But in his own right the good clinician is a good scientist. Obviously the social sciences can depend but to a limited extent on actual controlled experimentation; *but they can be clinical sciences* depending more on observation than on experimentation.

Finally, scientific thinking cannot be, except perhaps in suggesting problems, what nowadays most of us know well enough as wishful thinking. The scientist's own hopes and fears, his own standards of what he would like to have prevail on this earth must be kept as far as possible out of his work, and especially out of his observations of, or dealing with, facts. How far such hopes and fears and standards enter into his choice of conceptual schemes, how far they influence the kind of questions he asks, are difficult problems we may perhaps be permitted to dodge. Sufficient that the techniques of most of the established sciences provide a very effective check on the cruder forms of wishful thinking. History, which because it has been so long an art and a craft is perhaps the most respectable of the social sciences, provides in the technical training undergone by most professional historians a surprisingly effective and not wholly dissimilar check on the more violent forms of partisan writing and thinking.

All in all, there is no reason why we should feel that the natural scientist uses methods, set standards, forever quite unattainable by the social scientist. Natural science as the more innocent materialists of the last century saw it—exact, infallible, a cosmos built on what in modern folk-usage is called induction—must seem remote to a struggling economist or sociologist. But natural science as it has always been understood by its ablest practitioners and is now widely understood—natural science as expounded methodologically by a Poincaré—is no such thin substitute for Divine Providence, no such metaphysical abstraction. Only God is exact, infallible, omniscient, unchanging, and modern science has been content to leave the search for God to disciplines fitted by long success for such a search.

III. *The Application of Scientific Methods to This Study*

Of the bare elements of scientific thinking—conceptual scheme, facts, especially "case histories," logical operations, uniformities—the social sciences in general come out well on the score of facts. Even in the field of history, where neither laboratory nor questionnaire methods of research are available, our existing supply of facts is surprisingly good. You cannot draw Cromwell back to life, but neither can you call the dinosaurs back to life. What we know about Cromwell from the written record is in many ways as reliable as what we know about dinosaurs from the fossil record. To say that history is a fable agreed upon, or a set of tricks played upon the dead, is to slander, or at least to misjudge, the great body of industrious and sober workers who have carried on the study of history. Notably the last century or so has seen the formation of a body of research workers in history who, with all their faults, maintain standards comparable in some ways to those maintained by similar groups in the natural sciences. These research workers do not indeed uncover the simple raw material of facts. The humblest antiquarian arranges the facts he digs out of his documents into some kind of pattern. Such a process of arrangement, however, is not the conscious theorizing of the physical scientist. It was never even learned as the scientist learns the theoretical scaffolding of his science, but was acquired almost as the manual worker acquires a craft. It is this craftsman's technique for the gathering, winnowing, and assaying of facts about the behavior of men in the past that is the great strength of the professional historian. If you asked such a historian what a fact is, he would probably be greatly puzzled at the question, and usually quite unable to answer in adequate general terms. Any good philosopher could convict him of complete epistemological *naïveté*. But in his daily work the historian shows a very keen appreciation of the difference between a fact and a theory, and a real ability to interpret or generalize from a basis in facts.

We shall, then, rely on the historians to supply us with the necessary facts. For the English, American, and even for the French revolution, the body of reputable and reasonably detached historical writing is very large indeed. Passions still run high over the French Revolution, but they are being cooled slowly in an increasing flood of printer's ink; the chief trouble, indeed, is to choose from this enormous mass of material. The Russian Revolution is perhaps too near us to be regarded by professional historians as capable of the kind of treatment the guild likes to give. Its source material is scattered about, and much of it is still withheld from scholars. Language is a barrier not yet wholly overcome here in the West. Yet our supply of facts about the Russian Revolution is by no means so slight, or so poor in quality, as to hinder our enterprise hopelessly. Half a century is a long time, and the early stages of the Russian Revolution have been surveyed, if not *sine ira et studio*, at least with relative detachment. And then both lovers and haters of the present regime in Russia are almost equally articulate, and can be balanced off one against the other by anyone who cares to take the trouble.

Our conceptual scheme will give us a great deal more difficulty than will our supply of facts. In the social sciences, at least, the distinction between a conceptual scheme and a metaphor is still an uncertain one, and there is no great harm in looking at our present problem as a search for a metaphor to hold together the details of our revolutions. Yet one of the most obvious of such metaphors, that of a storm, has several faults. One can outline it readily: at first there are the distant rumblings, the dark clouds, the ominous calm before the outbreak, all this corresponding to what our textbooks used confidently to list as "causes" of the revolution; then comes the sudden onset of wind and rain, clearly the beginnings of the revolution itself; the fearful climax follows, with the full violence of wind, rain, thunder, and lightning, even more clearly the Reign of Terror; at last comes the gradual subsidence, the brightening skies, sunshine again in the orderly days of the Restoration. But all this is too literary and too dramatic for our purposes, too close altogether to the metaphor as used by prophets and preachers.

At almost the opposite side there is the conceptual scheme of a social system in equilibrium. The tender-minded are often annoyed by the term "equilibrium," which has for them mechanistic overtones damaging to the dignity of man. In modern science, however, the term has proved useful in fields such as chemistry and physiology, well outside of that of the mechanics in which it had its origin. Furthermore, the word as the practicing scientist uses it has no metaphysical connotations whatever. The concepts of a physicochemical system in equilibrium, a social system in equilibrium, John Jones's body in equilibrium, do not in the least prejudice the immortality of anyone's soul, nor even the ultimate victory of Vitalists over Mechanists. The concept of equilibrium helps us to understand, and sometimes to use or to control, specific machines, chemicals, and even medicines. It may someday help us to understand, and within limits to mold, men in society.

Its use in the study of revolutions is in principle clear. A society in perfect equilibrium might be defined as a society every member of which had at a given moment all that he could possibly desire and was in a state of absolute contentment; or it might be defined as a society like that of certain social insects such as bees or ants, in which every member responds predictably to given stimuli. Obviously any human society can be in but an imperfect equilibrium, a condition in which the varying and conflicting desires and habits of individuals and groups of individuals are in complex mutual adjustment, an adjustment so complex that no mathematical treatment of it seems possible at present. As new desires arise, or as old desires grow stronger in various groups, or as environmental conditions change, and as institutions fail to change, a relative disequilibrium may arise, and what we call a revolution break out. We know that in the human body, for instance, the disequilibrium we call disease is accompanied by certain definite reactions which tend to restore the body to something like what it was before the onset of the disease. It seems quite likely that in a social system in disequilibrium there is something of the same kind of reaction toward the old conditions, and that this helps explain why revolutions do not turn out entirely as revolutionists want them to. The old adjustments tend to re-establish themselves, and produce what in history is known as the reaction or the restoration. In social systems, as in the human organism, a kind of natural healing force, a *vis medicatrix naturae*, tends almost automatically to balance one kind of change with another and restorative change.

This conceptual scheme of the social equilibrium is probably in the long run the most useful for the sociologist of revolutions. It is for our present purposes, however, a bit too ambitious. It needs for full success a more accurate grasp of more numerous variables than we can at present manage. It is better suited to a complete sociology of revolutions, or a "dynamics of revolution," than to our modest study of the anatomy of four specific revolutions. We are here attempting merely a preliminary analysis, attempting to classify and systematize at a relatively low level of complexity.

Though it has one very grave defect, the best conceptual scheme for our purposes would seem to be one borrowed from pathology. We shall regard revolutions as a kind of fever. The outlines of our fever chart work out readily enough. In the society during the generation or so before the outbreak of revolution, in the old regime, there will be found signs of the coming disturbance. Rigorously, these signs are not quite symptoms, since when the symptoms are fully enough developed the disease is already present. They are perhaps better described as *prodromal* signs, indications to the very keen diagnostician that a disease is on its way, but not yet sufficiently developed to be the disease. Then comes a time when the full symptoms disclose themselves, and when we can say the fever of revolution has begun. This works up, not regularly but with advances and retreats, to a crisis, frequently accompanied by delirium, the rule of the most violent revolutionists, the Reign of Terror. After the crisis comes a period of convalescence, usually marked by a relapse or two. Finally the fever is over, and the patient is himself again, perhaps in some respects actually strengthened by the experience, immunized at least for a while from a similar attack, but certainly not wholly made over into a new man. The parallel goes through to the end, for societies which undergo the full cycle of revolution are perhaps in some respects the stronger for it; but they by no means emerge entirely remade.

This conceptual scheme may be used without committing its users in any sense to an organic theory of society. The word "society" is used in this study as a convenient way of designating the observed behavior of men in groups, their interactions, and that is all. We find it convenient to apply to certain observed changes in given societies a conceptual scheme borrowed from pathology. We should find it inconvenient and misleading to extend that conceptual scheme and talk of a body politic, with a soul, a general will, heart, nerves, and so on. When, for instance, we apply terms like "prodrome," "fever," "crisis," to the French Revolution, we are very definitely *not* thinking of a personified France which suffers all these. To some this distinction may seem only a verbal one, and unimportant. It is, however, based on one of the most important distinctions in human thinking—the essential distinction between metaphysics and science.

The really grave defect of this fever chart lies deeper, in the apparently unalterable fact that our ordinary language, to which words like "fever" and "disease" clearly belong, is only in small part logical. When a given act by a given person, John Doe, is referred to by five separate reporters as persevering, firm, determined, obstinate, or pig-headed, you obviously learn as much about the feelings of the reporters toward John Doe as about John Doe himself. The reporters are more successful in spreading abroad their own feelings than in describing John Doe. Many people from Thucydides through Bacon and Machiavelli to Pareto have understood this use of words. In our own day a dozen disciplines, from psychology and semantics to political theory, have made us keenly aware that propaganda lurks in every syllable, in every accent. This awareness seems not to have resulted in any appreciable drying up of propaganda.

Now nobody wants to have a fever. The very word is full of unpleasant suggestions. Our use of terms borrowed from pathology is likely, at the very least, to arouse in many readers sentiments which bar further understanding. We seem to be damning revolutions by comparing them with a disease. To those of liberal sympathies and hopes we shall seem to be condemning in advance such great efforts of the free human spirit as the French Revolution. To the Marxists our whole inquiry has probably been suspect from the beginning, and our conceptual scheme will appear to them simply the expected bourgeois dishonesty. Yet it seems too bad to offend even the Marxists unnecessarily. Protestations of good intent are probably useless, but we may nonetheless record that consciously at least we are aware of no feelings of dislike for revolutions in general. We do indeed dislike cruelty, whether in revolutions or in stable societies. But the thought of revolution sets up in us no train of unhappy associations. Of more persuasive force with the distrustful is perhaps the fact that, biologically, fever in itself is a good thing rather than a bad thing for the organism that survives it. To develop the metaphor, the fever burns up the wicked germs, as the revolution destroys wicked people and harmful and useless institutions. On close and fair inspection our conceptual scheme may even seem to have overtones of implication too favorable, rather than too unfavorable, to revolutions in general.

Facts and conceptual scheme being thus disposed of, it remains to consider the possibility of finding some kind of uniformities in the way in which our facts fit into our conceptual scheme. Most of us would assume that on the rough level of common sense some kind of uniformities can be discerned in history. But at least among many professional historians there is a tendency to deny that these uniformities are real and important, and we must therefore give the matter brief attention. In a review of W. C. Abbott's magisterial edition of Cromwell's speeches and writings, a learned and conventional English historian wrote:

> it is unfortunate that Professor Abbott has thought to elucidate the English revolution by comparing it with the American and French revolutions. Revolutionary technique undoubtedly interests a world familiar with the writings of Marx and Trotsky and the method of Lenin, but comparisons in history as elsewhere are odious and revolutions are more remarkable for their particular differences than for their common elements.

This is undoubtedly an extreme view. The English have for the last century and more been insistent that their revolution was unique—so unique as to have been practically no revolution at all.

A full consideration of the problem of historical uniformities would be very long, and might well end in the cloudland of metaphysics. We shall have to be content with the crude assertion that the doctrine of the absolute uniqueness of events in history seems nonsense. History is essentially an account of the behavior of men, and if the behavior of men is not subject to any kind of systematizing, this world is even more absurd than the existentialists would have it. History at least gives us case histories, is at least material for the clinician. But you have only to look at a page of Theophrastus or of Chaucer to realize that Greeks of more than two thousand years ago and Englishmen of six centuries ago seem in some ways extraordinarily like Americans of today. Comparisons may be odious, but they form the basis of literature as well as of science, and provide a good deal of the staple of everyday conversation.

As we have seen, an essential element in any attempt to work scientifically is the detachment of the scientist. In the historian, this is the ability to keep his observations of what has happened uninfluenced by what he would like to have had happen, or to happen. We have already encountered this difficulty in our discussion of a conceptual scheme, where to think of a revolution as a fever seems at first sight a way of condemning the revolution, of giving it a bad name. It must be repeated that in all the social sciences genuine scientific detachment is difficult to attain, and in any "absolute" or "pure" sense impossible of attainment. Even in the natural sciences, desire to prove an hypothesis or a theory of one's own may bring to the distortion or neglect of facts some of the most powerful sentiments in human beings. But the natural scientist does not want to improve a molecule or an amoeba—at least, not "morally." Upon the social scientist, however, there pours the full force of those sentiments we call moral as well as those we call selfish. He can hardly avoid wanting to change what he is studying: not to change it as the chemist changes the form of the elements he compounds, but to change it as the missionary changes the man he converts. Yet this is just what the social scientist must try to avoid as a better man would avoid the devil. One of the hardest things to do on this earth is to describe men or institutions without wanting to change them, a thing so hard that most people are not even aware that the two processes are separable. Yet separated they must be if we are to get anywhere with the social sciences.

In this study we shall make this attempt to describe without evaluating. It will not be a complete success, for here on this earth completion is rare. Absolute detachment is a polar region, unfit for human life; but one might well make an effort to get out of the steaming jungles, and come a bit closer to the pole. In less figurative language: it is impossible to study revolutions without having sentiments about them, but it is quite possible to keep your sentiments relatively more out of your study than in. And an inch gained here is worth several ells on less fertile frontiers of the mind.

iv. *Limitations of the Subject*

We shall, then, study four revolutions which on the surface seem to have certain resemblances, and deliberately avoid certain other types of revolution. Our four took place in the post-medieval Western world, were "popular" or "democratic" revolutions carried out in the name of "freedom" for a majority against a privileged minority, and were successful; that is, they resulted in the revolutionists becoming the legal government. Anything like a complete sociology of revolutions would have to take account of other kinds of revolution, and notably of three: the revolution initiated by authoritarians, oligarchies, or conservatives—that is, the "Rightist" revolution; the territorial-nationalist revolution; and the abortive revolution.

No doubt there are sentimental distortions involved in distinguishing our four revolutions as "popular" or "democratic," but even words heavily encrusted with sentiments have reference to concrete things; the English, French, American, and even the Russian revolutions were attempts to ensure a different kind of society from that aimed at in the Fascist revolutions in Italy and Spain and the National Socialist revolution in Germany, or, as it now looks, from that aimed at by recent revolutions in the "underdeveloped" lands of Asia and Africa. We meet here clearly one of our great difficulties with the Russian Revolution; it has in our Western eyes not proved "popular" or "democratic." But if in some respects Russian Communism has come to seem to us as totalitarian, undemocratic, the fact remains that the Russian Revolution started as the heir of the eighteenth-century Enlightenment, and the Italian and German revolutions started by repudiating that Enlightenment.

If, however, these Fascist revolutions seem too recent to be judged, or even to be catalogued, fairly, we may find in the time of troubles in Athens at the end of the fifth century B.C., less controversial evidence. Here the Revolution of 411 B.C. was the work of the conservative or oligarchic group, and was directed against the old democratic constitution under which Athens had been ruled since

Cleisthenes, if not since Solon. In the Council of Four Hundred set up by the successful revolutionists, the extreme oligarchs split with the moderates. After the assassination of the extremist Phrynicus, and the arrival of bad news from the front, the moderate Theramenes was able to take over power and set up a "mixed" constitution, seeking to combine the best of democracy and oligarchy. Then the fleet, in general strongly democratic, won the battle of Cyzicus, and paved the way to a fairly complete restoration of democracy in 410.

The final victory of Sparta led in 404 to a similar revolutionary cycle in Athens, beginning with the extreme oligarchic rule of the Thirty Tyrants and ending again with the restoration of democratic forms. In these movements, the sequence—to use perhaps misleading modern political analogies—is from Right to Center to Left, or from Conservative Extremists to Moderates to the Old Radical Gang, a sequence clearly quite different from that we shall encounter in England, France, and Russia. Those devoted to the concept of social equilibrium will note that in these Athenian revolutions the tendency seems to be toward the restoration of old habits and old institutions; and there is much here—the role of political clubs, for instance, and the varied uses of violence—familiar to any student of modern revolutions.

With the territorial-nationalist revolution, we Americans are familiar, for ours was in large part that kind of revolution. Men like John Adams and Washington were not attempting to overturn our social and economic system, but rather to set the English North American colonies up as an independent nation-state. So too with the Irish Revolution of 1916-1921. Nationalism, many good observers believe, is more important than is Communism in the recent revolution in China. But it is a rare territorial-nationalist revolution that is purely territorial, purely nationalist. Sam Adams, Tom Paine, Jefferson himself, were trying to do more than just cut us off from the British Crown; they were trying to make us a more perfect society according to the ideals of the Enlightenment. The Chinese Communists may be more Chinese than Communist, but they are certainly not mandarins, or even devotees of Sun Yat-sen.

The Algerian Revolution would seem to be a complex mixture of the territorial-nationalist revolution and the socioeconomic revolution.

Of abortive revolutions we have numerous examples. Needless to say, one hopes, abortiveness is not measured by the failure of revolutionary movements to live up to the ideals professed by their leaders. By abortive is meant simply the failure of organized groups in revolt. Thus the American Civil War is really an almost classical example of an abortive territorial-nationalist revolution. The European revolutions of 1848 were on the surface mostly abortive, though in many countries they helped bring about important and comparatively permanent administrative and constitutional changes. The Paris Commune of 1871 is an abortive social, though hardly socialist, revolution.

An abortive revolution may, of course, mold the defeated revolutionary group to an even more heroic determination, and pave the way to continued underground resistance, plotting, propaganda. This seems especially true of abortive nationalist revolutions. Our own "road to reunion" after the Civil War is a road not often followed, perhaps because those who suppress the abortive revolution will not usually allow that road to curve backward as much as with us the dominant Republicans did after 1876, indeed, earlier. The blood of martyrs has built council halls and presidential palaces as well as churches. The abortive revolution is especially important in the welding together of oppressed nationalities, which after a few heroic uprisings attain a pitch of exalted patriotism and self-pity that makes them almost unbeatable. Contemporary Ireland and Poland were born of a long series of revolutions that failed. Poland since 1945 has had to have a social and economic revolution imposed, apparently, largely from the outside—still another type of revolution.

Even a partial taxonomy of revolutions would list many others—the "palace" or "harem" revolution in societies the politics of which concern only a few, and in which therefore conspiracy can be readily successful; the revolution induced from the outside, as in at least some of the classically named republics on the French borders under the Directory; the revolution directed against "colonialist" masters in "underdeveloped" countries. What has happened among American Negroes in the last decade or so is often, and by no means altogether inaccurately, referred to as a revolution. And other kinds of revolution can readily be distinguished, none of which can be expected to fit exactly into the analysis which follows.

Three of our four revolutions—the English, French, and Russian, have courses in general surprisingly similar. All have a social or class rather than a territorial or nationalistic basis, though Oxford and Lancashire, the Vendée, and the Ukraine, suggest that one cannot wholly neglect these latter factors. All are begun in hope and moderation, all reach a crisis in a reign of terror, and all end in something like dictatorship—Cromwell, Bonaparte, Stalin. The American Revolution does not quite follow this pattern, and is therefore especially useful to us as a kind of control.

The American Revolution was predominantly a territorial and nationalistic revolution, animated throughout by patriotic American hatred for the British. On the other hand, it was also in part a social and class movement, and as time went on its social character came out more and more strongly. It never quite went through a reign of terror, though it had many terroristic aspects, usually soft-pedaled in school and popular histories. All in all, the American Revolution presents a number of interesting problems, and the attempt to integrate some of its aspects with our other three revolutions promises to extend, without unduly stretching, the limits of this study. But we must always remember that the American Revolution was as a social revolution in a sense an incomplete one, that it does not fit perfectly our conceptual scheme, that it does not show the victory of the extremists over the moderates. We must be even more cautious than with the other revolutions when we attempt to discern uniformities in the anatomy of the American Revolution.

We choose then, deliberately, to isolate four revolutions for analysis, quite aware that there are many other revolutions on record. We do not entangle ourselves unduly with the exact definition of "revolution," nor with the borderline between revolutionary change and other kinds of changes. At some point, the conflicts which are normal—or if you

regard conflicts as wholly bad, you may read "endemic"—
to any Western society boil over into violence, and there is
a revolution. The difference between a revolution and
other kinds of changes in societies is, to judge from many
past users of the term, logically nearer to that between a
mountain and a hill than to that, say, between the freezing
point and the boiling point of a given substance. The physicist can measure boiling points exactly; the social scientist cannot measure change by any such exact thermometer, and say exactly when ordinary change boils over
into revolutionary change. One might flirt with the notion
of a "revolt point" for different social systems; England's
being at, say, 200° in some conventional scale, France's at
150°, the United States at 300°, and so on. But this would
be nonsense of the type altogether too common in the
social sciences, which have long been in the habit of putting up mathematical false fronts. In actual practice, we let
use distinguish for us between a hill and a mountain, and
there is no harm in accepting the decision of use as to
what to call a revolution. The important element in
scientific definition is that the definition should be based
on facts, and enable us to handle facts better; precision
and neatness come definitely second, and are defects if
they are achieved by the neglect or distortion of facts.
Obviously in present usage the word "revolution" is a class
term covering quite a number of concrete phenomena,
from the introduction of the spinning jenny to the ejection
of Porfirio Diaz, and the job of the systematist is to cling to
the general term and devise useful subclassifications within
it.

To such simple truths are we reduced even before we
enter fully into the study of actual revolutions. Yet the
eally obvious, the really commonplace, does not often find
ts way into print. What gets there much more often is the
literary commonplace, the beliefs men have about things
and beings they never deal with directly.

The world of the pulp magazines is a world of literary
commonplaces. Many an intellectual in the world usually
rated above the pulps is driven by a no doubt commenda-
ble horror of the literary commonplace into an equal horror of the obvious. The scientist can afford himself no such

indulgence. The first job of the scientist is to be obvious, for only on a firm foundation in the obvious can he build securely the more complex fabric of a developed science. He may even have to be a bit insistent and repetitive about the obvious; for in this modern world of ours, where so much of our experience is the vicarious experience of sermons, books, pictures, plays, even the simple souls who love commonplaces have literary clichés fobbed off on them instead of the real thing.

We shall, then, hope that whatever uniformities we can detect in the revolutions we are analyzing will turn out to be obvious, to be just what any sensible man already knew about revolutions. We shall be genuinely disappointed if the anatomy of revolutions does not turn out to be a familiar one. It will seem a sufficient gain if these uniformities can be listed, recorded, as uniformities. Those whose appetites demand great discoveries are, then, warned in advance. Here they will find poor fare. Nor is this said in any spirit of mock humility. A literary saw, now almost folk wisdom, but still pretty literary, is scornful over the mountain which labored and brought forth only a ridiculous mouse. That mountain has perhaps never had due recognition for what is surely a rather remarkable biological feat. Moreover, the mouse was at least alive. Most mountains, when they go in for this sort of thing, produce nothing better than lava, steam, and hot air.

THE OLD REGIMES

1. *The Diagnosis of Preliminary Signs*

From France comes the phrase "old regime." Applied to the history of France, it refers to the way of life of the three or four generations preceding the Revolution of 1789. We may reasonably extend its use to describe the varied societies out of which our revolutions emerged. We shall look in these societies for something like a revolutionary prodrome, for a set of preliminary signs of the coming revolution.

Such a search must not be undertaken without one important caution. Disorder or conflict, as we have just noted, in some sense appears to be endemic in all societies, and certainly in our Western society. The historian can find evidences of disorders and discontents in almost any society he chooses to study. Sorokin, in an appendix to the third volume of his *Social and Cultural Dynamics*, lists for England—a classic land of political sobriety—one hundred and sixty-two "internal disturbances in intragroup relationships" between 656 and 1921. This averages roughly one such "disturbance" every eight years! They range in seriousness from the Great Rebellion and Civil War of the 1640's, which we shall take up in this book, to such comparatively trivial episodes as the insurrection of yeomanry in Wessex in 725. If a stable, or healthy, society is defined as one in which there are no expressions of discontent with the government or with existing institutions, in which no laws are ever broken, then there are no stable or healthy societies.

Our normal or healthy society, then, will not be one in which there are no criticisms of the government or the ruling class, no gloomy sermons on the moral decay of the times, no Utopian dreams of a better world around the corner, no strikes, no lockouts, no unemployment, no crime waves, no extremists, no attacks on civil liberties. All we can expect of what we may call a healthy society is that there should be no striking excess of such tensions, and perhaps also that most people should behave as if they felt that, with all its faults, the society were a going concern. Then we may look about for the kind of signs just described—discontents expressed in words or deeds—and try to estimate their seriousness. We shall, of course, very soon find that we are dealing with a large number of variables, that for given societies studied in their old regimes these variables combine variously and in different proportions, and that in some cases certain variables are apparently absent altogether or nearly so. We are surely unlikely to find in all the cases we study one clear, omnipresent symptom, so that we could say: when you find x or y in a society, you know that a revolution is a month, year, or decade away—or any time in the future. On the contrary, symptoms are apt to be many, varied, and by no means neatly combined in a pattern. We shall be lucky if, to borrow another medical term, they form a recognizable syndrome.

II. *Structural Weaknesses, Economic and Political*

As good children of our age, we are bound to start any such study as this with the economic situation. All of us, no matter how little sympathy we may have with organized Communism, betray the extent of Marx's influence in the social studies—and of the influences that worked on Marx—by the naturalness with which we ask the question: "What had economic interests to do with it all?" Since Beard's study of our Constitution, many American scholars have indeed seemed to feel this is the only question they need ask.

Now it is incontestable that in all four of the societies we are studying, the years preceding the outbreak of revolution witnessed unusually serious economic, or at least financial, difficulties of a special kind. The first two Stuarts were in perpetual conflict with their parliaments over taxes. The years just before 1640 resounded with complaints about Ship Money, benevolences, tonnage and poundage, and other terms now strange to us, but once capable of making a hero of a very rich Buckinghamshire gentleman named John Hampden. Americans need not be reminded of the part trouble over taxation played in the years just before the shot fired at Concord defied all the laws of acoustics. "No taxation without representation" may be rejected by all up-to-date historians as in itself alone an adequate explanation of the beginnings of the American Revolution, but the fact remains that it was in the 1770's a slogan capable of exciting our fathers to action. In 1789 the French Estates-General, the calling of which precipitated the revolution, was made unavoidable by the bad financial state of the government. In Russia in 1917 financial collapse did not perhaps stand out so prominently because the Czarist regime had achieved an all-round collapse in all fields of governmental activity, from war to village administration. But three years of war had put such a strain on Russian finances that, even with the support of the Allies, high prices and scarcity were by 1917 the most obvious factors in the general tension.

Yet in all of these societies, it is the *government* that is in financial difficulties, not the societies themselves. To put the matter negatively, our revolutions did not occur in societies with declining economies, or in societies undergoing widespread and long-term economic misery or depression. You will not find in these societies of the old regime anything like unusually widespread economic want. In a specific instance, of course, the standard against which want or depression is measured must be the standard of living more or less acceptable to a given group at a given time. What satisfied an English peasant in 1640 would be misery and want for an English farm laborer in 1965. It is possible that certain groups in a society may be in unusual want even though statistically that abstraction "society as a whole" is enjoying an increasing—and almost equally abstract—"national income." James C. Davies in the *American Sociological Review* (Volume XXVII) suggests that what provokes a group to attack a government is not simply deprivation or misery, but "an intolerable gap between what people want and what they get," and that revolutions often come during economic depressions which follow on periods of generally rising standards of living.

France in 1789 was a very striking example of a rich society with an impoverished government. The eighteenth century had begun to collect statistics about itself, and though these would not satisfy a modern economist they enable us to be very certain about the increasing prosperity of eighteenth-century France. Any series of indices—foreign trade, population growth, building, manufactures, agricultural production—will show a general upward trend all through the eighteenth century. Here are a few examples: wastelands all over France were being brought under the plow and in the *élection* of Melun alone in two years from 1783 to 1785 uncultivated land was reduced from 14,500 to 10,000 *arpents*; Rouen doubled its production of cotton cloth in a generation; the total French foreign trade had in 1787 increased nearly 100,000,000 *livres* in the dozen years since the death of Louis XV in 1774.

Even in our imperfect statistics we can distinguish short-term cyclical variations, and it seems clear that in some respects 1788-89 was a bad year. It was, however, by no means a deep trough year, as 1932 was for this country. If businessmen in eighteenth-century France had kept charts and made graphs, the lines would have mounted with gratifying consistency through most of the period preceding the French Revolution. Now this prosperity was certainly most unevenly shared. The people who got the lion's share of it seem to have been the merchants, bankers, businessmen, lawyers, peasants who ran their own farms as businesses—the middle class, as we have come to call it. It was precisely these prosperous people who in the

1780's were loudest against the government, most reluctant to save it by paying taxes or lending it money.

Yet the notion persists that somehow or other the men who made the French Revolution must have suffered serious economic deprivation. A very distinguished contemporary scholar, C. E. Labrousse, has sought to prove that there were sufficiently bad price squeezes on little and middling men so that they were spurred to revolution by actual want or at least hardship. Despite his hard work, his general thesis is not wholly convincing. At best, his thesis needs restating along the lines suggested by James C. Davies, and referred to on the preceding page.

In America, of course, with an empty continent available for the distressed, general economic conditions in the eighteenth century show increasing wealth and population, with economic distress a purely relative matter. There can be no talk of starvation, of grinding poverty in the New England of the Stamp Act. Even the minor fluctuations of the business cycle fail to coincide with the revolution, and the early years of the 1770's were distinctly years of prosperity. There were economic stresses and strains in colonial America, as we shall soon see, but no class ground down with poverty.

Nor is it easy to argue that early Stuart England was less prosperous than late Tudor England had been. There is rather evidence that, especially in the years of personal government which preceded the Long Parliament, England was notably prosperous. Ramsay Muir writes that "England had never known a more steady or more widely diffused prosperity and the burden of taxation was less than in any other country. The coming revolution was certainly not due to economic distress."

Even in the Russia of 1917, apart from the shocking breakdown of the machinery of government under war strain, the productive capacity of society as a whole was certainly greater than at any other time in Russian history; and to take again the long view, the economic graphs had all been mounting for Russia as a whole in the late nineteenth and early twentieth centuries, and the progress in trade and production since the abortive revolution of 1905 had been notable. Hardly any non-Marxist historian nowadays questions the fact that the Russia of the first three Dumas (1906-12) was on its way upward as a Western society. In comparison with the West, Russia was "backward" in 1917, but it was progressing rapidly toward economic maturity.

Our revolutions, then, clearly were not born in societies economically retrograde; on the contrary, they took place in societies economically progressive. This does not, of course, mean that no groups within these societies cherished grievances mainly economic in character. Two main foci for economic motives of discontent seem to stand out. First, and much the less important, is the actual misery of certain groups in a given society. No doubt in all our societies, even in America, there was a submarginal group of poor people whose release from certain forms of restraint is a very important feature of the revolution itself. But in studying the *preliminary signs* of revolution, these people are not very important.

French republican historians have long insisted on the importance of the bad harvest of 1788, the cold winter of 1788-89, and the consequent sufferings of the poor. Bread was relatively dear in that spring when the Estates-General first assembled. There was apparently a tightening up of business conditions in America in 1774-75, but certainly nothing like widespread distress or unemployment. The local sufferings of Boston, considerable under the Port Bill, were really a part of the revolution itself, and not a sign. The winter of 1916-17 was certainly a bad one in Russia, with food rationing in all the cities.

The important thing to note, however, is that French and Russian history are filled with famines, plagues, bad harvests, sometimes local, sometimes national in sweep, many of which were accompanied by sporadic rioting, but in each case only one by revolution. In neither the English nor the American Revolution do we find even this degree of want or famine. The worst famine in modern Western history, the Irish potato famine of the 1840's, heightened an abiding bitterness among the Irish people, but produced no revolution. Clearly, then, the economic distress of the underprivileged is not one of the symptoms we need dwell upon. This the subtler Marxists themselves recognize, and Trotsky has written: "In reality, the mere existence of privations is not enough to cause an insurrection; if it were, the masses would always be in revolt."

Of much greater importance is the existence among a group, or groups, of a feeling that prevailing conditions limit or hinder their economic activity. We are especially aware of this element in our American Revolution. A. M. Schlesinger, Sr., has shown how the prosperous merchants, their immediate interests damaged by the new imperial policy of the British government, led an agitation against the legislation of 1764 and 1765 and helped stir up a discontent among the less well-to-do which these merchants later found a bit embarrassing. No doubt, too, that many of the firm spots in the very uneven and wavering policy of the British government—the Stamp Act and subsequent disorders, the announced intention of enforcing the Navigation Act, and so on—did have momentary ill effects on business, did throw men out of work.

The working of economic motives to revolt among possessing classes normally inclined to support existing institutions is especially clear among the aristocrats of tidewater Virginia. Largely dependent on a single crop (tobacco), used to a high standard of living, increasingly indebted to London bankers, many of the planters hoped to recoup their fortunes in the western lands they regarded as clearly belonging to Virginia. George Washington's own involvements in western land speculations make one of the favorite topics of the debunkers. By the Quebec Act of 1774, however, the British government took the trans-Allegheny lands north of the Ohio from Virginia and other claimant colonies, and incorporated them with Canada. This act gave a grievance to others besides the planter-speculator. The closing of this frontier was also an offense to a class perhaps normally more inclined to revolt—the restless woodsmen and fur traders, and the only slightly less restless small pioneer farmers who had already occupied the Appalachian valleys, and were ready to pour over into the Kentucky and Ohio country. The Quebec Act in itself does not, of course, explain the American Revolution; but taken with a long series of other acts, the Stamp Act, the Navigation Act, the Molasses Act, it accounts for the feeling so evident among active and ambitious groups in America that British rule was an unnecessary and incalculable restraint, an obstacle to their full success in life.

In France the years preceding 1789 are marked by a series of measures which antagonized different groups. With striking awkwardness, the government offered with one hand what it withdrew with the other. Tax-reform efforts, never completely carried through, offended privileged groups without pleasing the underprivileged. Turgot's attempted introduction of laissez-faire offended vested interests; his failure to make his reforms stick offended the intellectuals and the progressives generally. The famous tariff reduction treaty with England in 1786 directly affected French textiles for the worse, increased unemployment in Normandy and other regions, and gave the employer class a grievance against the government. So, too, in seventeenth-century England, there is no doubt that the attempt to revive obsolete forms of taxation seemed to London or Bristol merchants a threat to their rising prosperity and importance.

Thus we see that certain economic grievances—usually not in the form of economic distress, but rather a feeling on the part of some of the chief enterprising groups that their opportunities for getting on in this world are unduly limited by political arrangements—would seem to be one of the symptoms of revolution. These feelings must, of course, be raised to an effective social pitch by propaganda, pressure-group action, public meetings, and preferably a few good dramatic riots, like the Boston Tea Party. As we shall see, these grievances, however close they are to the pocketbook, must be made respectable, must touch the soul. It may be argued that the American income tax is now as "bad" a tax as any in France of the old regime, and clearly many Americans are infuriated by it. Yet, in spite of Edmund Wilson's diatribe, they do not seem for the most part morally outraged by the tax. Men may revolt partly or even mainly because they are hindered, or, to use Dr. George Pettee's expressive word, *cramped*, in their economic activities; but to the world— and, save for a very few hypocrites, also to themselves— they must appear *wronged*. "Cramp" must undergo moral transfiguration before men will revolt. Revolutions cannot do without the word "justice" and the sentiments it arouses.

All this, however, is rather less than what the Marxists seem to mean when they talk about the revolutions of the seventeenth, eighteenth, and nineteenth centuries as deliberately the work of a class-conscious bourgeoisie. Not having the benefit of the writings of Marx to go by, nor indeed those of the still little-known Adam Smith, even eighteenth-century revolutionists and discontented spirits used a very non-economic vocabulary. Of course the Marxist, aided by Freud, can reply neatly that economic motivation drove these bourgeois at an unconscious or subconscious level. If, however, we confine ourselves to what these bourgeois said and did, we find plenty of evidence that separate groups—the American merchants, for instance—felt specific economic grievances, but no signs that bourgeois, entrepreneurs, businessmen, were aware that as a class their interests in free economic expansion were blocked by existing "feudal" arrangements. Indeed, in France a great many businessmen were more annoyed by the semifree trade treaty of 1786 with England than by any other governmental step. Certainly one finds no trace of men in England or America or France saying: "Organized feudalism is preventing the triumph of middle-class capitalism. Let us rise against it." Nor, as a matter of fact, were there in these countries just before the revolutions any unusual *economic* barriers to prevent the clever lad, even in the lower classes, from making money if he possessed the money-making gifts. Dozens of careers—a Pâris-Duverney, a Voltaire, an Edmund Burke, a John Law, a John Hancock—show this. Certainly one cannot deny that class antagonisms existed in these countries; but so far as we can judge, these class antagonisms do not seem to have a clear and simple economic basis. In twentieth-century Russia, of course, these antagonisms were expressed in the language of Marxist economics, even though here we shall probably also find that human sentiments as well as human interests are involved.

To sum up so far, as we look at economic life in these societies in the years preceding revolution, we note first, that these societies have been on the whole prosperous; second, that their governments are chronically short of money—shorter, that is, than most governments usually are; third, that certain groups feel that governmental policies are against their particular economic interests; fourth, that, except in Russia, class economic interests are not openly advanced in propaganda as a motive for attempting to overturn existing political and social arrangements. It is interesting to note here that R. B. Merriman, in a study of six seventeenth-century revolutions in England, France, the Netherlands, Spain, Portugal, and Naples, finds that they all had in common a financial origin, all began as protests against taxation.

If we now turn from the stresses and strains of economic life to the actual workings of the machinery of government, we find a much clearer situation. Here, again, we must not posit perfection as a normal condition. Government here on earth is at best a rough-and-ready thing, but there are obviously degrees of governmental inefficiency, and degrees of patience on the part of the governed. In our four societies the governments seem to have been relatively inefficient, and the governed relatively impatient.

Indeed, the near bankruptcy of a government in a prosperous society might be regarded as good *a priori* evidence of its inefficiency, at least in the old days when governments undertook few social or "socialized" services. France in 1789 is a striking example of a society the government of which simply no longer works well. For generations French kings and their ministers had fought the particularistic tendencies of the provinces to get out of the control of Paris by devising a whole series of agencies of centralization, which may be said in a sense to run from the *missi dominici* of Charlemagne to the *intendants* of Richelieu and Louis XIV. Almost as if they had been Anglo-Saxons, however, they destroyed very little of the old in the process, so that France in 1789 was like an attic stuffed full of all kinds of old furniture—including some fine new chairs of Turgot's that just wouldn't fit in the living room. We need not go too deeply into the details of the situation, which can perhaps be summed up graphically by saying that in the sense in which you could make a map of the

United States showing all our administrative areas—townships, counties, states—you could not possibly make *one* map of the administrative areas of old France. Even the confusion added to an administrative map of the United States by the various, and relatively new, federal commissions, bureaus, agencies, administrations, does not begin to equal that of France in 1789. You would need at least half-a-dozen maps to show the crisscross units of *paroisse, seigneurie, baillage, sénéchaussée, généralité, gouvernement, pays d'état et d'élection, les cinq grosses fermes, pays de grande et de petite gabelle*—and this is but a beginning.

All this means that in eighteenth-century France it was very hard to get action from the government, a difficulty which is one of the most important forms of Dr. Pettee's "cramp." There is told about Louis XV one of those revealing anecdotes the actual historical truth of which is unimportant, since they reflect contemporary opinion of a concrete condition. Traveling in the provinces, his majesty saw that a town hall or some such building in which he was to be received had a leaky roof. "Ah, if I were only a minister, I'd have that fixed," he remarked. A government of which such a tale could be told was perhaps despotic, but most certainly inefficient. In general, it would seem the inefficiency is more readily recognized by those who suffer from it than is the despotism.

The incompetence of the English government under the first two Stuarts is much less clear, but one can safely say that the central government was not as well run, especially under James I, as it had been under Elizabeth. What is most striking in the English situation is the total inadequacy to modern government of a tax system based on the modest needs of a feudal central government. For the government of James I was beginning to be a modern government, to undertake certain elementary social services, and to rest on a bureaucracy and a professional army and navy that had to be paid in cash. The chronic need for money which confronted James I and Charles I was by no means a result of riotous living and courtly extravagance, but was for the most part brought on by expenses no modern government could have avoided. And yet their income was on the whole determined and collected by old-fashioned medieval methods. The Stuarts needed money; but their attempts to fill their coffers were awkward, hand-to-mouth expedients that brought them into sharp quarrels with the only people from whom they could in those days readily collect money—the gentry and the middle class. Their struggles with Parliament threw the whole machinery of English government out of gear.

In America the failure of the machinery was a double one. First, the central colonial administration in Westminster had been allowed to grow in the hit-or-miss fashion Anglophiles have long regarded as the height of political wisdom. In this crisis, however, muddling through clearly was not enough. The attempted reform in colonial administration after the Seven Years' War only made matters worse, as did Turgot's attempted reforms in France, since it was carried out in a series of advances and retreats, cajolings and menaces, blowings-hot and blowings-cold. Second, within most of the colonies the machinery of government had never been properly adjusted to the frontier. The newer western regions of many colonies complained that representation, courts, administrative areas, were rigged in favor of the older seaboard settlements.

The breakdown of Czarist administration is now so much a commonplace that one is tempted to suspect that it has been a bit exaggerated. Looking at the decades preceding 1917—for in all these countries, we have been considering the background of the revolutions and not their actual outbreaks—it seems possible to maintain that the government of Russia in peacetime, at least, was perhaps a bit more of a going concern than the other governments we have been studying. From Catherine the Great to Stolypin a great deal of actual improvement can be seen in Russian government. But one thing is clear from the hundred years preceding 1914. Russia could not organize herself for war, and failure in war had, especially in 1905, brought with it a partial collapse of the machinery of internal administration. We must be very careful here to stick to facts and to avoid judgments which have so insinuated themselves into our awareness of Russia that we regard them as facts. For our purposes, it is sufficient to note that the Russian *governmental* breakdown, clear in 1917 or even 1916, was by no means clear, say, in 1912.

Finally, one of the most evident uniformities we can record is the effort made in each of our societies to reform the machinery of government. Nothing can be more erroneous than the picture of the old regime as an unregenerate tyranny, sweeping to its end in a climax of despotic indifference to the clamor of its abused subjects. Charles I was working to "modernize" his government, to introduce into England some of the efficient methods of the French. Strafford was in some ways but an unlucky Richelieu. George III and his ministers were trying very hard to pull together the scattered organs of British colonial government. Indeed, it was this attempt at reform, this desire to work out a new colonial "system," that gave the revolutionary movement in America a start. In both France and Russia, there had been a series of attempted reforms, associated with names like Turgot, Malesherbes, Necker, Witte, and Stolypin. It is true that these reforms were incomplete, that they were repealed or nullified by sabotage on the part of the privileged. But they are on the record, an essential part of the process that issued in revolution in these countries.

III. *The Transfer of Allegiance of the Intellectuals*

So far we have fixed our attention on the machinery of economic and political life, and have tried to distinguish signs of any approaching breakdown. Let us now turn to the state of mind—or better, feeling—of various groups within these societies. First we may ask the question, does the disorganization of the government find a counterpart in the organization of its opponents? We shall have later to deal with what are nowadays well known as "pressure groups," men and women organized in societies with special aims, societies which bring all sorts of pressure, from propaganda and lobbying to terrorism, to the attaining of their aims. Such pressure groups in one form or another are apparently a constituent part of all modern states, and the mere fact of their existence cannot be taken as a symptom of revolution, or we should have to regard

the Society for the Prevention of Cruelty to Animals, the
Authors Guild, or anti-billboard associations as signs of a
coming second American revolution. There seems to be no
simple and sole test to determine when and under what
conditions the existence of pressure groups may be taken
as a symptom of approaching political instability. The
prerevolutionary decades in our four societies do show,
however, an intensity of action on the part of pressure
groups, an action more and more directed as time goes on
toward the radical alteration of existing government. Certain groups, indeed, begin to go beyond lobbying and
propaganda, begin to plan and organize direct action, or at
least a supplanting of the government in some dramatic
way. They are the beginnings of what we shall later know
as the "illegal government."

In America the merchants' committees organized to resist measures for imperial control did a great deal of quite
modern pressure-group work, from straight propaganda to
stirring up popular demonstrations and to intercolonial
cooperation through resolutions, conferences, and so on.
They form the prelude to those efficient revolutionary cells,
the correspondence committees Sam Adams handled so
well in the 1770's. Similar organizations are to be found
lower down the social scale, where they edge over into
boisterous tavern parties. In many of the colonies, the legislatures could be used for pressure-group work against the
imperial government in a way not possible in the other
societies we are studying. The New England town meeting
provided a ready-made framework for this kind of agitation.

In France, the work of Cochin has shown how what he
called the *sociétés de pensée*, informal groups gathered
together to discuss the great work of the Enlightenment,
gradually turned to political agitation and finally helped
steer elections to the Estates-General of 1789. Though the
official school of historians in the Third Republic always
distrusted the notion that their great revolution was
planned at all in advance, it is difficult for an outsider not
to feel that Cochin has put his finger on the essential form
of group action which turned mere talk and speculation
into revolutionary political work. Freemasonry, even

French republican historians admit, had a place in the preparation of the revolution. Masonic activity in eighteenth-century France was clearly no dark plot, but it certainly was far from being purely social, recreational, or educational.

In Russia, organized groups of all degrees of hostility to things as they were had long flourished. Nihilists, anarchists, socialists of all stripes, liberals, westernizers, and antiwesternizers, expressed themselves in various ways from bomb-throwing to voting at Duma elections. One gathers from a consideration of the last years of the Czarist regime that the diversity and cross-purposes of its opponents did much to keep that regime in the saddle. Certainly the Russian Revolution had plenty of advance publicity, and the role of pressure groups in its preparation is singularly clear.

England here is a less clear case. Nevertheless there are definite indications of systematic opposition of merchants and some of the gentry to measures like Ship Money, and the parliamentary majorities which were rolled up against Charles after the period of personal government were the product of embryo pressure groups, as a glance at the very prolific pamphlet literature of the time will show. Moreover, the English Revolution was the last of the great social overturns within the active domination of specifically Christian ideas. In a sense, the pressure groups most obvious in seventeenth-century England are simply the Puritan churches, and especially the churches called Independent. Their very existence was as much a menace to Charles as was that of the Bolshevik party to Nicholas.

It must be noted that some of these pressure groups, the American merchants' committees, the French *sociétés de pensée* and freemasons, for instance, would not in the heyday of their action have admitted they were working for a revolution, certainly not for a violent revolution. What perhaps separates them from pressure groups like the A.S.P.C.A. or anti-billboard associations—which we can surely agree are not to be taken as symptomatic of revolution—is their basic aim at a radical change in important political processes. Thus the American merchants were really aiming to reverse the whole new imperial policy of

Westminster; the French who prepared the elections to the Third Estate were aiming at a new "constitution" for France. On the other hand, some of the Russian organizations were from the very start violently revolutionary; but these were not the important elements in the Russian situation from 1905 to 1917, any more than the antinomians or anarchistic religious sects were in England before 1639.

There were, then, pressure groups with purposes more or less revolutionary in all these societies. Their activity is seen against a background of political and moral discussion which in these societies seems particularly intense. We come now to a symptom of revolution well brought out in Lyford P. Edwards's *Natural History of Revolution,* and there described as the "transfer of the allegiance of the intellectuals." Intellectuals in this context we may define without undue worry over preciseness as the writers, artists, musicians, actors, teachers, and preachers. Further subdivision into the small group of leaders who initiate, or at least stand prominently in the public eye, and the larger group who grind over material they get from the leaders, is not of major importance here.

What is important and somewhat puzzling, is the general position of such intellectuals in our Western society since the Middle Ages. Clearly we must not posit agreement among its intellectuals before we decide that a given society is reasonably stable. In modern times we expect the intellectuals to disagree among themselves, and certainly to disagree with the non-intellectuals, the vulgar, the Philistines, the Babbitts, the *booboisie*—or whatever other name the intellectuals may coin for them. Moreover, for a number of reasons, writers, teachers, and preachers are to a large degree committed by their function to take a critical attitude toward the daily routine of human affairs. Lacking experience of action under the burden of responsibility, they do not learn how little *new* action is usually possible or effective. An intellectual as satisfied with the world as with himself, or at least, with his ideas and ideals, would simply not be an intellectual.

Quantitatively, we may say that in a society markedly unstable there seem to be absolutely more intellectuals, at any rate comparatively more intellectuals, bitterly attacking existing institutions and desirous of a considerable alteration in society, business, and government. Purely metaphorically, we may compare intellectuals of this sort to the white corpuscles, guardians of the bloodstream; but there can be an excess of white corpuscles, and when this happens you have a pathological condition.

Qualitatively, we may discern a difference of attitude, partly, no doubt, produced by the numbers and unity of these intellectuals in attack, but partly produced by a subtler reality. Victorian England, for instance, was a society in equilibrium, an equilibrium that looks in retrospect a bit unstable, but still an equilibrium. Here Carlyle upbraided a generation addicted to Morison's Pills instead of to heroes, Mill worried uncomfortably over the tyranny of the majority, Matthew Arnold found England short of sweetness and light, Newman sought at Rome an antidote for the poison of English liberalism, Morris urged his countrymen to break up machines and return to the comforts of the Middle Ages, and even Tennyson was worried over his failure to attain to anything more useful than a high, vague, and philosophical discontent.

Many, though by no means all, Victorian intellectuals were in disagreement among themselves, united apparently in nothing but a profound dislike for their environment. If, however, you look at them carefully you will find a curious agreement that not too much is to be done right away to remedy matters. It is not, as we are told so often of the scholastic intellectuals of the Middle Ages, that these Victorians were in agreement on fundamental metaphysical and theological assumptions. They weren't in any such agreement. It is rather that they were in agreement about the less dignified but in some ways more important routines and habits of daily life, and they did not expect the *government* to change such matters. They were in a sense *alienated* intellectuals, but not intellectuals who had transferred their allegiance to an existing group, party, or cause directed against an existing government.

The difference between the intellectual atmosphere of a group like the Victorians, writers who cannot be said as a whole to have transferred allegiance, and a group which has so transferred its allegiance will be clear in a moment if we look at that famous group in eighteenth-century France which stood at the center of the great Enlightenment. One has first the impression of immense numbers of intellectuals, great and small, all studying matters political and sociological, all convinced that the world, and especially France, needs making over from the tiniest and more insignificant details to the most general moral and legal principles. Call the roll—Voltaire, Rousseau, Diderot, Raynal, d'Holbach, Volney, Helvétius, d'Alembert, Condorcet, Bernardin de St. Pierre, Beaumarchais—rebels all, men leveling their wit against Church and State or seeking in Nature a perfection that ought to be in France. You will hardly find active literary conservatives like Sam Johnson or Sir Walter Scott, or even literary neutrals, men pursuing in letters a beauty or an understanding quite outside politics. Even the now almost forgotten opponents of the *philosophes*, even the pessimists who deny the doctrine of progress, are for the most part doctrinaire intellectuals, as unreasonable devotees of *la raison* as the radicals.

Literature in late eighteenth-century France is overwhelmingly sociological. If you look in the yellowing remains of French eighteenth-century journalism, if you try to reconstruct the chatter of salons and clubs, you will find the same chorus of complaints and criticisms of existing institutions. There is both a bitterness and a completeness in this chorus of complaint that you will not find in Victorian complaints. There is, however, a reforming zeal, a basic optimism, that you will by no means find in the merely alienated intellectuals of the twentieth-century Western world. Not even de Sade sounds quite like Céline, or, indeed, Henry Miller.

Russia, too, is a clear example of this transfer of allegiance of the intellectuals. There is certainly much more than political propaganda in the series of novelists who have made Russian literature a part of the education of us all. But there is unmistakably political and social criticism of Czarist Russia even in the work of the most detached and Olympian of them, Turgenev. The impression one gets from a cursory view of Russian intellectual life in the nineteenth and early twentieth centuries is unmistakable; to write or teach in those days meant being against the government. It did not in those days necessarily mean to be Marxist.

America is not so neat an instance. In Boston, for instance, in the 1760's and 70's, a good many of the kind of people we are discussing—"intellectuals" will have to do—were as firmly as many such people are now against so un-Bostonian an activity as sedition. It is clear that Harvard was by no means unanimous against the Crown, let alone in favor of the democratic machinations of her alumnus, Sam Adams. But if the literary and journalistic output in the colonies between 1750 and 1775—and even if we include the sermons—could be statistically assigned as either for or against the actual policies of the imperial government, there seems little doubt as to the very considerable balance against these policies. The Enlightenment, especially through Locke and Montesquieu, had come to the American colonies. The natural and inalienable rights of man were in this country, as in Europe, concepts introduced by intellectuals.

England may seem at first sight an exception to this attitude of the intellectuals. Lovelace, Suckling, even Donne seem hardly preoccupied with sociology. Yet at a second glance it is quite clear that English literature under the first two Stuarts is far from being the chorus of loyal praise it was in the days of Elizabeth I. A glance into Grierson's *Cross Currents in English Literature in the Seventeenth Century* will show how much that literature was a dissolvent of the merry England of the Renaissance. Even more important is the fact that in those days there were no real newspapers. The pamphlet took their place. Now the pamphlet literature of the early seventeenth century in England, quantitatively enormous, even by modern standards, is almost wholly preoccupied with religion or politics—better, religion *and* politics—and is about as good an example of the transfer of allegiance of the intellectuals as could be found. Indeed, as Professor Gooch has written, in the reign of James I "proclamation followed proclamation against the sale of 'Seditious and Puritan books,' and there was 'much talk of libels and dangerous writings.'"

There is such talk now, in the United States, in the mid-twentieth century. This simple statement should remind us of the difficulties of diagnosis of impending revolutions, of the need of considering all aspects of the syndrome, and not a single aspect, not even that fascinating one we have called here "transfer of the allegiance of the intellectuals." For American intellectuals have been complaining about the failures of our society for decades. In 1922 Harold Stearns edited a book, *Civilization in the United States*, a symposium with such distinguished contributors as H. L. Mencken, Lewis Mumford, Conrad Aiken, Deems Taylor, Zachariah Chafee, Jr. The gist of the book was simple: there is no civilization in the United States in 1922. Yet the United States does not seem in this century ripe for revolution, does not seem to be a society in marked disequilibrium. Perhaps twentieth-century American intellectuals, like the Victorians we have just considered, are protesting from a sound background of basic, though nonverbal, agreement with their own Babbitts. Yet there is a bitterness in many American writers, a sense of being cut of things in a country run by nonintellectual businessmen, which one does not quite feel even in the Matthew Arnolds, the Morrises, the Carlyles. American intellectuals tend to cling together as a class against other classes, which perhaps is why they show no signs of being about to inspire a revolution. We must not, however, be here led astray into the difficult and still poorly understood problems of the sociology of knowledge involved in the behavior of the intellectual classes of contemporary America. Sufficient that from Dreiser and Lewis to Hemingway, Farrell, Leslie Fiedler and Norman Mailer most of our widely read writers have been hostile to things as they are in the United States, and yet things as they are have remained quite unthreatened by revolutionary overturn.

To what did our successfully revolutionary intellectuals transfer allegiance? To another and better world than that of the corrupt and inefficient old regimes. From a thousand pens and voices there are built up in the years before the revolution actually breaks out what one must now fashionably call the foundations of the revolutionary myth—or folklore, or symbols, or ideology. We might even say simply, the revolutionary ideal. Some such better world is contrasted with this immediate and imperfect world in all the ethical and religious systems under which Western men have lived, and notably in Christianity. It is not quite accurate to assert that for medieval Christianity the other, ideal world is safely put off to heaven. Yet it is clear that with the Reformation and the Renaissance men began to think more earnestly about bringing part of heaven, at any rate, to this earth. What differentiates this ideal world of our revolutionaries from the better world as conceived by more pedestrian persons is a flaming sense of the immediacy of the ideal, a feeling that there is something in all men better than their present fate, and a conviction that what is, not only ought not, but need not, be. And, one must add, a gut-deep hatred for the way the things are.

Perhaps, indeed, it is the lack of any such immediate better world in the minds of American intellectuals that explains why they are not playing now the kind of role the Voltaires and the Lockes played in the eighteenth century. American intellectuals have never really shared the Marxian dream; if they have a dream, theirs—witness Parrington—has been the old eighteenth-century dream, which nowadays cannot be really revolutionary.

We shall later meet these revolutionary ideals in their fully developed forms. Here we need only notice that in the writings and preachings of the English Puritans—and to a lesser extent the constitutional lawyers—in those of the eighteenth-century *philosophes,* in those of the nineteenth- and twentieth-century Marxists, the evil, and indeed illegitimate, existing regime is very effectively contrasted with the good, and indeed inevitable, rule of right to come. In England, America, and in France, the essential principle to which men appealed against present conditions was nature, with its clear and simple laws. Ship Money in England, Stamp Act in America, patents of nobility in France, were all contrary to the law of nature. Even in England and America, where there was also much appeal to rights to be found in Magna Carta or the common law, the final appeal was always to a law of nature "engraved in the hearts of men." As the Puritan Henry Parker wrote in England, the common courts were "furnished only with rules of particular justice, which rules being too narrow for so capacious a subject [the relation of Crown to People] we must refer to those that the original laws of nature hold out to us." By the eighteenth century this kind of language had become almost universal among intellectuals. That nature always counseled what the intellectuals in revolt wanted is an observation we must in these days feel bound to make.

For the Russian writers and agitators of the Czarist regime, nature did not play quite so prominent a part. Not that nature is lacking in the pages of Tolstoy and his fellows, and the contrast between "artificial" society and "natural" instincts was not disdained even in Socialist propaganda. For the liberals, a rather heady mixture of advanced Western thought from the Renaissance to Darwin gave them enthusiasm rather than firm standards. But the official ideology of the successful radicals in Russia was Marxism, and Marxism finds that the existence of capitalists, the rule of the bourgeoisie, is altogether natural. Only, its destruction by the proletariat is also natural, and this destruction is determined by forces quite beyond capitalistic control. The inevitable march of economic forces scientifically understood would then for the Marxists accomplish what the English Puritan expected from God and the French *philosophe* from nature and reason. The essential thing all these prerevolutionary agitators have in common, the essential ingredient, intellectually at least, in the revolutionary myth, is this abstract, all-powerful force, this perfect ally.

One special point is here worth our attention for a moment. Not only does God, nature, or dialectical materialism make the victory of the present underdog certain. The present upperdog can be shown—perhaps for propaganda purposes *must* be shown—to have acquired his preponderance by an accident, or a particularly dirty trick, while God or nature was temporarily off duty. Thus in the English Revolution the royalist and indeed the gentry as a whole were labeled "Normans," descendants of a group of foreign invaders with no right to English soil. John Lilburne, the Leveller, goes so far as to assert that the whole common law was a badge of slavery imposed upon the free people of England by the Norman Conquest. American hatred of absentee British government hardly needed such artificial fanning. The French were told by no less a person than Siéyès that all their trouble came from the usurpations of the Franks over a thousand years ago. French noblemen in 1789 were descendants of barbarous Germans, while French commoners were descendants of civilized Gauls and Romans. Marxism explained the exploiting class without recourse to such pseudo-historical notions. And yet there is plenty of reference in Russian revolutionary agitation to the usurpation of land by the nobles, to their Varangian, or Tartar, or Western, or at any rate foreign origins. Present evil as well as future good needs the strengthening force of what Sorel called the "myth." Satan is as necessary as God.

Finally, a great deal of energy has been expended on the question as to whether these revolutionary ideas "cause" revolutionary action, or whether they are merely a sort of superfluous decoration with which the revolutionists cover their real acts and real motives. Most of this discussion is in the highest degree futile, since it is based on a crude notion of causation altogether untenable in fruitful scientific work beyond a very simple level. There is no more point disputing whether Rousseau made the French Revolution or whether the French Revolution made the reputation of Rousseau than in disputing whether egg or chicken came first. We note that in our prerevolutionary societies the kind of discontents, the specific difficulties about economic, social, and political conditions on which hard-boiled moderns focus are invariably accompanied by a very great deal of writing and talking about ideals, about a better world, about some very abstract forces tending to bring about that better world. It is, indeed, the *expression* of ideas, rather than particular ideas—which may vary enormously in different revolutions—that makes the uniformity. We find that ideas are always a part of the prerevolutionary situation, and we are quite content to let it go at that. No ideas, no revolution. This does not mean that ideas *cause* revolutions, or that the best way to prevent revolutions is to censor ideas. It merely means that ideas form part of the mutually dependent variables we are studying.

IV. *Classes and Class Antagonisms*

Certain groups in our four societies of the old regimes nourished feelings of dislike, mixed or unmixed with contempt, for other groups. If we avoid the narrow economic connotations of the term, we may call these groups classes; if we realize the struggle was not simply one between two contending classes, feudal vs. bourgeois or bourgeois vs. proletariat, we may even speak of class struggles. This type of struggle in one form or another seems endemic in the stablest of Western societies. It is, however, a struggle usually carried on under rules, or at least without overt violence.

Here again therefore we must not postulate for the normal society with which we contrast our prerevolutionary societies, a lying down together of the lion and the lamb. Perhaps, indeed, we should postulate for the relation between the privileged, upper, or ruling class and the rest of the people a relation Toynbee calls "mimesis," a sharing of ideals, a looking up from the lower to the higher groups, the sort of relation Burke and John Adams—perhaps even Plato—sought to express. Here again we are on most difficult diagnostic ground, for we cannot be quite sure what actual health is. Something less than perfect mimesis seems to prevail in most Western societies, even in that fifth-century Athens and thirteenth-century Western Europe which seem now such golden ages. The cry

> When Adam delved and Eve span
> Who then was the gentleman

seems always ready to arise. But even so, it will soon appear that these class hatreds are stepped up, exacerbated in a noticeable degree in the old regimes. Class distinctions are seen, not as barriers the clever, brave, or ambitious can cross, let alone as a heaven-decreed order not to be tampered with, but as unnatural and unjust privileges, established by wicked men against the express intention of Almighty God, nature, or science. These class struggles are by no means simple; there are groups within groups, currents within currents. We must try and analyze some of these currents.

In the first place, what may be called the ruling class seems in all four of our societies to be divided and inept. By ruling class we understand, it may be too generously, the people who run things, the people in the public eye—the politicians, the important civil servants, the bankers, the men of affairs, the great landowning nobles, the officers of the armed forces, the priesthood, perhaps even some of the intellectuals. Formal nobility of the blood has in the Western world usually been a much too narrow test of membership in a ruling class. Even in early modern times, the ruling class was something like what we have outlined above—the minority of men and women who seemed to lead dramatic lives, about whom the more exciting scandals arose, who set the fashion, who had wealth, power, position, or at least reputation, who, in short, ruled. They are Mosca's "political class." Indeed, in a socially stable society it seems likely that the great masses of poor and middling folk, as also the obscure and unsuccessful people who by birth and training might seem to be in the ruling class, really accept the leadership of those at the top of the social pyramid, and dream rather of *joining* them than of *dislodging* them—though this statement will seem to the idealist a rather thin reduction of Toynbee's "mimesis."

Now the ruling classes in our societies seem, and not simply *a posteriori* because they were in fact overthrown, to have been unsuccessful in fulfilling their functions. It is unlikely that short of Sparta or old Prussia the simpler military virtues alone are enough for a ruling class. Such a class ought not, however, to shrink from the use of force to maintain itself, and it ought not to value wit and originality in its own members too highly. Wit, at any rate, it can usually hire adequately enough from other sources. A mixture of the military virtues, of respect for established ways of thinking and behaving, of willingness to compromise, and if necessary, to innovate, and a willingness to recruit new members from the properly gifted of other classes is probably an adequate rough approximation of the qualities of a successful ruling class.

When numerous and influential members of such a class begin to believe that they hold power unjustly, or that all men are brothers, equal in the eyes of eternal justice, or that the beliefs they were brought up on are silly, or that "after us the deluge," they are not likely to resist successfully any serious attacks on their social, economic, and political position. The subject of the decadence of a ruling class, and the relation of this decadence to revolution, is a fascinating and, like so much of historical sociology, a relatively unexplored subject. We can here do no more than suggest that this decadence is not necessarily a "moral" decadence if by "moral" you mean what a good evangelical Christian means by that word. Successful ruling classes have not infrequently been quite addicted to cruel sports, drinking, gambling, adultery, and other similar pursuits which we should no doubt all agree to condemn.

The Russians here provide us with a *locus classicus*. To judge from what appears of them in print, Russian aristocrats for decades before 1917 had been in the habit of bemoaning the futility of life, the backwardness of Russia, the Slavic sorrows of their condition. No doubt this is an exaggeration. But clearly many of the Russian ruling classes had an uneasy feeling that their privileges would not last. Many of them, like Tolstoy, went over to the other side. Others turned liberal, and began that process of granting concessions here and withdrawing them there that we have already noticed in France. Even in court circles, it was quite the fashion by 1916 to ridicule the Czar and his intimates. As Protopopov, a hated Czarist minister, wrote:

> Even the very highest classes became *frondeurs* before the revolution; in grand salons and clubs the policy of the government received harsh and unfriendly criticism. The relations which had been formed in the Czar's family were analyzed and talked over. Little anecdotes were passed about the head of the state. Verses were composed. Many grand dukes openly attended these meetings. . . . A sense of the danger of this sport did not awaken until the last moment.

Finally, when those of the ruling classes who had positions of political power did use force, they used it sporadically and inefficiently. We shall have more to say about this general problem of the use of force when we come to the first stages of actual revolution. In this connection it will be sufficient that the Russian ruling classes, in spite of their celebrated Asiatic background, were by the late nineteenth century more than half ashamed to use force, and therefore used it badly, so that on the whole those on whom force was inflicted were stimulated rather than repressed. The line in actual practice of government between force and persuasion is a subtle one, not to be drawn by formulas, by "science" or textbooks, but by men skilled in the art of ruling. One of the best signs of the unfitness of the ruling class to rule is the absence of this skill among its members. And this absence is recorded in history in the cumulated minor disturbances and discontents which precede revolution.

Russia remains the classic instance of an inept ruling class, but France is almost as good a case. The salons in which the old regime was torn apart—verbally, of course —were often presided over by noblewomen and attended by noblemen. Princes of the blood royal became freemasons, and if they did not quite plot the overthrow of all decency, at least sought to improve themselves out of their privileges and rank. Perhaps nowhere better than in France is to be seen one of the concomitants of the kind of disintegration of the ruling class we have been discussing. This is the deliberate espousal by members of the ruling class of the cause of discontented or repressed classes— upperdogs voluntarily siding with underdogs. It is not altogether cynical to hazard the guess that this is sometimes an indication that there is about to be a reversal in the position of the dogs.

Once again, however, it is necessary to point out that the existence of rebellious radicals in the upper classes is only one symptom in a complicated syndrome. Such upper-class mavericks must be relatively numerous as well as conspicuous in a society in disequilibrium. They, as well as the wasters and the cynics, must *set the tone* for the class. Individual "misguided superiors," as Lothrop Stoddard called these upperdogs on the side of the underdogs, were by no means uncommon in so stable a society as Victorian England; but they did not set the tone of the society. Nor

do they in America today, where rebels like Corliss La-
mont are rare indeed among the great families. A Franklin
Roosevelt, a John Kennedy, cannot—save in the eyes of
jaundiced ultra-conservatives—be made into "misguided
superiors," traitors to their society. They are clearly pillars
of their society.

In eighteenth-century America this decadence of a
ruling class is not a prominent symptom of the coming
revolution. Our native ruling class was still young, still in
the process of formation, and seen as a class exhibited
none of the ineptness we have noted in Russia and France.
But of course a large part of our ruling class espoused the
American Revolution, which is probably *one* of the reasons
why our revolution stopped short of a full-blooded Reign
of Terror. As far as the ruling class in Great Britain at the
time of our revolution is concerned, it was very far from
being capable of a resolute course toward America.

Even in seventeenth-century England this sort of symptom is to be discerned. In the English aristocracy of Jaco-
bean times there is not, of course, exactly the same mixture
of weariness, doubt, humanitarian hopes, and irresponsibil-
ity we have found in Russia or in France. Yet most of
these elements can be found in the group later known as
Cavaliers. Picturesque, romantic, appealing though the
Cavaliers seem to us now in literature and tradition, it
would be hard to maintain that they displayed the solidarity and balance necessary to a ruling class. And the Cavalier legend is not wholly a product of the years after the
Great Rebellion. The Cavaliers were romantic even to
themselves, and in a harsh world of Puritans and money-
making had already begun that search for a golden past so
characteristic of the *émigrés* of later revolutions. Nor are
the enlightened or inspired, the Lafayettes or the Tolstoys,
altogether lacking in the English ruling classes of the time.
Even though you accept the nineteenth-century evaluation
of the English as always hard-headed, practical, compro-
mise-loving, you will do well to recall that a Tudor gentleman gave the word "Utopia" to political thought, and that
Harrington's famous Utopia, *Oceana*, is a seventeenth-century product.

Still, what conceals from us the extent to which many

able and ambitious English gentlemen had transferred allegiance from the established order in early Stuart times is that they had espoused the cause of God and the way of salvation. Puritanism, in one or another of its many forms, proved attractive not merely to humble men, or even to traders and bankers, but to many of the gentry and the nobility. Do not forget that Cromwell himself was a gentleman. Finally, what we may call the politico-legal opposition to the first two Stuarts—though separation of political and religious for that time is purely a matter of analysis, the two being inextricably mixed in the feelings of contemporaries—this politico-legal opposition was, as far as leadership went, almost wholly recruited from gentry and nobility. Men like Hampden and Essex resemble Washington in that they are essentially conservatives driven to rebellion by the ineptness of their immediate rulers; they are not, like Lafayette, sentimental deserters of their class.

Except perhaps in America, we find the ruling classes in the old regimes markedly divided, markedly unsuited to fulfill the functions of a ruling class. Some have joined the intellectuals and deserted the established order, have indeed often become leaders in the crusade for a new order; others have turned rebels, less because of hope for the future than because of boredom with the present; others have gone soft, or indifferent, or cynical. Many, possibly even most of the rank-and-file of the ruling classes, the English squire, the French and Russian country nobleman, retained the simple faith in themselves and their position which is apparently necessary to a ruling class. But the tone of life in the upper classes was not set by such as these. Fashion had gone over to the intellectuals. The sober virtues, the whole complex series of value-judgments which guards a privileged class from itself and others, all these were out of fashion at Whitehall, at Versailles, at the old court of St. Petersburg. *Esprit de corps* is a subtle thing, difficult, indeed impossible, to analyze with the methods of the chemist or the statistician. The intricate balance of sentiments and habits which hold men together in any such group as those we have been discussing may be altered by changes apparently insignificant, and extremely difficult to trace. But the fact of the alteration is clear. The very wit, refinement, the cultural graces so evident in what we know of the Cavaliers, the French aristocrats of Versailles and the salons, the Russian upper classes of the ballet, the opera, the novel, are signs of the decadence, not necessarily moral, but certainly political, of a ruling class.

Nor is it possible, even for those who find the simple forms of the economic interpretation of history inadequate and misleading, to deny that in three of our societies—England, France, and Russia—there are clear signs that the ruling classes were in a very shaky economic position. In each case there had been a notable rise in the standards of living of the nobility and gentry; finer houses, finer clothes, the luxuries brought by the decorative arts, by sculpture, painting, and music all cost a great deal of money, and were not in a purely economic sense good investments. Though the prohibitions against a gentleman's making money in business were by no means as absolute, even in France, as they sometimes appear in textbooks of history, it is a fact that most gentlemen had neither the gifts nor the training for such money-making. Most of them lived from agricultural rents, which could not be stretched to meet their rising costs, and from pensions, sinecures, and other aids from the government, which were at least as inelastic in view of the increasing financial difficulties of these governments. Indeed, Louis XIV actually exploited his new nobility by frequently revoking his patents of nobility and reselling them. Notably for the French and Russian upper classes, it is clear that some of the discontent which undermined their *esprit de corps* at the outbreak of the revolution had its origin in their economic difficulties.

In France, class tensions had by 1789 been greatly increased by a strengthening of the expectations and of the actual political role of a part of the aristocracy, the nobility of the robe. Many of these men come close to the role of the "misguided superior" we have noted above; but as Franklin Ford has shown, the main drive of the nobility of the robe was to weaken the powers of the Crown, to head what French historians call the *"réaction nobiliaire."* These men largely helped make the "aristocratic revolution" of 1787-89 which paved the way for the real revolution. In spite of their temporary success, the work of these often very able aristocrats was a failure. Some link with the many, some sense of what the country demanded, escaped them. They do not disprove our generalization that the ruling class in a pre-revolutionary society fails to act as a ruling class should act to preserve its power.

So much for the upper or ruling classes. The classes immediately beneath them in the social structure display in England, France, and Russia, and to a lesser degree in America, a more than ordinary dislike for their superiors. Here once more we are confronted with the problem of what is normal in class relationships in Western societies. The view that in a normal society there are no class antagonisms is as much to be rejected as the Marxist view that in such societies—at least up to the present—the class struggle has been unceasingly and equally bitter and ferocious. The existence of antagonisms among classes is a fact, however much it may be to the interest of the ruling class or classes to deny it. But in a normal society the various antagonisms, by no means purely economic, which set class against class are subordinated to other concerns, wider or narrower, cut across by other conflicts, subdued by other interests. At any rate they are not concentrated, embittered, strengthened by an almost unanimous support from the intellectuals, as we shall find they were in the old regimes we are studying.

In England, where we have usually been taught to believe that class hatreds were minimized by the good relations between country gentlemen and villagers, by the absorption of younger sons of the nobility in the gentry and even in the middle classes, by some English sense of solidarity and decency, the seventeenth century saw a bitter class struggle. The following quotation from Mrs. Lucy Hutchinson is not only a fair specimen of the feelings of a middle-class Puritan toward the nobility; it can stand as a sample of the kind of intense, and always highly moral, atmosphere of such class antagonisms in other pre-revolutionary societies:

The court of the King [James I] was a nursery of

lust and intemperance . . . the nobility of the land was utterly debased. . . . The generality of the gentry of the land soon learned the court fashion, and every great house in the country soon became a sty of uncleanness. Then began murder, incest, adultery, drunkenness, swearing, fornication, and all sorts of ribaldry to be countenanced vices because they held such conformity to the court example.

We need hardly labor the point that both the French and the Russian middle classes hated, and envied, and felt morally superior to their aristocracies, and that their writings are filled with passages indicative of the strength and spread of these sentiments. At fourteen years Manon Phlipon—later as Madame Roland something of an Egeria to the Girondins during the French Revolution—told her mother after a week spent with a lady of the suite of the Dauphine, "Another few days and I shall detest these people so much that I shan't be able to control my hatred." And to her mother's question as to what harm these aristocrats did her she answered, "It's just feeling the injustice, thinking every moment about the absurdity of it all." The higher the French bourgeois rose, the closer he came in his way of life to the aristocracy, the more vividly in some respects he felt the gap which separated him from his neighbor with four quarters of nobility.

> It wasn't the taxes [wrote Rivarol in his memoirs], nor the *lettres de cachet,* nor all the other abuses of authority; it wasn't the vexations of the *intendants,* nor the ruinous delays of justice which most irritated the nation; it was the prejudice of nobility. What proves this is that it was the bourgeois, the men of letters, the financiers, in fine all those who were envious of the nobility, who raised against the nobility the petty bourgeois of the towns and the peasants in the country.

Elinor Barber has shown that until quite late in the eighteenth century French bourgeois with wealth and ambition wanted to *join* the aristocracy rather than *abolish* it. The aristocratic reaction of the last few decades before 1789 probably made the realization of such ambitions more difficult; the spread of the ideas of the *philosophes*, perhaps even more those of Rousseau, Bernardin de St. Pierre and others by no means strictly *philosophes*, helped create the state of mind exemplified by Manon Phlipon. Whatever the cause, by 1789 the kind of feeling she displayed was "typical" enough. Let us repeat that there is no good way to measure such feelings in any society. But once more we may take refuge in a comparison with our own society. There are tensions indeed in that society. The assassination of President Kennedy, culminating a sorry record of verbal and physical violence backed up by extremist ideas inspired many editorials pointing with fear to the possibility of widespread instability if not actual revolution in this country. Senator Goldwater's aphorism about the virtues of extremism worried the commentators greatly. But somehow all this alarmist writing rang false. Something that must exist in the social tensions, the class struggles of a society really on the eve of revolution, seems to be missing in the United States. No one who has even vicariously plunged into a really unstable society can feel that ours is as yet such a society.

How far the lower classes or the proletariat really were stirred against their betters in these societies is not wholly clear, save perhaps in Russia. In England there can be little doubt that the more prosperous artisan classes in the big cities, and in regions like East Anglia the peasantry, were won over to Puritanism; and this meant hostility to the Anglican upper classes. Mixed inextricably with the religious fervor and phrases of the pamphlet literature is a great deal of social hatred, which later came out fully as the revolution moved toward its radical extreme. The French peasantry in many, perhaps most regions, showed by acts in 1789 that they hated their absentee landlords, or the institutions of land tenure, but conclusive evidence that this hatred was much stronger and more universal than it had been for several hundred years has not yet been produced. We cannot be sure whether they hated individuals or a status. Certainly the old notion, evident even in the work of Taine, that the French peasantry were in 1789 smarting under a sharpened double oppression from government and from *seigneurs*, is a revolutionary myth rather than an historical fact. A great deal of work remains to be done in the objective study of the actual sentiments of suppressed or oppressed classes at the bottom of the social scale.

The relatively small Russian proletariat, at least in the cities, had certainly been exposed to several generations of Marxist propaganda, and had acquired, so far as its elite goes, a sense of mission against nobles and middle class alike. Just how the Russian peasants felt toward classes above them is a difficult problem. We may assume a good deal of variety, as also in eighteenth-century France, depending on local conditions, the character of the landlord, the prosperity of the peasants themselves. There is some indication that by the twentieth century one can risk the generalization: the more prosperous the peasants, the more discontented. But here, as throughout the range of our study, trustworthy materials of one kind are scarce: neither historians nor sociologists have paid sufficient systematic attention to the *sentiments* toward other groups which seem to prevail in a given social group or class. Certainly the Russian peasants in 1917 wanted the land— but for themselves, not for a Marxist proletarian dictatorship.

We have noted the ineptness of the ruling classes, and the existence among the middle and parts of the lower of more than normally strong sentiments hostile to the ruling classes. It remains to consider how far these class lines were rigid, how far, in particular, the "career open to talents" existed in these societies. One might well argue *a priori* that in Western societies any approach to a rigid caste system which would bar the possibility of rise to the able but low-born, any serious stoppage of what Pareto calls the *circulation of the elites,* and we call the career open to talents, or social mobility, would be a very important preliminary symptom of revolution. Able men do seem to get born in the humblest ranks, and an accumulation of able and discontented men would provide splendid natural leaders for groups restive and ready for revolt. Yet this test of the career open to talents is one of the hardest to apply to our societies. The normal standard for a Western society is here very difficult indeed to sketch, even as roughly as we have done for our other variables.

One might start with a characteristic American assumption, and say that in this country at least we have full freedom of opportunity. Very well, let us take at random some self-made twentieth-century Americans—Ted Williams, Henry Ford, Harry Truman, Bob Hope, Theodore Dreiser. It would be comforting to be able to say confidently that in the societies of the old regimes men like these would have been kept down by hard-and-fast caste lines, condemned to obscurity or to revolt. Unfortunately, it would not be true. We must not, indeed, be indecently sure about such hypothetical matters. The professional athlete as such could probably not have attained in any other society than our own the wealth Mr. Williams has or as much honor—public attention, if you prefer—save perhaps in the Rome of the gladiators. Yet in early feudal society sheer physical strength and skill might have won him knighthood, and even in later societies noble patronage might have carried him far. Ford may be taken as the entrepreneur-inventor, and though one doubts whether any other society than our own would have made him a national hero, it is likely that in eighteenth-century France or in early twentieth-century Czarist Russia he could have secured substantial financial success. Mr. Truman is the gifted politician risen from the ranks, a type not unknown in the most aristocratic societies in the West. Mr. Hope is the man who amuses, and Western society has usually rewarded adequately, and sometimes highly, those who could amuse it. Perhaps aristocracies have never quite concealed their contempt and democracies have made no attempt to conceal their admiration for those who amused them. Yet actors, musicians, jesters and their like seem not, in spite of the example of Beaumarchais' Figaro, to have been greatly irked by their social status in the past. Certainly the French eighteenth century was kind enough to them, and paid them well in money and attention. As for Dreiser, he would presumably have been in his element among the *philosophes,* and with proper national and racial adjustments, among the Gorkis and the Chekhovs. He would have made proportionately quite as much money, and have been even more honored.

We are dealing with very subtle variables of human sentiments. At all times and in all societies, probably, some men feel that they have abilities which are denied free play by existing social, political, and economic restrictions. Perhaps, indeed, the freer a society as regards social mobility, the more numerous will be those who feel they have not had the success they should have had. Yet it is very difficult to put one's finger on those kinds of activity, those fields of distinction, where this restraint is most felt, and where it is most likely to breed social conflict. Here as elsewhere the given situation is always a complex of restraints, no one or two or three of which would, without additional elements of disturbance, be anything but a quite normal social fact. Moreover, there are other elements besides restraint. Men conditioned to loyalty may put up with great hardships. Fact and feeling seem to vary independently. Thus in Western society there has always been—say in comparison with Hindu caste society—a very high degree of the "career open to talents." The circulation of the elites has always gone on. We can here but glance at our societies and see whether there were any special limitations to that circulation in the years prior to the revolution.

In eighteenth-century France, the way to wealth and fame was open practically unrestricted to businessmen, adventurers, adventuresses, actors, artists, writers—to Samuel Bernard, to Pâris-Duverney, to Cagliostro, to Mesmer, to Mme. Du Barry, to Fragonard, to Beaumarchais, to Voltaire. The way to political power was much harder, though the Abbé Dubois, an apothecary's son, could attain its highest peak. On the whole, substantial political power, the power of making programs and policies, was open to the courtier talents even more than to noble birth; administrative power was almost entirely in the hands of the *noblesse de robe,* an hereditary, conscientious, and capable bureaucracy. Social position, the highest honors, we are frequently told, went only to those who could show four quarters of nobility. Moreover, there are signs that under the leadership of the *noblesse de robe* the French nobility of the eighteenth century was actually tightening its lines, making access to the top more difficult for ambitious non-nobles. Certainly a privileged nobility did exist, and was disliked in the abstract by many a bourgeois who had no concrete experience of it—and who, as Elinor Barber has made very clear, greatly desired to acquire some evidence of being himself noble, if only by conferring the once noble *particule* "de" on himself. Thus Danton appears at least once as d'Anton before the Revolution.

Twentieth-century Russia is in many ways a close parallel in these respects. A privileged nobility topped the social system, and closed the very highest social honors to plebeian talent. This class was disliked, and bitterly disliked, by those who saw it from the outside; and no doubt many of its individual members were insufferably haughty, overbearing, dissolute, vain, empty-headed, and the rest, just as if they had come from the pages of *A Tale of Two Cities*. Yet the way to fame and fortune was far from closed in pre-revolutionary Russia, with new industries rising, with an active theatrical, ballet, and musical life, with university and administrative positions open to ambitious and able young men even from the villages. Rasputin you may perhaps regard as an unhealthy example of the career open to talents, but you can hardly deny that the Siberian monk reached the top.

One clue to this problem of the circulation of the elite may lie in a stoppage of that circulation in a particular and very delicate spot, such as the professions, and especially the "intellectual" professions; that is, among people especially liable to the feeling of frustration, of being excluded from good things. One is struck in studying French society in the years just preceding the revolution with a kind of jam in the stream of bright young men descending on Paris to write and talk their way to fortune. Mercier in his *Tableau de Paris* tells how every sunny day young men might be seen on the quays, washing and drying their only shirts, ruffled and lacy symbol of high social status. Later leaders of the French Revolution as different temperamentally and morally as Brissot (incidentally, Brissot *de War-*

ville) and Marat had failed, before 1789, at literature and science, respectively. There are also in Russia signs of pressure in competition in the ranks of what we Americans should call "white-collar men," intellectuals, bureaucrats, clerks, and the like. We know that a similar stoppage in the society of the Weimar Republic had a great deal to do with the Nazi Revolution of 1933. This symptom is, like most others that indicate strong social tensions, nearly lacking in eighteenth-century America, and extremely difficult to trace, partly for lack of proper historical materials, in the English Revolution. Naturally enough, a stoppage in the circulation of the elite into success in journalism, literature, and such professions is likely to be rapidly reflected in the alienation, and perhaps in the transfer of allegiance, of the intellectuals.

Finally, social antagonisms seem to be at their strongest when a class has attained to wealth, but is, or feels itself, shut out from the highest social distinction, and from positions of evident and open political power. This, broadly speaking, does describe the situation of the Calvinist gentry and merchants in seventeenth-century England, the colonial aristocracy and merchants of America, at least in relation to the British ruling class, the French bourgeois of the eighteenth and the Russian bourgeois of the nineteenth and early twentieth centuries. Individuals in each society might rise from ranks even lower than the middle class, and surmount all these barriers. Even as a class, the bourgeoisie in all four societies really had a determining voice in major political decisions even before the revolutions. But the countries were "run" by other, and privileged, beings, and from the highest social distinctions the bourgeoisie as a class were hopelessly excluded. Moreover, this exclusion was symbolized, manifested continuously in all but the most remote rural districts. Long before Marx, long before Harrington's *Oceana*, practical men knew that political power and social distinction are the handmaids of economic power. Where wealth, certainly the second or third generation of wealth, cannot buy everything—everything of this world, at any rate—you have a fairly reliable preliminary sign of revolution.

v. Summary

In summing up, the most striking thing we must note is that all of these preliminary signs—government deficits, more than usual complaints over taxation, conspicuous governmental favoring of one set of economic interests over another, administrative entanglements and confusions, transfer of allegiance of the intellectuals, loss of self-confidence among many members of the ruling class, conversion of many members of that class to the belief that their privileges are unjust or harmful to society, the intensification of social antagonisms, the stoppage at certain points (usually in the professions, the arts, perhaps the white-collar jobs generally) of the career open to talents, the separation of economic power from political power and social distinction—some, if not most of these signs may be found in almost any modern society at any time. With the wisdom of hindsight, we can now say that in four, or at least in three, of our societies these—and no doubt other signs we have omitted to consider—existed in some unusual combination and intensities before revolution ensued. But clearly we must infer from what we have just done that in its earlier stages diagnosis of revolution is extremely difficult, and certainly cannot be reduced to a neat formula, a recipe, a set of rules. This is also true of the diagnosis of human illnesses. The best diagnosticians, we are told on good authority, could not possibly analyze out and put into formal logical sequence all the steps they take in the clinical diagnosis of disease.

We are not, however, left altogether helpless before some mystical gift for short-term prophecy in the successful diagnostician. His methods are not those of magic, but rather the gift for making what is, until familiarity has made it easy, the difficult and rarely explicit synthesis of past experience and present observation into a successful generalization—or hunch if you prefer. And we can in this instance hazard something further as to signs of revolution in our four societies. In all of them, and especially in France and in Russia, there is, as the actual outbreak of revolution approaches, increasing talk about revolution, increasing consciousness of social tension, increasing "cramp" and irritation. Prophets of evil there always are, and we need not lay much stress on any specific prediction of a given revolution, such as the Marquis d'Argenson made forty years before the French Revolution. But when such fears—or hopes—become something like common property, when they are, to use a very aged metaphor to which the invention of the radio has given an ironic twist, in the air, then it is fairly safe to take this general sentiment as a pretty conclusive sign of revolution. Even then, however, we have a sign difficult to use. For people never seem to expect revolution for themselves, but only for their children. The actual revolution is always a surprise. This is true even for Russia, where the revolution had long been in the air.

It must, however, be really in the air, and not simply in the mouths of professional seers or timid conservatives. It must, above all, go beyond the intellectuals. For, valuable as the transfer of allegiance of the intellectuals is as a sign, *if found with others,* it is always difficult to distinguish from mere alienation of the intellectuals. After all, one of the great functions of the intellectuals in Western society has always been to shake ordinary mortals out of their unthinking optimism, and Cassandra has perhaps as much claim as Plato to be founder of a great academic tradition. But Cassandra's successors have not yet quite achieved her unhappy infallibility.

Chapter

3

FIRST STAGES OF REVOLUTION

1. *The Eternal Figaro*

There is in the *Marriage of Figaro* of Beaumarchais, first performed at Paris in 1784, a famous soliloquy by Figaro in which much of what we have laboriously analyzed in the previous chapter is dramatically focused. Figaro himself is the able young man unjustly kept down by the pressure of a social system built on privilege. As the scene opens he is waiting to surprise in an assignation his bride and his master, the Count Almaviva. His first reflections on feminine inconstancy pass over rapidly into a violent attack on his noble master. "Because you are a great lord, you think you are a great genius! . . . nobility, fortune, rank, appointments; all this makes a man so proud! But what have you done to deserve so many good things? You took the trouble to get born!" Then he looks back on the struggles that have filled his life—his obscure birth, his education in chemistry, pharmacy, surgery, all barely sufficing, because of his lack of high birth, to give him the privilege of practicing veterinary medicine; his venture in playwriting, and his inevitable clash with the censor; his turn to writing on state finance, and the resulting prison term; another essay in literature, this time in journalism, and another suppression; rejection as candidate

for a government job, since unfortunately he was fitted for
the post; a turn as gambler, when his noble patrons took
most of his profits; and his final return to his old trade as
barber-surgeon.

Scattered throughout the soliloquy are a train of epi-
grams which delighted fashionable audiences and were
taken up throughout the country. Indeed, families would
come up to Paris chiefly to see the *Marriage of Figaro*, and
hear French wit at its best directed against a wicked government. Here are a few of Beaumarchais' most famous
jibes: "Not being able to degrade the human spirit, they
get revenge by mistreating it." "Only little men fear little
writings." "For the job an accountant was necessary; a
dancer got it." "To get on in this world, *savoir faire*
[know-how] is worth more than *savoir* [knowledge]."
And, of course, that bitter jibe at the Count's attainments
—"*qu'avez-vous fait pour tant de biens? vous vous êtes
donné la peine de naître.*" Here in this one speech are so
many indications of the coming revolution that, with the
wisdom of after-the-fact that comes so naturally to the
historian, we can say the revolution is already almost full-
blown in Figaro. Including, of course, the fact that, after a
long vacillation, the censor *did not stop* Beaumarchais'
play.

The years just preceding the actual outbreak of revolution witness a crescendo of protests against the tyranny of
the government, a hail of pamphlets, plays, addresses, an
outburst of activity on the part of interested pressure
groups. Facing all this, the government certainly does not
live up to the reputation its opponents seek to make for it.
Its tyrannous attempts at suppressing the rebellious opposition may perhaps fail because that opposition is too
strong, resourceful, and virtuous; or its attempts may fail
because they are carried out half-heartedly and inefficiently by governmental agents more than half won
over to the opposition. The fact remains that they do fail.

Even the period of the personal rule of Charles I which
preceded the English Revolution was not altogether as
quiet and successful as it seemed on the surface to be.
Many Puritan divines escaped Laud s attempt to drive
them from the Established Church, and the others found

plenty of independent pulpits and printing presses. Strafford might write in 1638 that "the People are in great quietness and, if I be not much mistaken, well-satisfied if not delighted with His Majesty's gracious government and protection"; but he was much mistaken. At the very least these eleven years of personal government were but the calm before the storm.

In our other three societies we do not even find this deceptive calm, but a steady growth of revolutionary agitation. In America hardly a colony escaped some form of rioting in the period between the Stamp Act and Lexington, and all of them saw a steady growth of agitation through merchants' committees, correspondence committees, Sons of Liberty, and similar groups. The French government in the 1780's drew nearer and nearer to bankruptcy, and with each expedient to avoid bankruptcy brought nearer the calling of the Estates-General and the signal for revolution. As for Russia, it was a society strikingly conscious of the possibilities of revolution. Upper-class Russians had for more than a generation been turning their uneasiness into the smooth coin of conversation: "sitting upon a volcano," "after us the deluge," "the storm is rising." In 1905 and 1906, under pressure of defeat by the Japanese, a kind of dress rehearsal of the great revolution took place. The patriotic enthusiasms of 1914 for a while stilled conspicuous preparation for revolution, but military defeat in 1915 and 1916 brought back conditions that grew daily more and more like those of 1905.

II. *The Events of the First Stages*

The Russian Revolution began more dramatically and definitely with a single event—street riots in Petrograd in March, 1917—than did any of our other revolutions. History and patriotic ritual have singled out dramatic episodes—the Concord fight, the fall of the Bastille—as beginning revolutions. But though contemporaries were aware of the dramatic quality of such events, they were not always sure that they had turned revolutionary agitation into revolution. The first steps in revolution are by no means always clear to the revolutionists themselves, and the transition from agitation to action is not a sudden and definite thing in these four revolutions.

Charles I came to the throne in 1624, and almost immediately found himself engaged with the House of Commons in a struggle chiefly over taxes. Out of the conflict there emerged the Petition of Right of 1628, in which the Commons forced the King's consent to a statement of definite limitations on the royal power: Charles promised not to raise forced loans, not to quarter soldiers on unwilling householders, not to permit officers to exercise martial law in time of peace, not to send anyone to prison without showing cause why he had done so. Emboldened by this success, the Commons under the leadership of the emotional Sir John Eliot went on to refuse to grant the King the usual form of customs revenue—tonnage and poundage—and to insist in an aggressive and indeed revolutionary way on their privileges. At a final debate on March 2, 1629, two men, Denzil Holles and Valentine, held down the Speaker in his chair by force while Eliot proposed a ringing declaration on the illegality of paying tonnage and poundage without a grant from Parliament. Conservatives pushed forward to free the Speaker. There followed a riotous debate fully worthy of the standards set later by the National Assembly in France, but somehow or other in the confusion Eliot's resolutions were put through before the royal order dissolving the Parliament could be carried out. The Parliamentarians had made a grand gesture of protest. From that day, no Parliament met in England for eleven years. Eliot, jailed for rioting, maintained that the King had no power over a member of the House of Commons. He died a most effective martyr in 1632.

In the years of personal rule Charles, aided by his two great supporters, Strafford and Laud, did his best to organize the government of England in accordance with notions of efficient centralization and expert rule which were the chief political heritage of the Renaissance. He did a job in some ways surprisingly good. But he may, as nineteenth-century liberal historians fondly believed, have been going against the basic grain of the English character, English history, and the basic mold of English institutions; he was most certainly going bankrupt. A clash with the Scotch Presbyterians probably merely hastened the inevitable. Charles called a Parliament in the spring of 1640, but dissolved it after less than a month. A Scottish army now invaded England, and Charles had to buy it off. To get money he had to call another Parliament. The Short Parliament was, therefore, but a breaking of the ground for the Long Parliament, which met on November 3, 1640, was dissolved on April 20, 1653, and was brought briefly to life again in 1659, just before the restoration of the Stuarts. The life of this extraordinary assembly thus spans almost completely the twenty years of the English Revolution.

The Long Parliament got to work at once, for on November 11, 1640, a week after it first met, Pym moved the impeachment of Strafford for high treason. The impeachment, held up by the more conservative House of Lords, was turned early in 1641 into a bill of attainder. Impeachment involved at least the forms of judicial action, whereas attainder was a simple legislative act. The Lords were willing enough to abandon Strafford, if not to try him, and on May 12th he fell under the executioner's ax. Less than eight years later that ax was to reach his royal master.

Parliament voted by a majority of eleven the Grand Remonstrance, a long summing-up of all the grievances accumulated against the King in the seventeen years of his reign. Charles replied to this vote of want of confidence by attempting to arrest six members of Parliament: Lord Kimbolton in the Lords; Pym, Hampden, Haselrig, Holles, and Strode in the Commons, who had compromised themselves by entering into technically treasonous negotiations with the invading Scottish army. Charles rashly came down to the House of Commons himself with armed men and attempted to seize the members. The threatened members fled to the City of London, and Charles was again checkmated. The Commons were now so aggressively successful that they decided to take over the military by naming officers in the militia and trainbands. Charles, in turn, began to build up his own army, and set up his standard at Nottingham in August, 1642. The Civil War had begun.

Where in this long and closely knit series of events you wish to say the English Revolution fairly began is partly subjective matter. Somewhere between the calling of the Long Parliament in 1640, and the outbreak of the war two years later, the first critical steps in the revolution were undertaken. Perhaps the execution of Strafford is a good dramatic date, or Charles's futile attempt to seize the five members in the Commons. At any rate, by the summer of 1642 the English Revolution had taken on unmistakable form in civil war.

Events in America moved hardly more rapidly. In a sense, you can maintain that the American Revolution really began in 1765 with the Stamp Act; or at any rate that the agitation which culminated in the repeal of that Act was a kind of rehearsal for the great movement of the seventies. The imperial government was determined to do something about the American colonists, and Townshend's mild duties on tea, glass, lead, and a few other articles imported into America were accompanied by an attempt to collect them. The result was a series of clashes with increasingly well-organized groups of Americans. Tarring and feathering of informers, stealing sequestered goods from under the noses of customs officers, jeering at British troops, led up to the more dramatic incidents enshrined in the textbooks: the seizure of the *Gaspee* at Providence, the Boston Massacre of 1770, the Boston Tea Party, the burning of the *Peggy Stewart* at Annapolis.

The closing of the port of Boston, the dispatch of Gage and his troops to Massachusetts, the Quebec Act itself, were all really measures taken by the imperial government against colonies already in revolt. You may, if you are interested in such matters, discuss at length the question as to just when the American Revolution is to be considered as formally beginning. You may go as late as the first Continental Congress in 1774, or the battles of Lexington and Concord in 1775, or even the most famous Fourth of July in 1776. But the complex group-struggles out of which revolutions actually grow only later turn into formal sources for patriotic ritual.

The French Revolution of 1789 may be said to have been incubating for several decades. Overt and definite resistance to the royal government, as in the parliaments of Charles I and in the American colonial assemblies, is not to be found in France, which was wholly without such representative bodies. The nearest thing to such a body was the *parlement de Paris*, a kind of supreme court composed of judges who were nobles and held their positions by heredity. It was precisely this *parlement*, followed by the provincial *parlements*, that began in the 1780's an open quarrel with the Crown, which culminated in a dramatic defiance of royal power and the forced exile of the judges. Popular opinion, at least in Paris, was overwhelmingly with the judges, and privileged nobles though they were, they became heroes and martyrs for a day and their "aristocratic revolution" an important step in the revolutionary process.

Approaching bankruptcy had forced the King to call in 1787 an Assembly of Notables, a kind of hastily gathered special commission of prominent persons, from whom Louis XVI in good eighteenth-century style no doubt expected enlightenment. This he certainly obtained, for the Assembly contained many upper-class intellectuals, like Lafayette, who were convinced that France must cease to be a "despotism," must endow itself with an up-to-date constitution of the kind the new states of the American union were making fashionable. The Assembly of Notables was clear that further consultation with the nation was necessary. The Crown finally yielded, brought back into the government the Swiss commoner, Necker, who had a reputation as a financial wizard, and summoned a meeting of the Estates-General for the spring of 1789.

An Estates-General had last met in 1614, and there was some uncertainty as to how one went about electing one. The antiquarians came to the rescue, however, and three hundred representatives of the First Estate, or clergy, three hundred of the Second, or nobility, and six hundred of the Third, or commons, were chosen, practically in time for the first meeting. The double representation of the Third Estate had no precedent in 1614 or earlier. It was, in fact, a revolutionary step, an admission that in some way or another the Third Estate was more important than the others. In the old constitution, however, final decisions—they were merely advisory to the Crown—were made by the orders as units. When the Estates met in May, 1789, the great question was whether to follow the old constitution and vote by orders, or to vote in one great assembly of twelve hundred members in which the doubled Third Estate, plus the "liberals" among the other two orders, would have a clear majority. Louis and his ministers had characteristically permitted this problem to remain vague and unsettled, and only after the Third Estate had insisted on one great assembly did the Crown insist on three separate ones.

The issue out of which the French Revolution formally grew was this simple one of vote by orders or vote by individuals in one assembly. The Third Estate stood pat, and refused to transact any business until the other orders joined it in what was to be called—and the name was a sound piece of propaganda for the revolutionists—the National Assembly. There are certain dramatic moments in a two-months' struggle which was essentially parliamentary. Shut out by a royal blunder from their usual meeting place, the Third Estate on June 20, 1789, met hastily in a large indoor tennis court, and swore not to disperse until they had endowed France with a constitution.

Thanks partly to David's famous painting, which is more symbolic than realistic, this episode is now second only to the taking of the Bastille in the patriotic ritual of the French Republic. At a dramatic session on June 23rd Mirabeau is said to have made his famous reply to a request from the King's Grand Master of Ceremonies that they in turn withdraw: "We are assembled here by the will of the nation, and we will not leave except by force." Shortly afterward the King yielded, though probably not to Mirabeau's rhetoric. By the beginning of July the National Assembly had been duly constituted. The first steps in the French Revolution had been taken.

Those who insist that you must have violence before you can label revolution as begun will date the great French Revolution from July 14, 1789, when a Paris mob, aided by soldiers who had gone over to the popular side, took the gloomy fortress-prison of the Bastille on the eastern edge of the city. Bastille Day is the French republican Fourth of July, a great holy day in one of the best organized of our contemporary nationalist religions. As such it has been surrounded by legends, endowed with a martyrology, safely withdrawn from the unedifying touch of history. To an outsider, the taking of the Bastille seems an involved and confusing process, at least as much the result of the weakness of the royal governor, De Launay, as of the strength of the besiegers. What is important for us is that Paris was in the hands of a mob for three days, and that this mob was clearly shouting against the Court, and shouting for the National Assembly. After the rioting had died down, the National Assembly—or rather, the revolutionary majority in the Assembly—could proceed in the useful assurance that the people were on its side, could feel that it had *carte blanche* to neglect royal protests as it went about its task of remaking France.

The revolution in Russia got under way with great speed. As we have seen in a previous chapter, there were plenty of precedents for a Russian uprising, and several generations of Russians had been discussing the inevitable coming of the storm. The first steps which led up to the February Revolution of 1917, however, took even advanced leaders like Kerensky somewhat by surprise. Socialist parties the world over had been used to celebrating March 8th as Women's Day. On that day—February 23rd of the old Russian calendar, whence the name, February Revolution, by which it has gone down in history—crowds of women workers from the factory districts poured into the streets of Petrograd calling for bread. Each day thereafter crowds increased. Orators of the radical groups harangued at street corners. Soldiers from the large wartime garrison mingled with the crowds, seemed indeed to sympathize with them. Even the Cossacks were not hostile to the people, or at any rate, seemed to lack stomach for fighting.

Meanwhile the authorities were consulting, and as piecemeal measures failed to work, they decided on March 11th to repress the troubles in accordance with a fine neat plan already drawn up on paper for just such emergency. But the plan didn't work. The soldiers of the garrison, anxious not to be sent to the front, began to waver. On March 12th the first of the mutinies broke out, and one after another the famous regiments of the Imperial Army poured out of the barracks, but to join, not to shoot on, the crowds. Obscure leaders, sergeants, factory foremen and the like arose and directed their little groups at strategic points. Out of all the confusion and madness which makes the detailed record of events in this week the despair of the historian, one clear fact came out. There was no imperial government left in the capital, no formal government at all. Gradually there emerged the nucleus of the Petrograd Soviet government to come, organized through trade-unions, Socialist groups, and other working-class sources. The Czar and his advisers, too bewildered and incompetent to control the movement, did prevent the legal duma from taking control. Instead, moderates of all sorts got together to form the nucleus of the provisional government to come. In such a chaotic condition, indeed, it would seem that the action of the moderates is a uniformity of revolutions. Their sentiments and training impel them to try and put a stop to disorder, to salvage what they can of established routines.

Socialists and liberals alike were agreed that the Czar must abdicate. Nicholas himself had started from Army headquarters for his palace at Tsarskoe Selo near Petrograd, but was held up at Pskov by the increasing disorders. Here, on March 15th, he decided to abdicate in favor of his brother, the Grand Duke Michael. What centralized power there was in Russia seems to have been in the hands of a committee of the duma, and this committee waited on Michael in person. The Grand Duke refused the crown. Russia was to be a republic. Michael's own decision to refuse seems to have been dictated by personal cowardice. One of the nice problems of history-in-the-conditional centers around the question of what would have happened had this Romanov been a man of courage, decision, and ability. No one can say, but the question reminds us that even in its most sociological moments, history cannot neglect the drama of personality and chance.

With Michael's abdication on March 16, 1917, the Russian Revolution had clearly begun. There were repercussions in the provinces, and in some remote spots the fall of the Romanovs was not known for weeks. But the work of those eight days had destroyed a centralized bureaucratic government at its most vital point—its head and nerve center. Much in Russia was unchanged by the February Revolution, but politically a week had done what it had taken months to do in England, America and France. The Romanovs had gone much more rapidly than the Stuarts, the Hanoverians and the Bourbons.

III. *Spontaneity or Planning?*

Even from the foregoing sketch of the first steps in four revolutions, it should be clear that to the narrative historian the differences in the four are striking. The English Revolution was begun in one of the oldest, best established of parliamentary bodies; the American Revolution began chiefly in New England, among people used to town meetings and colonial legislatures; the French Revolution developed out of the meetings of a legislative body with no immediate precedents, staffed by men unused to parliamentary life; the Russian Revolution started in street riots in the capital city, and went on without benefit of any parliamentary body, since even the old duma met only through an emergency committee. There are differences of personality, differences of time and place. Charles raising his standard in hope at Nottingham in 1642 seems worlds apart from the abject Nicholas, buffeted about the northern plains in a railroad train at the mercy of striking workers and troops in revolt, drearily abdicating in the provincial gloom of Pskov. There may even be racial differences. The orderly and almost chivalrous Civil War of the English seems at first sight something quite unlike the madness of July 14th, or the tragicomic spectacle of metropolitan Petrograd in the hands of a mob without even a good slogan.

Yet this last should give us pause. At the informal level of mere dramatic or narrative likenesses, these early stages of revolution have similarities as striking as their differences. Speaker Lenthall defying Charles's attempt to seize the five members, Mirabeau thundering his challenge to the bewildered Grand Master of Ceremonies at the royal session of June 23rd, Patrick Henry warning a king of the unfortunate fate of certain other rulers—these seem to be speaking the same language, assuming the same effective postures. The English House of Commons in the pandemonium of its final session in 1629 seems much like the French National Assembly during its frequent heated moments, and not worlds apart from certain important sessions of the Petrograd soviet.

For the emotions of men in groups, and the rhetoric and gestures necessary to bring out and make effective for action these emotions, are more uniform than the romantic—or merely conventional—historian likes to think them. Any representative body of several hundred responds in definite ways to certain definite stimuli, and it does this the more certainly and invariably because it cannot respond to logic, cannot confront a new situation with complete experimental freedom. Especially are excited representative bodies much alike, whether they are composed of "irresponsible" Russians, "excitable" Frenchmen, or "sensible" Englishmen. We need not be surprised if in these early stages of revolution there are clear parallels in the behavior of men in such groups.

It is, however, more important for us to see whether there are not in these four revolutions uniformities which can be grouped together, related to the whole course of the movements, given a place in our conceptual scheme of the fever. What evidence have we here that we are dealing with a process which has definite and common stages? Do these first steps in revolution take place under conditions sociologically similar even if dramatically dissimilar?

One uniformity is crystal-clear. In all four of our societies, the existing government attempted to collect monies from people who refused to pay. Three of our four revolutions started among people who objected to certain taxes, who organized to protest them, and who finally reached the point of agitating for the elimination and replacement of the existing government. And even in Russia in 1917 the financial problems were real and important. This does not necessarily mean that those who resisted taxation foresaw or wished a radical revolution. It does mean that the transition from talking about necessary great changes—for in all our societies, as we have seen, something was in the air—to concrete action, was made under the stimulus of an unpopular form of taxation.

A second uniformity is quite as clear, though the consequences that derive from it are much more obscure. The events in this stage, these first steps in revolution, do most certainly bring out of the confused discontents of the old regime two parties into clear opposition, and indeed into preliminary violence. These parties we may call briefly the party of the old regime and the party of the revolution. Moreover, by the end of this period of the first stages, the party of the revolution has won. The muddy waters of doubt, debate and agitation are momentarily cleared. The revolution, hardly begun, seems over. In England after the Long Parliament had disposed of Strafford and wrung concessions from the King, in America after Concord, and that greatest of moral victories, Bunker Hill, in France after the fall of the Bastille, in Russia after the abdication, there is a brief period of joy and hope, the illusory but charming honeymoon of that impossible pair, the Real and the Ideal.

That our four revolutions ran through some such early stage as this, in which the opposition between old and new crystallized dramatically, and the new won a striking victory, is too evident for the most old-fashioned narrative historian to deny. Over the reasons why this stage developed as it did, however, there is still a running dispute among writers who concern themselves with such matters —historians, political theorists, sociologists, essayists. The heart of the dispute is a matter which must be got straight before anything like a sociology of revolutions is possible. Briefly, one set of disputants maintains that these glorious first steps in revolution are taken almost spontaneously by a united nation rising in its might and virtue to check its oppressors; another maintains that these first steps are the fruition of a series of interlocking plots initiated by small but determined groups of malcontents. By and large the first view is that taken by persons favorable to a given revolution, the second by persons hostile to it, or at least loyal to the memory of the old regime. For Russia, Lenin's firm belief in the role of a militant minority undeterred by bourgeois legalistic scruples, has consecrated the "planning" theory as the official one. In contrast, American and French tradition, and even the English, hold firmly to the belief that their revolutions were spontaneous risings of outraged peoples. There are, however, all sorts of variations on the theme, and different commentators have differently balanced these elements of spontaneity and planning.

This opposition is clearest, and in some ways quite adequately typical for our purpose, in the historiography of the French Revolution. Augustin Cochin used to describe this opposition as that between the *thèse des circonstances* and the *thèse du complot*, the explanation by circumstances and the explanation by plot. Those who on the whole regarded the revolution as a good thing maintained that the people of France, and especially the people of Paris, were goaded into revolt by the oppression of King and court, that the circumstances of their social, political, and economic life in 1789 are in themselves adequate explanation of what happened. Given such circumstances, and men and women of French blood, you have revolution as naturally, as *automatically*, in a sense, as you have an explosion when a spark strikes gunpowder.

This figure may be applied to specific steps in the revolutionary process. The Bastille riots, according to French republican tradition, were not planned in any sense. "Paris" heard of the dismissal of Necker, noted that the King was concentrating troops around the city, and in a million forgotten conversations spread the fear that the King and his party were about to dismiss the revolutionary National Assembly and rule by armed force. Paris therefore rose in its might, and with a sure instinct seized on the Bastille as a symbol of the hated old regime, and destroyed it. In an excellent general study of the Revolution published in 1963, Norman Hampson can write that in July 1789 the majority in the National Assembly "were saved by the spontaneous action of the middle class in most French towns, and notably in Paris." The sovereign people were self-guided in all this, moved if you like by a natural force, by a hatred of injustice, and were led by hundreds of small men, by noncommissioned officers of the revolution, but not by any general staff, not by any small group who had deliberately planned an aggression.

The opposite theory maintains that the whole revolutionary movement in France was the work of a scheming and unprincipled minority, freemasons, *philosophes*, professional agitators. These people in the second half of the eighteenth century got control of the press and the platform, and persistently indoctrinated the literate part of France with a hatred for established institutions, and especially for the Church. As the government found itself in increasingly bad financial straits, these plotters wormed their way into its councils, and finally secured the promise of an Estates-General. By clever electioneering in a populace not used to representative assemblies, they filled the Third Estate with members of their sect, and succeeded in penetrating even the ranks of the First and Second Estates. They had been used to working together, and thanks to years of discussion of political reform, they knew what they wanted. The more determined and initiated of these plotters could therefore control the actions of the large and shapeless National Assembly, though they were a minority of its twelve hundred members.

Bastille Day seems very different to the writers of this school. Louis was concentrating troops to protect, not to dissolve, the National Assembly, to protect it from the minority of wild radicals who were abusing its machinery. Fearing defeat, these radicals stirred up Paris in a hundred ways: they sent orators to street corners and cafés; they distributed radical news-sheets and pamphlets; they sent agents to spread discontent among the royal troops, and especially among the French Guard; they even subsidized prostitutes to get at the soldiers more effectively. Everything was planned ahead for a more propitious moment, and when the dismissal of Necker afforded that moment, the signal was given and Paris rose. But not spontaneously. Somewhere a general staff—Mirabeau was on it, in the Orleanist interest, and most of the popular figures in the National Assembly—was working, carefully sowing the seeds of rebellion.

With the appropriate changes, this sort of opposition between spontaneity and planning can be made out in all our revolutions. To the Stuart partisans—and they still find their way into print—the Great Rebellion was an unhappily successful conspiracy of gloomy money-grubbing Calvinists against the Merry England of tradition. More commonly, since the Whigs gave the tone to modern England, the Parliamentarians are seen as liberty-loving children of Magna Carta, who rose quite naturally and spontaneously against unbearable Stuart tyranny. American Loyalists always maintained that the best of the country was with them, that the Whigs had won by superior organization and chicanery. Most of us, of course, were brought up to regard George III as a personal tyrant, a hirer of Hessians, a man who wished to grind the Americans into unmanly submission. The American Revolution was to us the spontaneous reply of injured freemen to British insolence.

Finally, some Russian *émigrés* still seem to believe that a minority of unscrupulous Bolsheviks somehow engineered *both* the February and the October revolutions. Marxism attaches no shame to revolution, and admits the importance of planning and leadership in revolutionary movements. Therefore, though official Communist explanations by no means soft-pedal Czarist guilt and oppression, though they insist that the people of Russia in February, 1917, wholeheartedly and nearly unanimously rose against the Czar, still they admit, and indeed glory in, the role of leaders consciously planning a revolution. At least, this was the explanation accepted in orthodox Marxist circles, and it is classically stated in the first volume of Trotsky's *History of the Russian Revolution.*

Indeed, that these two conflicting, and in their exaggerated form antithetical, explanations of the first steps in revolution should arise is in itself a clear uniformity to be got from the comparative study of our revolutions. Very early indeed these two interpretations arise, the victorious revolutionists attributing their success to the rise of the many against intolerable tyranny, the defeated supporters of the old regime attributing their failure to the unscrupulous tactics of a minority of clever, wicked men. Neither explanation is devised as an objective interpretation of facts; both are aimed at satisfying human sentiments. It is interesting to note that even the revolutionists' explanation seeks to gloss over violence, seems in a way ashamed of the fact of revolution. This again is perfectly natural, since once in power the revolutionists wish to stay in power. A useful help to this end is a general feeling among the governed that it is wrong to resist those in authority.

It is, however, possible for us to go further than simply noting this division of opinion among the lovers and the haters of a given revolution. We may venture the generalization that there is some truth in both the explanation by circumstances and the explanation by plot. This may seem to many today a characteristically liberal and wishy-washy solution, a stupid adherence to an outdated notion of a golden mean. But it does seem to have a more satisfactory relation with the facts than either extreme explanation.

Bastille Day may again serve as an example. There is plenty of evidence that organized groups did help stir up trouble in Paris in those July days. We know that the radical groups, the "patriots" in the Assembly at Versailles, had close connections with Paris politicians. A kind of skeletal political organization had been left over from the Paris elections to the Third Estate, and these Parisian electors helped greatly to bring a new municipal organization, and a new National Guard, out of the confusion of the riots. Most of the Royalist description of agents circulating in the crowds, of inflammatory pamphleteering, even perhaps of subsidized prostitutes, is substantially true. What is not true is that these elements of planning can be traced to any one or two small plotting groups, to the Duc d'Orléans, or to a few freemasons. The word "plot" is indeed a bad one—except for the purposes of Rightist propaganda, where it proves very useful indeed. Rather we must say that there is evidence of the activities of a number of groups of the kind any careful observer of societies knows well—pressure groups, embryo political parties, semireligious sects, gatherings on the lunatic fringe. There is, however, no evidence that these very dissimilar groups were in July, 1789, managed from any one center, controlled by a small scheming directorate.

On the contrary, there is every evidence that once the dismissal of Necker got these various groups excited, what followed was in a sense spontaneous mob action. No one has yet said the final word on the psychology of crowds, but it is fairly well accepted that the behavior of crowds cannot be completely gauged in advance by the cleverest of mob leaders. Actually it is clear that in Paris in those days there was not one mob, but at least several dozen. People came out in the street because their neighbors were already out. They paraded up and down, shouting and singing, stopping now and then for another drink, or to hear another street-corner orator. Self-constituted leaders of little groups certainly supplemented any planned action. The decision to march on the Bastille seems to have been taken independently in several quarters. No one knows for sure who first had the brilliant idea of going to the Invalides Hospital to secure small arms. The rioting seems to have died out less because the Bastille fell than because the rioters were tired out. Three days is a long time to be riotous, or drunk, or both.

What holds for the taking of the Bastille holds for the general preparatory work and the first stages of revolutions as we have discussed them in this chapter. The Russian February Revolution centered in Petrograd in one week and seems like the Bastille riots on a larger scale. Trotsky has done some of his best writing in his description of the February Revolution and in his balanced accounting of what must be considered spontaneous popular risings and what must be attributed to conscious revolutionary tactics. Kerensky writes flatly that the revolution "came of its own accord, unengineered by anyone, born in the chaos of the collapse of Tsardom." Trotsky admits that no one planned or expected the revolution when it did come, that it developed out of ordinary Socialist manifestations and a mild bread riot. But that development, he adds, was led by "conscious and tempered workers, educated for the most part by the party of Lenin." We may question the last part of this statement, but there can be no doubt that in the last few days of the Petrograd riots leaders of the coming city soviet and leaders of the coming provisional government combined to force out the Czarist government.

The role of the pressure group is especially conspicuous in the early stages of the American Revolution. As early as April, 1763, the merchants of Boston organized a "Society for Encouraging Trade and Commerce with the Province of Massachusetts Bay" with a standing committee of fifteen to watch trade affairs and call meetings. Accounts of their activities were sent to merchants in other colonies. To combat the Stamp Act the radicals organized themselves as "Sons of Liberty," a mass organization which met at times openly, at times secretly, to promote opposition to the Crown. Their vigilance committees "maintained a sort of Holy Inquisition with the sales and purchases of every man of business, into the outgoings and incomings of private households, and with the reported opinions of individuals." Town and county in the North, the county in the South, provided a framework for public meetings and resolutions. The Committees of Correspondence, organized originally as private pressure groups, were later skillfully manipulated by Sam Adams until they had partly supplanted the more conservative town meetings. Adams called into meeting in 1773 a joint committee for Boston, Dorchester, Roxbury, Brookline, and Cambridge which was able to swamp the now fairly conservative merchant vote. Throughout the movement, violence was employed whenever it seemed necessary, from grand affairs like the Boston Tea Party to isolated beating of Tories.

Yet the most "realistic" of our modern historians will hardly go so far as to assert that the American Revolution was plotted by a tiny minority. The net effect of a dozen years of British mistakes, of concessions and retractions, blowings-hot and blowings-cold, together with a great variety of American agitation, was to produce in 1775 a widespread popular backing for the Continental Congress in its resistance to George III. The American Revolution was, like the others, in part the result of an active, able, and far from infinitesimal minority working on a substantial group with grievances enough to be stirred up effectively when the right time came.

To sum the matter up in a metaphor: the school of circumstances regards revolutions as a wild and natural growth, its seeds sown among tyranny and corruption, its development wholly determined by forces outside itself or at any rate outside human planning; the school of plot regards revolutions as a forced and artificial growth, its seeds carefully planted in soil worked over and fertilized by the gardener-revolutionists, mysteriously brought to maturity by these same gardeners against the forces of nature. Actually, we must reject both extremes, for they are nonsense, and hold that revolutions do grow from seeds sown by men who want change, and that these men do do a lot of skillful gardening; but that the gardeners are not working against nature, but rather in soil and in a climate propitious to their work; and that the final fruits represent a collaboration between men and nature.

IV. *The Role of Force*

A final uniformity to be discerned in these first stages of our revolutions is perhaps the clearest and most important of all. In each revolution there is a point, or several points, where constituted authority is challenged by the illegal acts of revolutionists. In such instances, the routine response of any authority is to have recourse to force, police or military. Our authorities made such a response, *but in each case with a striking lack of success.* Those of the ruling class responsible for such responses in all our societies proved signally unable to make adequate use of force. Let us first look at the facts of our case histories.

In England there was no considerable standing army, and of course nothing like a modern police force. Indeed, the question of control over what standing army there was had been one of the big issues between the first two Stuarts and their Parliaments. The Crown had been obliged to quarter its soldiers on private citizens in order to keep any kind of army together, and this quartering was one of the grievances most strongly held against Charles I. When a Scottish army crossed the border, Charles was obliged to call the Long Parliament to get money to buy this armed force off. When the actual break between Royalists and Parliamentarians drew near, both sides tried to constitute an armed force. Charles had the benefit of a devoted noble officer-class, and enough tenant-followers of noblemen and gentry to constitute what was by far the strongest effective and available armed force controlled by the government, or conservatives, or party-in-power side in any of our four revolutions. Yet the Civil War proved that he didn't have enough good soldiers, in comparison with the human resources available to the Parliament. Charles was beaten in the first instance because he lacked decisive military power.

Similarly in the American Revolution, neither the American Loyalists nor the British armies were quite strong enough, as in the actual event they used their armed strength to try to suppress the revolutionists. Notably in the earlier stages, the British undertook to introduce what they knew to be unpopular governmental changes with what now seems an amazing disregard of police necessities. No doubt the long tradition of British loyal self-government made it hard for a British colonial administrator to conceive of any other methods. But the fact remains that these forces in North America in 1775 were quite inadequate to enforce authority. How many more men than Gage actually did have would have been necessary to keep royal order in Massachusetts Bay is a matter of guesswork, of perhaps unprofitable history-in-the-conditional. It is, however, unduly complimentary to rugged Yankee love of independence to suppose that no armed force could have been large enough to control Massachusetts. In America also an important initial failure of the government was its failure to use force adequately and skillfully.

Louis XVI had in 1789 a fairly trustworthy armed force. His French troops were open to propaganda by the patriots. But he had important household troops, mercenaries recruited from foreign peoples, chiefly Swiss and German, and not readily accessible to French agitators. That the Swiss would die for him, or for their duty, was proved three years later at the storming of the Tuileries. He had, especially in the artillery, a capable set of officers, most of whom could be relied upon at this stage. Yet at the decisive moment, the rioting in Paris in July, he and his advisers failed to use the military effectively. Again we edge into history-in-the-conditional, but one cannot avoid wondering what would have happened had a few disciplined troops with street guns attempted the reduction of Paris in

July, 1789. Napoleon was later to show that such a force could readily beat down civilian resistance, and this fact was to be amply confirmed in June, 1848, and in 1871. Louis might have failed. But the point is that, French republican and socialist historians to the contrary notwithstanding, he didn't really try. Once again a government failed to make adequate use of force.

Petrograd in 1917 is the most perfect example of this important role of the military and the police. Everyone, from Czarist to Trotskyite, admits that what turned somewhat chaotic and aimless street demonstrations into a revolution was the failure of the elaborate government plan to restore order in Petrograd in case of uprisings. And that plan failed because at the critical moment the soldiers refused to march against the people, but regiment by regiment came over instead to join them. Again, such is the advantage which a disciplined force with modern artillery possesses over even the most inspired civilian revolutionists, there can be little doubt that if the Cossacks and a few of the famous regiments of the line, the Preobrazhensky, for instance, had been warmly loyal to the government, even the somewhat incompetent rulers of Petrograd could probably have put down the disturbance. We may, however, note parenthetically that the nowadays common view that modern weapons have for the future made street-risings impossible is probably wrong. Modern weapons have to be used by police or soldiers, who may still be subverted, even in the atomic age.

This striking failure on the part of the rulers to use force successfully is not, however, likely to be an isolated and chance phenomenon. Indeed, it seems initmately bound up with that general ineptness and failure of the ruling class we have noticed in the previous chapter. Long years of decline have undermined the discipline of the troops, bad treatment has given the private soldiers a common cause with civilians, many of the brightest officers have lost faith in the conventional and stupid military virtues. There is no co-ordinating command, no confidence, no desire for action. Or if there are some of these things, they exist only in isolated individuals, and are lost among the general incompetence, irresolution, and pessimism. The conservative cause—even the cause of Charles I—seems a lost cause from the start. The American case is somewhat different. Here we have an inept *colonial* government in London, but not an inept native ruling class.

We can then with some confidence attribute in part the failure of the conservatives to use force skillfully to the decadence of a ruling class. After all, we are dealing with fairly large groups of the kind we are accustomed to treating as subjects for sociological generalization. When, however, we attempt to bring the four crowned heads of our societies under some such general rule, we can hardly help feeling that we have no adequate statistical basis. Yet Charles I, George III, Louis XVI, and Nicholas II display such remarkable similarities that one hesitates to call in chance as an explanation. Trotsky confidently asserts that a decaying society will inevitably head up into the kind of incompetence displayed by these monarchs. Unsupported by a belief in dialectical materialism, we here dare not display quite as much confidence, but we must bring forward these uniformities in the behavior of four men as a valid part of our observed uniformities. At any rate their being what they were had an important part in that process through which the revolutionists won their preliminary and decisive victories over incompetent authority.

For our revolutions, then, we may put this last uniformity very simply: they were successful in their first stages; they became actual revolutions instead of mere discussions, complaints, and rioting, only after revolutionists had beaten, or won over, the armed forces of the government. We cannot here attempt to erect uniformities for other revolutions or for revolutions in general. But we may suggest in very tentative and hypothetical form the generalization that no government has ever fallen before attackers until it has lost control over its armed forces or lost the ability to use them effectively—or, of course, lost such control of force because of interference by a more powerful foreign force, as in Hungary in 1849 and in 1956, and conversely that no revolutionists have ever succeeded until they have got a predominance of effective armed force on their side. This holds true from spears and arrows to machine guns and gas, from Hippias to Castro.

v. *The Honeymoon*

The first stage of revolution ends in all four of our societies with the victory of the revolutionists after what is rather dramatic than serious bloodshed. The hated old regime has been conquered so easily! The way is open to the regeneration men have been so long talking about, so long hoping for. Even the Russian February Revolution, though it broke out in the midst of the misery and shame of defeat at the hands of Germans and Austrians, was cradled in the hope and joy that seems a natural heritage in our four revolutions. Russians all over the world heard the good news with delight. Liberals were as happy as their ancestors had been in '76 and '89. Now Russia was washed clean of the stain of absolutism, could take her place with confidence in the ranks of her sister democracies of the West, join with a new effectiveness in the crusade against the sole remaining forces of darkness, the Hohenzollerns and the Hapsburgs.

The honeymoon stage of revolution is most perfectly developed in France, where the revolution came in peacetime, and at the end of a great intellectual movement called the Enlightenment which had prepared men's minds for a new and practical miracle. Wordsworth's lines are familiar:

> France standing on the top of golden hours,
> And human nature seeming born again.

But poets in a dozen languages set to work to celebrate the regeneration of France and of mankind. And not only poets. Sober businessmen, professional men, country gentlemen, people who in the twentieth century tend to regard revolution with horror, joined in the rejoicing. Far away in unenlightened Russia noblemen illuminated their houses in honor of the fall of the Bastille. The Danish man of letters Steffens tells how his father came home one night in Copenhagen, gathered his sons about him, and with tears of joy told them that the Bastille had fallen, that a new era had begun, that if they were failures in life they must blame themselves, for henceforth "poverty would vanish, the lowliest would begin the struggles of life on equal terms with the mightiest, with equal arms, on equal ground." Americans and Englishmen rejoiced that the ancient enemy had come to join the self-governing peoples. Frenchmen themselves were for a brief happy moment almost unanimous. The King had seen the error of his ways, had embraced the paladin Lafayette, had come freely to his good city of Paris to hear the cheers of the heroes of the Bastille.

Yet the honeymoon period even in France was brief, briefer yet in Russia, in England and in America never quite so clear and so definite. In the first stages, and at the critical moment when the test of force comes, the old regime is faced by a solid opposition. The opposition is indeed composed of various groups, is never quite that oversimplification a "united people." But it is welded by the necessity of effectively opposing the government into a genuine political unit, into something more than a chance coalition of contradictory elements. Its victory is, if we are willing to take the terms critically and not sentimentally, the victory of the "people" over its "oppressors." It has shown itself stronger and abler than the old government in this time of crisis. It has now become the government, and is facing a new set of problems. When it actually gets to work on those problems the honeymoon is soon over.

4

TYPES OF REVOLUTIONISTS

1. *The Clichés*

It would clearly be helpful in our inquiry if we could at this point isolate the revolutionist as a type. To pursue our analogy of the fever perhaps unduly far, may it not be that certain individuals act as "carriers," and that they can be classified, labeled, described in economic and sociological terms as well as in those of psychology or common sense? This is at any rate a lead which seems worth following.

There are, however, several ways in which such a pursuit might lead us astray. We must beware of regarding revolutionists, and revolutionary leaders in particular, as literally bearing disease germs of revolution. Here as throughout this study, our conceptual scheme must never be allowed to lead us into fantasy. It must be a convenience, not an obsession. We must more than ever avoid using terms of praise or dispraise, which lurk in every corner of this particular field. For the simple word "revolutionist" is likely to call up in the minds of most of us a relatively uncritical personification, the sort of loose change of daily intercourse that serves us well enough to get on with "poet" or "professor" or "Frenchman."

Even the subtlest thinker, the most delicate and conscientious artist in words, has to come down in daily life to something very close to the clichés that serve the man in the street. You and I, of course, do not picture poets as long-haired, delicate, bohemian, and tubercular, or professors as impractical, absent-minded, kindly, and bearded, or Frenchmen as polite, dapper, wax-mustached, ladies' men. But we cannot go into Proustian intricacies with ourselves when we use such words, nor can we use them as rigorously as a scientific systematist. We get along with them as best we may, adjusting them roughly to our experience and our sentiments.

Now what "revolutionist" means at this level to various persons and various groups is in itself an important element in a full sociology of revolutions. What all sorts of people feel about revolution is perhaps most easily studied in the clichés which arise out of words like "revolutionist" and "revolutionary," or their more concrete parallels, "Jacobin," "Communist," "red," and the like. We cannot attempt such a study here, but we must look a bit further into a few of these clichés, if only as a warning and a contrast.

Probably for most Americans in the twentieth century the word "revolutionist" carries unpleasant overtones. At the level of the press of the Radical Right, a revolutionist appears as a seedy, wild-eyed, unshaven, loud-mouthed beatnik, given to soapbox oratory and plotting against the government, ready for, and yet afraid of, violence. Even at slightly more sophisticated levels, one suspects many of our countrymen feel much the same about revolutionists, or at any rate are convinced that they are pronouncedly queer people, failures under prerevolutionary conditions, sufferers from inferiority complexes, envious of their betters, or just downright ornery disturbers on principle and by disposition. Other and more favorable pictures of the revolutionist no doubt arise in other minds. To judge by some of our proletarian writers—not themselves proletarians—the revolutionist is a sturdy, broad-shouldered steelworker, uncorrupted by the falsities the bourgeois call education, but well-versed in Marx and Lenin, strong, kindly, a warrior-spirit with just a redeeming touch of Shelley about him.

Now the social uses of beliefs of this sort are plain enough. In an old bourgeois society like the United States, sentiments hostile to revolutionists are probably important factors in maintaining social stability. Revolutionists were all right in 1776, but not now. Any society that is a going concern must apparently contain large numbers of people who feel this way about revolutionists. Even in Russia, where memories of violent revolution are still comparatively fresh, a concerted effort is being made by the government to discredit living, flesh-and-blood revolutionists and certainly to discredit what such men are doing in China. Revolution was all right in 1917, but not today; or at the very least, revolution now in Russia, as in the days of the Kirov trials of the 1930's, is "counter-revolutionary." On the other side, it is clear that the radicals and extremists who think of revolutionists as fine fellows, as heroes and martyrs, are also adding to their own social discipline, strengthening themselves for the fray.

The social scientist, however, cannot let the matter rest there. He must attempt an objective classification of revolutionists, as complicated as his data about them makes necessary. We can say with confidence that even a hasty review of the four revolutions with which we are concerned is very far from confirming either set of clichés we have outlined. And notably, since the derogatory set is commoner in this country, such a review by no means confirms the notion that our revolutionists were seedy, loud-mouthed, bomb-throwing failures in the old regimes. If we include, as we must, those who took the first steps in revolution as well as those who ruled in the reign of terror, our type becomes still less simple, becomes in fact, types, not a type.

Let us take a random list of names as they come to mind: Hampden, Sir Harry Vane, John Milton, Sam Adams, John Hancock, Washington, Thomas Paine, Lafayette, Danton, Robespierre, Marat, Talleyrand, Hébert, Miliukov, Konovalov, Kerensky, Chicherin, Lenin, Stalin. All are revolutionists; all opposed constituted authority with force of arms. The list includes great nobles, gentlemen, merchants, journalists, a student for the priesthood, a professor of history, lawyers, a political boss, a ward-heeler. It includes several very rich men and one or two poor men. It includes many who would by conventional Christian standards seem to have been good men; and it includes several who would by such standards seem to have been very wicked men. It includes some who were important people in their prerevolutionary days, some who were quite unknown, and two, perhaps three, who were apparent failures in life until the revolution gave them a chance to rise. Surely it is no easy task to find a least common denominator for a list like this.

No doubt we shall be aided by making a distinction between the men who dominate in the early stages of a revolution—on the whole the moderates—and those who dominate in the crisis stage—on the whole the extremists. But it will not do to say that only our extremists are real revolutionists. After all, even George Washington had taken an oath of loyalty to the British Crown, and his breaking that oath would have been treason had the American Revolution failed. We have been taught by Whig historians to believe that Essex and Pym were defending the sacred laws of England, and that therefore they weren't real revolutionists. This was not, by any means, the current opinion in Europe in the 1640's, where the Parliamentarians were regarded as shocking rebels against their king; and monarchy was in seventeenth-century Europe as solidly rooted in the sentiments which give force to law as the American Constitution seems rooted with us in this country at the present time. No, we must list the moderates among our revolutionists, even though they were defending the higher law against the lower, and weren't just nasty anarchists and rebels.

II. *Economic and Social Position: Rank and File*

One of the most useful approaches to the problem of the personnel of revolutionary movements is from the relatively objective indications of the economic and social status of those who take part in the uprising. Now it is very difficult to find out much about rank and file of the revolutionists. Like the private soldier in war, the ordinary revolutionist is inarticulate and nameless. For the French Revolution, however, some such study is not impossible. In the surviving records of the Jacobin clubs, which served as centers of revolutionary action, and resemble the English Independents, the Russian soviets, and the American corresponding committees, we have a large number of lists of members—imperfect, of course, but still lists. Some years ago the present writer made a study of these lists, and, aided by tax rolls and other documents in French local archives, was able to arrive at certain rough statistical generalizations about these revolutionists. Some of these generalizations must be here summarized from the author's *The Jacobins: A Study in the New History.*

In general, it is possible to arrive at some statistical approximation of the social and economic positions of these Jacobin revolutionists in prerevolutionary France. There are tax rolls extant for various years between 1785 and 1790, and on these many of the Jacobins can be found, with the sums they were assessed at. As these were direct taxes not too far out of proportion to income, it is possible thus to get a rough estimate of Jacobin wealth. Occupations are usually given, and this is a useful indication of social position. Finally, it is also possible to study certain clubs at specific moments in the revolution, so that a sample can be taken during the early or moderate period, and another during the later rule of the extremists. Here, briefly, are some of the results.

For twelve clubs, with a total membership of 5,405 over the whole course of the revolution, 1789-95, in both its moderate and its violent phases: 62 per cent of the members were middle class, 28 per cent working class, 10 per cent peasants. For twelve clubs in the moderate period, 1789-92, with a membership of 4,037: 66 per cent were middle class, 26 per cent working class, 8 per cent peasants. For forty-two clubs in the violent period, 1793-95, with a membership of 8,062: 57 per cent were middle class, 32 per cent working class, 11 per cent peasants. The tax rolls confirm what occupational and social classification suggests. In eight clubs considered over the whole period of revolution, club members paid an average tax of 32.12 *livres,* where the average tax for all male citizens paying this direct tax in the towns considered was 17.02 *livres;* in twenty-six clubs considered in the violent period only, club members paid 19.94 *livres,* male citizens 14.45 *livres.* Thus, though there was certainly a tendency for the clubs to be recruited in the violent period from social strata a bit lower, on the whole one is forced to the conclusion that "the Jacobin was neither a nobleman nor a beggar, but almost anything in between. The Jacobins represent a complete cross-section of their communities."

Other relatively objective indices help us a bit. It was often possible to list the ages of members of the clubs during the revolution. As far as the rank and file of these clubs went, the notion that revolutionists are recruited from the young and irresponsible was not borne out. For ten clubs the average age varied from 38.3 years to 45.4 years, and for all ten together came to 41.8 years. These were clearly not foolhardy youngsters. Nor were they footloose itinerants, shock troops imported from revolutionary urban centers like Paris. Out of 2,949 members of fifteen clubs, only 378, or 13 per cent, had moved into the towns since the outbreak of trouble in 1789. The actual membership of the clubs varied as the revolutionary movement grew more and more extreme—or in modern terms, went more and more to the Left. Many moderates emigrated or were guillotined, many disreputable extremists, often though by no means always from the lower classes, only "made" the clubs later on. Yet in six clubs with a total membership from 1789 to 1795 of 3,028, something over 31 per cent managed to stay on the books for the whole period, to have been successively good monarchists, good Girondists, good Montagnards. It is not true that the personality of these clubs became dominantly lower or working class after the fall of the monarchy in 1792, nor even that their newer recruits were largely from the proletariat. And it is quite clear that these people are not on the whole failures in their earlier environment; rather they represent the abler, more ambitious, and successful of the inhabitants of a given town. It is as if our present-day Rotarians were revolutionists.

A similar statistical study could probably not be made for the English Revolution since lists corresponding to the

Jacobin membership lists are not available. The material certainly exists for such a study in the actual membership of the soviets in, say, the crucial year 1917, but it would have to be put together from scattered sources available only in Russia. We know a good deal about the membership of our own American revolutionary groups, from merchants' committees and corresponding committees to continental congresses. Even for the English Revolution we have enough scattered material to permit some generalizations about the personnel of the movement.

In the early stages of the English Revolution there can be no doubt about the respectability and economic prosperity of the men who backed Parliament. Baxter, somewhat exaggeratedly, but with a kernel of truth, writes that when the Great Rebellion broke out "it was the moderate Conformists and Episcopal Protestants who had long been crying of Innovations, Arminianism, Popery, Monopolies, illegal taxes and the danger of arbitrary government, who raised the war." The merchants of London, Bristol and other towns, great lords, small landowning gentry, all rose in sedition against their king. Even in what we may call the extremist or crisis period of the English Revolution, which begins in 1646 or 1647 when the tension between the New Model Army and the Presbyterians becomes acute, your revolutionists are very far from riffraff. Even Baxter reports of that army—which was to the English Revolution what the Jacobins were to the French and the Bolsheviks to the Russian revolutions—that "abundance of the common troopers and many of the officers I found to be honest, sober, orthodox men, and others tractable, ready to hear the truth, and of upright intentions." A historian has estimated that when the New Model "took the field in 1645, of its thirty-seven chief officers, nine were of noble, twenty-one of gentle birth, and only seven not gentlemen by birth." The English lower classes, or at least the more proletarian and peasant elements as opposed to independent artisans, on the whole stood aloof from the conflict. Even the wilder sectarians seem to have been recruited from humble, but by no means poverty-stricken people, men who had taught themselves to follow the theological disputes, men on the whole representing the more active and ambitious of their class. The poorer peasants, especially in the North and West, actually sided with the King and against the revolutionists.

In America we have already pointed out the well-known fact that it was the merchants who first organized opposition to the Crown. This opposition was echoed by many planters in the southern coastal plain, and by many very respectable yeoman farmers of the Piedmont. It is quite true that there are numerous signs of the pretty active participation of what a good conservative would regard as the dregs of the population. The Boston Sons of Liberty, who performed most of the actual work of violence there, were recruited from workingmen and actually met habitually in the counting room of a distillery. The Tories, whom it is now more fashionable to call Loyalists, naturally saw their opponents as a pretty shabby lot. Hutchinson writes of the Boston town meeting that it is "constituted of the lowest class of the people under the influence of a few of the higher class, but of intemperate and furious dispositions and of desperate fortunes. Men of property and the best character have deserted these meetings, where they are sure of being affronted."

Actually the line between Tory and Whig is a very irregular one, depending on much besides economic status, as can be seen from J. F. Jameson's *The American Revolution Considered as a Social Movement*. If the rich gentlemen of "Tory Row" in Cambridge sided with the Crown, there were plenty of sober respectable farmers, merchants, and lawyers, who turned revolutionist. A good sign of the respectability of revolution is the adhesion of the clergy, which save for the Episcopalians was in most colonies general. As a disgruntled Loyalist put it:

> The high sons of liberty include the ministers of the gospel, who instead of preaching to their flocks meekness, sobriety, attention to their different employments, and a steady obedience to the laws of Britain, belch from the pulpits liberty, independence, and a steady perseverance in endeavoring to shake off their allegiance to the mother country. The independent

ministers have ever been . . . the instigators and abettors of every persecution and conspiracy.

To sum up we shall have to agree with Jameson that the strength of the revolutionary movement in the long run lay with the plain people—not with the mob or "rabble," for American society was rural and not urban—but with country artisans, small farmers, and frontiersmen. But we shall also have to agree with Alexander Graydon that "the opposition to the claims of Britain originated with the better sort: it was truly aristocratical in its commencement."

The February Revolution in Russia seems to have been welcomed by all classes save the most conservative of conservatives—a few army officers, a few members of the Court and the old nobility. No one knows who made the February Revolution, but there can be no doubt as to its popularity. Almost everyone, liberal noble, banker, industrialist, lawyer, doctor, civil servant, *kulak*, and workingman, was glad to co-operate in giving the Czarist regime its final blow. Even the Bolsheviks, whose sudden victory in the October Revolution of 1917 makes the time-scheme of the Russian Revolution so very different from those of the English and French revolutions, were by no means what confirmed haters of revolution call riffraff, rabble, "the masses." They seem to have been recruited chiefly from the more enterprising, able, and skilled workingmen in the factories of Petrograd, Moscow, and specialized industrial centers like Ivanovo-Vosnessensk or the Don basin. Their most important leaders were largely drawn from the middle class. One might perhaps argue that the Kadets, led by Miliukov, were so early discouraged that they may not be counted as a revolutionary party. But the Mensheviks and S-R (Socialist-Revolutionary) party, later scorned as "Compromisists" by triumphant Bolshevik historians, are most certainly revolutionary elements. The Mensheviks may have been mostly intellectuals, but the S-R were also recruited from the prosperous peasants, from the people who ran the cooperatives, from small shopkeepers and the like.

III. *Economic and Social Position: Leaders*

Hitherto we have been considering the main bodies of the revolutionists, and have found that on the whole they by no means represent the dregs of society, even in the great proletarian uprising. Marxist theory of course recognizes that the *Lumpenproletariat* is not revolutionary; the idea that the very oppressed and poor are important as initiating and maintaining revolutions is a bourgeois one.

Let us now see what we can make of the leaders, judging them first by the comparatively objective standards of their social origins and economic status. With the Jacobins the present writer was able to make some study of the purely local leaders, the men who normally don't get into general history. From the careers of dozens of these subalterns of revolution, a conclusion seemed clear: "the leaders are substantially of the same social standing as the rank and file. Possibly there are, among the leaders during the Terror, more men who seem definitely, in 1789, failures, or at least at odds with their environment. Yet the proportion of these village Marats is not striking."

As for the national leaders in the French Revolution, they are, judged by these standards, a varied lot. In the years 1789-92 they include noblemen like the King's cousin, the Duke of Orléans, Mirabeau, the Lameths, Lafayette; lawyers in vast numbers, from well-known Parisian lawyers like Camus to obscure but thoroughly respectable provincial lawyers like young Robespierre from Arras (who had once written his name de Robespierre), or rising barristers like Danton (who had once written his d'Anton); men of science like the astronomer Bailly, the chemist Lavoisier, and the mathematician Monge; and, nursed by the new power of the press, journalists like Marat and Desmoulins, publicists like Brissot, a provincial bourgeois of Chartres, and Condorcet, a marquis and a *philosophe*. After 1792, extremely few new leaders came to the top. The men who ran France in 1793-94 were, perhaps, somewhat less refined or distinguished than the hopeful intellectuals of Mme. Roland's circle; and they would have seemed very out-of-place at Versailles in 1783. They were not, however, of very different social origins from the men who really ran the old France—the literate upper bourgeoisie from which were ultimately recruited the bureaucracy.

Of the striking respectability and excellent social standing of the men who signed our Declaration of Independence most Americans are fully aware. Of its fifty-six signers thirty-three held college degrees in an age when few ever went to college; only about four had little or no formal education. There were five doctors, eleven merchants, four farmers, twenty-two lawyers, three ministers. Twelve were sons of ministers. Nearly all were affluent. Sam Adams, who seems among the more radical of our leaders, came from a merchant family of some means, and graduated from Harvard in 1740. Even the Loyalists, though they flung words like "rabble" about very freely, could consistently reproach the revolutionary leaders with nothing worse in this respect than being amateurs in the art of governing. "From shopkeepers, tradesmen, and attorneys they are become statesmen and legislators. . . . Almost every individual of the governing party in America fills at present, in his own fancy, a station not only superior to what he had ever filled before, but to what he had ever expected to fill," writes a conservative, or moderate, in the *Middlesex Journal* for April 6, 1776.

We need not go into the social origins of the leaders of the moderates in the English Revolution. They are clearly among the highest in the land. The immoderates present an interesting spectacle, a mixture of gentlemen of good breeding, of self-educated careerists, and of humble men inspired by a fury as yet divine, as yet without benefit of psychoanalysis. Cromwell himself, of course, was an East Anglian country gentleman, whose family tree ramified into a good deal of the new wealth originating in Tudor confiscations. Ireton, who became his son-in-law, was of similar antecedents, as were many other Independent leaders in old and new England. Ludlow the regicide was a son of Sir Henry Ludlow of Wiltshire, and went to Trinity, Cambridge. Even John Lilburne the Leveller is described as "of good family" dating back to the fourteenth century, and seems to have been typical of the lesser gentry whose sons not infrequently passed over into trade. We know little of the social origins of such men as Winstanley the Digger or Edward Sexby, a soldier of Cromwell's regiment who appears later as a kind of international agent of republicanism. Robert Everard, with Winstanley a leader of the curious communistic group known as the Diggers, was a captain in the army and is described as a "gentleman of liberal education." John Rogers the Millenarian was the son of a royalist Anglican clergyman.

Russia presents a case more nearly parallel to our other countries in respect to the social origins of the leaders of her revolution than might at first sight seem likely in a proletarian revolution. Perhaps the moderates in Russia held power so briefly and so uncomfortably that they hardly count. Kadets like Miliukov, an historian of good family, Tereschenko, a Kiev sugar millionaire, the Octobrist Guchkov, a wealthy Moscow merchant, and poor old Prince Lvov remind us of the rich Puritan lords and merchants of the English Revolution, the wellborn Feuillants of the French Revolution. The Menshevik and Social-Revolutionary leaders were mostly intellectuals, petty officials, trade-union and co-operative leaders; some of their most eloquent orators came from Georgia, "the Gironde of the Russian revolution." Kerensky was a radical lawyer of provincial bureaucratic stock from the little Volga town of Simbirsk, now called Ulianovsk, in memory of a greater man than Kerensky who also hailed from Simbirsk. As a matter of fact, V. I. Ulianov, better known by his revolutionary name of Lenin, came from the same social class as Kerensky. His father was an inspector of schools at Simbirsk, a position of much more social standing in bureaucratic Czarist Russia than it would seem to us to be—very definitely in the superior bourgeoisie.

The other Bolshevik leaders are a varied lot: intellectuals like Trotsky and Kamenev, both educated men; Felix Dzerzhinsky, of noble Polish-Lithuanian stock; Sverdlov, by training a chemist; Kalinin, whom one might call a professional peasant; Stalin (born Djugashvili) of Georgian peasant-artisan stock, destined by his mother for the priesthood, and actually for some time a student in a seminary; Chicherin, of stock sufficiently aristocratic to hold himself at least as wellborn as Lord Curzon; Antonov-Ovseënko, Red Army leader with the fine bourgeois inheritance of a hyphenated name. The negotiations at Brest-Litovsk, however, afford a neat synopsis of Bolshevik leadership and proof of its non-proletarian character. When the first Russian delegation was sent to that town to meet the Germans it included as samples of the proletarian achievements of the revolution one specimen each of sailor, worker, and peasant. The peasant is said, no doubt by malicious enemies of the working class, to have distinguished himself chiefly by his interest in the liquor supply. When, however, the negotiations really got going after a recess, the Russians dropped their ornamental sailor, worker, and peasant, and were represented by men of course not the social equals of the high-born Germans opposite them, but, one suspects, their cultural superiors— Joffe, Kamenev, Pokrovsky, Karakhan—and by a somewhat neurotic lady-Bolshevik Mme. Bitzenko, who had won her spurs by shooting a Czarist official in the bad old days. But, it must be noted once more, Marxism is willing to admit that the proletariat cannot lift itself by its own bootstraps, and that its leaders must therefore come from classes sufficiently privileged to have had an education fitting them to interpret the subtleties of Marxist theology.

Finally, the inexperience, the "newness," of the revolutionary leaders has generally been exaggerated in our textbooks. They had, especially in Russia, had a long training in the direction of dissenting and persecuted little societies, the revolutionary groups. And revolutionists as a group in a society really ripe for revolution are so much like any other human beings that to learn the art of leading them is to have gone a long way in political apprenticeship. Even in France, the members of the National Assembly were not as politically innocent as they are supposed to have been. Many had had business experience, or had been diplomatists, or civil servants, or had taken part in local politics in provinces which had their own Estates. All of them were used to the politics of pressure groups. These revolutionary leaders are mostly far from academic, unworldly, pure theorists; they do not step suddenly from the cloister to the council hall. Their training may have subtly unfitted them for leading a stable society; but that is another, and at present insoluble, problem. They are certainly fitted for leadership in an unstable society.

We have, then, found that both rank and file and leaders of active revolutionary groups cannot be catalogued neatly as coming from any one social or economic group. They are not even strikingly, precociously, young. These leaders are usually in middle age, the thirties and forties, and thus younger than most of the politically prominent in stable societies, which naturally incline to the rule of the old. But the St. Justs and the Bonapartes, the boys in their twenties, are the exception, not the rule. The leadership of the Russian Revolution which, with the distortion that comes from contemporaneousness, we are likely to regard as the most "radical," was on the average the oldest in years of all our revolutions. The revolutionists tend to represent a fairly complete cross section of their communities, with a sprinkling of the very highest ranks of their societies, men like Lafayette, for instance, and, as far as the active ruling groups go, extremely few of the submerged, down-trodden, lowest ranks. This is as true of the Bolsheviks as of the Puritans and the Jacobins. Bums, hoboes, the mob, the rabble, the riffraff, may be recruited to do the street fighting and the manor burning of revolutions, but they emphatically do not make, do not run, revolutions— not even proletarian revolutions.

IV. *Character and Dispostion*

We now face a much more difficult task, one where our information is neither so objective nor so readily catalogued as our information about the social and economic status of revolutionists. This is the problem—psychological at bottom—of seeing how far these revolutionists belong to types which are normally viewed by John Jones as queer, eccentric, or downright mad. We here assume, contrary to Marx and Durkheim, that some reduction from sociology to psychology is possible and significant. Now one might quite justifiably argue *a priori* that a wholly contented man could not possibly be a revolutionist. But the trouble is that there are so many ways of being discontented, as well as contented, on this earth. Indeed, the cruder Marxists, and the cruder classical economists, make an almost identical error: they both assume that economics deals exhaustively with whatever makes men happy or miserable. Men have many incentives to action which the economist, limited to the study of men's rational actions, simply cannot include in his work. They observably do a great deal that simply makes no sense at all, if we assume them to be guided *wholly* by any conceivable rational economic motive: nearly starving in the British Museum to write *Das Kapital,* for instance, or seizing deserts under the comforting illusion that trade follows the flag, or making the world quite safe for democracy. Yet clearly a man who takes part in a revolution before it is demonstrably successful is a discontented man, or at least a man shrewd enough to estimate that there are enough discontented men to be forged into a group that can make a revolution. We must make some effort to study the nature of such discontents as seen in individuals.

For here the method of statistical study of large groups of revolutionists, like the Jacobins, will not work. At most these rank and file are names, with profession and perhaps some other indication of social status. Modern interest in social history and the common man has indeed made available a certain number of old diaries and letters of common men, and the Russian Revolution has done its best to keep alive the memory of worker this of the Putilov factory or sailor that of the *Aurora.* Trotsky himself is very eloquent about the role of these heroic workers, sailors, and peasants in his *History of the Russian Revolution,* yet he manages to spend as much of his time on the great names as if he were a mere bourgeois historian. We have, of course, the blanket denunciations—they are hardly descriptions— of one side by another. These are much too emotional as a rule to have any evidential value, except as to the intensity of emotions evoked during revolutions. Even in our own presumably mild revolution one notes a Loyalist who is reported to have said, "It would be a joy to ride through American blood to the hubs of my chariot wheels."

If we cannot for these reasons do much with the political and social psychology of large groups of revolutionists, we can at least look over some of the leaders, hoping that the list we decide upon will not be too unrepresentative. Here at least we can count upon quite a bit of biographical information. Thanks to those admirable works, the *Dictionary of National Biography* and the *Dictionary of American Biography*, we can even sample some of the lesser leaders, the noncommissioned officers of revolutions. The French are now at work on their biographical dictionary, which promises to be even more inclusive than its Anglo-Saxon prototypes, but as it has only just conquered the letter "D," it is not of much use to us. Russia is very difficult indeed from this point of view; there are plenty of brilliant comments on Lenin, Trotsky, and Stalin, but they are also very contradictory. On the lesser figures there is not much trustworthy biographical writing available in the Western languages. We may note here, however, that the extraordinary proliferation of assumed names in the Russian Revolution—Lenin, Stalin, Molotov, Trotsky and so on —probably does not stem with most of these pseudonymous heroes from any feelings of shame for a criminal or disgraceful past. Their crimes were no doubt many, but crimes only against Czarist oppression. Perhaps there was originally some mildly melodramatic notion that these aliases were useful against the Czarist police, but soon they became a mere fashion, a revolutionary fad.

At this point there is some danger of our falling into a dreary catalogue. We shall have to group our facts as we go along under certain human types or characters. This is a process which has been done successfully by a great many shrewd observers of human behavior, from Theophrastus through Molière to Sainte-Beuve and Bagehot. It is perhaps in some respects a more useful way of classifying men than formal psychology or formal sociology has yet worked out. These are not, one hopes, imaginary characters. If they are one-tenth as real as Alceste or Harpagon they are more real than anyone the average sociologist ever dealt with.

We may begin with the gentleman-revolutionist, the "misguided superior," the man born on top, but perversely unwilling to stay there. He is by no means a simple person, and indeed sometimes manages to combine an astonishing number of revolutionary traits. It must be admitted that with many of these misguided superiors in our four societies, dislike for the ways of their class is apparently partly motivated by their inability to succeed in certain activities honored in that class. You need not be a debunking historian to admit that Lafayette revolted against the Court of Louis XVI and Marie Antoinette partly because he was not at home there. And so today, when you find in one of our colleges a well-nurtured youth turned Marxist, or at any rate, existentialist, you can be almost certain that he is not captain of the football team or a fraternity leader. He may indeed be Phi Beta Kappa. This condition we need not here either applaud or condemn, but simply note.

It would, however, be cynical—and hence quite unscientific—to deny that many of these misguided superiors are also moved by what we shall have to call sincere idealism. Their own social group comes to seem to them dissolute, or dull, or cruel, or heartless. They see the possibilities of a better world. They are influenced by the writings of the intellectuals, who have begun their desertion of the established order. They begin to feel acutely their differences from their fathers and grandfathers; they are a generation in revolt. They come to struggle for God's kingdom on this earth. They are usually, of course, uncomfortable on this earth, but for a great many reasons, many of which cannot be simply dismissed as being in the province of the psychiatrist. Shelley, who never actually got a chance at revolution outside poetry, is a familiar example of this sensitive, and often neurotic, type. Dzerzhinsky, the Polish aristocrat who gave life to the terrible Cheka, was a delicate and sincere fanatic. The Marquis de St. Huruge, who figures disreputably in the disorders and street fighting of the French Revolution, was apparently pretty crazy, and not even a gentleman. Condorcet, also a marquis, was a gentleman and scholar, and if he had a good deal of the vanity that goes naturally enough with both, and very little of the sense that sometimes goes with either, he was at heart a kind and sensitive man.

Others desert their class and join the revolution for the ignoble but sometimes socially very useful reason that they think the signs point to the victory of the revolution

Sometimes these men are like the Comte de Mirabeau, rather shady characters who have for some time compromised themselves by irregular lives. Sometimes they are men like Talleyrand, also of the high nobility, careful, sensible men whose main desire is to keep in a position of honor and affluence, and who have no sense of loyalty to abstract notions of right and wrong—or to throne and altar either. And, of course, in the early stages of our revolutions, even the Russian, plenty of rich and influential men of no extraordinary intelligence or stupidity joined the revolution because the revolution was fashionable, and an apparent success. Often these men, who had not been directly in political power, were flattered by the prospect of political power—men like the Duc d'Orléans or Bailly or Tereschenko or Konovalov. But they were essentially fairly ordinary human beings, no fitter subjects for hagiography—Christian, Freudian, or Marxist—than you or I.

If we leave the superiors, those who belong by birth or upbringing to the ruling classes, and who yet side with revolt, and turn to leaders who come from classes below the ruling one, we shall find the same very great variety of what we must tritely call human nature. We shall find fools, scoundrels, idealists, professional revolutionists, diplomatists, lunatics, cowards, and heroes.

Now it would be useless to deny that among those who come to the top in the troubled times of revolution are many who probably never would have been heard of in normal times. Some of these were certainly failures in the old society, men who were unable to attain the objects of their ambition. Marat was a self-educated man of humble stock, with a habit of presenting himself with academic degrees and honorary distinctions his biographers—and even his contemporaries—were not always able to confirm. He tried very hard to storm the Parnassus of the *philosophes,* but was never admitted. Marat, rejected by these admired leaders of opinion, was in 1789 full to the brim with envy and hatred of everything established and esteemed in France. Soon revolutionary journalism was to give him an ample outlet. He became the watchdog of the revolution—a mad watchdog, always in his *l'Ami du Peuple* at work scenting plots against the people, always hating those in power, even when they were of his own party, always crying for blood and revenge. A most unpleasant fellow, no doubt.

Yet the failures are by no means all of the relatively simple type of Marat. Sam Adams was certainly a failure when judged by the standards of thrifty, sober New England. Yet Adams could do certain things extremely well, and if these things were not in the 1770's as financially rewarding as they are now, Adams at least reaped less tangible rewards in his own time—and he did become governor of Massachusetts. Adams's gifts, of course, as they are deftly analyzed in Mr. J. C. Miller's study, are those of the expert propagandist and organizer. It is hard to believe that today the advertising business would leave a man of his parts undiscovered and unrewarded.

Thomas Paine, who managed to involve himself in two revolutions, the American and the French, is still another revolutionist who amounted to very little before his revolutions. When he sailed for America in 1774 he was thirty-eight, certainly no longer a young man. He came from East-Anglian Quaker artisan stock, and had picked up an eighteenth-century education, chiefly in the sciences and in the philosophy of the Enlightenment, while pursuing half-a-dozen different occupations from privateering to staymaking and shopkeeping. He had made an unsuccessful marriage, been in and out of the excise service twice, acquired a reputation as the town "atheist" of Lewes in Sussex, and had led an unsuccessful and somewhat premature attempt at lobbying in the interest of his fellow excisemen. Paine arrived in Philadelphia like many another European, an unsuccessful man looking for a new start. The revolution gave it to him, and *Common Sense* made him a distinguished publicist. Paine was the professional radical, the crusading journalist, the religious rationalist, a man who in quiet times could hardly have been more than another Bradlaugh.

On the other hand, revolution not infrequently brings to the top men of very practical abilities, men of the kind that even cautious and hard-headed conservatives must recognize as worthy of respect. Such men may have lived in obscurity simply because they had not been disturbed;

or they may have been the victims of some such stoppage in the circulation of the elite, the career open to talents, as we noted in a previous chapter. Cromwell is a classic example of a man who might have remained a simple country gentleman with an undistinguished career in the House of Commons had it not been for the Puritan Revolution. Of Washington himself a similar generalization can be made. We shall come back again to this question of the soundness of revolutionary leadership.

So far we have said nothing of the men of blood, of Carrier and the *noyades* of Nantes, of Collot d'Herbois and the *mitraillades* of Lyons, of those to us nameless agents of the Cheka, or of those English agents of the so-called Cromwellian settlement of Ireland who for long-time effectiveness perhaps hold the record among terrorists. We shall later come to the problem of terroristic methods during the crisis period of our revolutions. Here we are simply interested in pointing out that among the personnel of the revolutionists are a number of men who have been singled out by posterity as examples of the kind of monster that comes to the surface in revolutions. No one can deny the fact of such emergence, nor the fact that such men can hardly be understood save with the help of criminology and abnormal psychology.

Carrier himself is a perfectly good example of these men. However much republican apologists may try to soften down the melodramatic accounts his enemies have left of his activities at Nantes, the fact remains that he did so speed up the revolutionary courts that it became much easier to drown convicted persons in batches in the river Loire than to wait for the slow-moving guillotine. Carrier was a provincial lawyer who had got himself elected to the Convention by joining his local club and repeating the stock phrases of the Enlightenment. He was sent as a representative on mission to Nantes, and there power seems to have gone to his head. Moreover, Nantes was on the edge of the always dangerous Vendée, and Carrier may well have been driven to cleaning up his enemies in a group by fear of conspiracy against his own life. He certainly put up a bold front, swaggered about town, gave entertainments, talked big, and left behind him festering hatreds that brought his downfall and condemnation to death after the Terror was over.

Carrier reminds one of gangsters as they appear in American folklore. There is the bravado, the consciousness of life lived at the level of melodrama, the new, crude sense of power, the constant haunting fear of reprisals, the childish immediacy of purpose. What one does not find in Carrier is a specific pathological love of bloodshed, a diseased mind of the sort linked with the name of the Marquis de Sade. Indeed, this latter kind of insanity is more often found among the jailers, thugs, and hangers-on of revolution than among its leaders, even leaders at the level of Carrier. And of course to many people the most revolting acts in general are the acts of revolutionary mobs—the September massacres at Paris in 1792, for instance, which are very closely paralleled by the history of lynching in America. Here there crop up some of the most shocking instances of human cruelty; but they are by no means specifically to be associated with revolutions. Pogroms and lynchings are at least as bad. Revolutions and mobs are not interchangeable terms; you can and usually do have one without the other. The kind of cruelty more properly associated with revolutions is the cruelty—to some people more revolting than the cruelty of mobs—of judicial murders done in cold blood, and on principle, as in the recrudescence of terror in Russia after the assassination of Kirov in 1934 (the "Yezhov period").

There is another type commonly, but erroneously, held to come to the top in revolutions. This is the crackbrained schemer, the fantastic doctrinaire, the man who has a crazy gadget which will bring Utopia. Briefly, perhaps, in the honeymoon stage the lunatic fringe has its innings, and in the English Revolution rather more than its innings, at least in print. But revolutions are a serious business, not to be distracted by eccentricities. Once the line of revolutionary orthodoxy is established—and though as we shall see it is a grim and rigid line, it is not a crazy and aberrant one—once this orthodoxy is established the lunatics, mild or serious, are pretty well kept down. There are Marxist revolutions, natural-rights revolutions, but none for the Single Tax, Social Credit, Theosophy, Vegetarianism, or

Extra Sensory Perception. It is only your very stable societies, like Victorian England, that can afford to turn a Hyde Park over to the lunatic fringe. Even if you think Cromwell, Washington, Robespierre, Napoleon, Lenin, and Stalin all belong to this lunatic fringe, you will have to admit that in their day of power they clamped down pretty hard on other and discordant lunatics.

Nor is it possible to isolate a revolutionary type labeled "criminal," "degenerate," and neatly conforming to some anthropometric standards. Attempts to do this sort of thing have certainly been made. There are probably those who hold that revolutionists have a fixed cephalic index, or that they are predominantly dark-haired. Certainly there are many revolutionists who, like Carrier, behave as criminals behave in stable societies; but the proportion of such revolutionists does not seem extraordinarily high.

A more characteristic revolutionary type is the disputatious, contrary-minded person who loves to stand out from the crowd of conformists. Indeed, one of our revolutionary groups, the English Puritans, was filled with this especially rugged anarchism. Not only do individuals stand out in this respect; the group as a whole sets itself off deliberately from the great and the fashionable. As a social historian has written:

> Whatever was in fashion is what the Puritan would not wear. When ruffs were in vogue, he wore a large falling band; when pickadillies [ruffs] were out of request [1638], and wide falling bands of delicate lawn edged with fine lace came in, he wore a very small band. Fashionable shoes were wide at the toe; his were sharp. Fashionable stockings were, as a rule, of any color except black; his were black. His garters were short, and, before all, his hair was short. Even at the end of Elizabeth's reign, short hair was a mark of Puritanism.

The type is seen most clearly, however, in certain individuals. John Lilburne, the English Leveller, is virtue incarnate and uncomfortable. He seems to have come of a family of rugged individuals, for his father, a gentleman of

Durham, is said to have been the last Englishman to have recourse to the feudal right to ask for judgment through ordeal by combat in a civil suit. John was steadily addicted to contention, and attacked Presbyterians and Independents as bitterly as he had earlier attacked the Court. He seems to have preserved a good deal of social pride along with that intellectual and spiritual pride which is one of the marks of the English Puritan. On trial in 1653, he told his judge, a self-made man of artisan background who had risen with Cromwell, that "it was fitter for him [the judge] to sell thimbles and bodkins than to sit in judgment on a person so much his superior." Henry Marsten, the regicide, who ought to have been a good judge of such matters, said that if the world were emptied of all but John Lilburne, Lilburne would quarrel with John and John would quarrel with Lilburne.

Lilburne's motives were no doubt of the highest. He believed in absolute democracy, and his platform of manhood suffrage, biennial parliaments, religious tolerance, equality before the law, was one day to secure pretty complete acceptance in England. But in 1645 only a very doctrinaire person, only a fanatic, could have held this platform possible of immediate realization. Lilburne was not only a disputatious man; he was what the world commonly calls an idealist, and suggests a consideration of a type which occurs very frequently in these revolutions. It does not seem altogether wise to single out any one type as the perfect revolutionist, but if you must have such a type, then you will do well to consider, not the embittered failure, not the envious upstart, not the bloodthirsty lunatic, but the idealist. Idealists, of course, are in our own times the cement of a stable, normal society. It is good for us all that there should be men of noble aspirations, men who have put behind them the dross of this world for the pure word, for the idea and the ideal as the noblest philosophers have known them. But in normal times such idealists do not seem, at least in Western society, to occupy positions of power and responsibility. In normal times today we look up to our idealists, and occasionally give them prizes and honorary degrees, but we do not choose them to rule over us. We notably refuse to let them make our foreign policies.

Indeed, one of the distinguishing marks of a revolution may well be that in revolutionary times the idealist at last gets a chance to try and realize his ideals. Revolutions are full of men who hold very high standards of human conduct, the kind of standards which have for several thousand years been described by some word or phrase which has the overtones that "idealistic" has for us today. There is no need for us to worry over the metaphysical, nor even the semantic, implications of the term. We all know an idealist when we see one, and certainly when we hear one.

Robespierre would have been an idealist in any society. There is a familiar story of how the young Robespierre resigned a judgeship rather than inflict the death penalty, which ran counter to his humanitarian eighteenth-century upbringing. Historians have pretty well destroyed that story, as they have so many others from Washington and the cherry tree to Alfred and the cakes. But, except in the very narrowest and least useful senses of the word, such stories are in many important ways usually "true." This story about Robespierre suggests that he was a good child of the Enlightenment. One need only read some of his speeches, full of the simplicities, the moral aphorisms, the aspirations of that often innocent age, to realize that he was quite capable of resigning, or buying, a judgeship rather than abandon his ideals. One of his most famous bits of oratory is: "Let the colonies perish rather than a principle!" (*Périssent les colonies plutôt qu'un principe!*) He did, indeed, kill for his ideals.

Those ideals, as they got formed by 1793, may seem to us somewhat less than heroic, and they were certainly bolstered by a good deal of personal ambition and sheer vanity in Robespierre. But there they were: Robespierre wanted a France where there should be neither rich nor poor, where men should not gamble, or get drunk, or commit adultery, cheat, or rob, or kill—where, in short, there would be neither petty nor grand vices—a France ruled by upright and intelligent men elected by the universal suffrage of the people, men wholly without greed or love of office, and delightedly stepping down at yearly intervals to give place to their successors, a France at peace with herself and the world—but surely this is enough? Robespierre's personal rectitude is now hardly questioned even by historians hostile to what he stood for; in his own day, and especially immediately after his fall, he was accused of almost every possible crime and moral delinquency. He seems actually not even to have had any of the fashionable vices—no drink, no gaming, no women. Modern historians claim to have evidence that for a brief time in Paris he kept a mistress. If he did, one supposes it must have been out of motives of fancied hygiene; or possibly for a few weeks the country lawyer had ideas of living as did the fashionable Parisians. The Robespierre of the Terror, however, had certainly put such ideas behind him, and was, as the Incorruptible, a living symbol of the Republic of Virtue in his public and private life.

Now this idealist type is by no means simple. Cromwell should clearly not be listed primarily under this category, and yet there is something of the puritanical "seeker" in Cromwell, something that makes his tortuous policy—indeed his double-dealing—very hard to understand if you insist on seeing human beings as logically consistent wholes. Both Lenin and Trotsky are strange compounds of idealism and realism. This coupling of idealism and realism does not mean simply that they both on occasion could use realistic methods to attain ends dictated by their ideals. Robespierre, Cromwell, Gladstone, or Woodrow Wilson could do that. It means that they were also capable of pursuing realistic immediate ends. Lenin, of course, was a very skillful propagandist and organizer, with a great deal of what we shall have to call executive ability. But, at least in 1917, he seems to have thought that world-wide revolution was just around the corner, and that absolute economic equality could be introduced immediately in Russia. The New Economic Policy of 1921 is a clear indication that Lenin would not pursue his ideals to the bitter end of defeat and martyrdom.

Trotsky had one of the best critical minds of any Marxist, was even capable, at moments, of a kind of skepticism about his own aims. The Civil War of 1917-21 in Russia gave convincing proof of his abilities both as an orator and as an executive under pressure. Yet the Trotsky of the exile years seemed to be howling for the moon, which is one definition, perhaps too unkind, of idealism. Had Trotsky remained in power he might indeed have made his peace with bureaucracy, inequality, socialism-in-one-country, Thermidorean decadence, personal rule, and all the other evils he later associated with the name of Stalin. And yet it seems not unlikely that this intransigence of Trotsky's, this insistence on bringing heaven immediately to earth, this unwillingness to accommodate his aims to human weakness, or if you like, to human nature, help to explain why he did not last in post-revolutionary Russia.

Sentimental idealism was of course distinctly out of fashion in the Russia of 1917. The harsh realities, or at any rate the harsh *formulas*, of Marxist Socialism had replaced the naïve hopes with which the French Revolution had set out to make this a better world. In both Lenin and Trotsky you can trace this desire to seem to be hard-boiled, and it will not do to imply that they did not in some ways succeed. It is quite clear that Stalin so succeeded. There is one pure idealist among the earlier Russian leaders, however, one who presents us with still another variant of the type. That is Lunacharsky, long Commissar for Education, the artist and man of culture of the movement. Lunacharsky, in spite of his past as a revolutionary agitator, was unquestionably a softie. He possessed the ability to talk movingly about life and education and art, and carried over into a century where it seemed a little strange something of Rousseau or of *Paul et Virginie*. The world should be grateful to him, however, for he helped greatly to prevent the wholesale destruction of works of art identified offhand with a dissolute capitalistic and Christian past.

Mr. Eric Hoffer in his interesting book on mass movements, *The True Believer*, concludes that revolutions are prepared by "men of words"—in our terms, the intellectuals who have transferred allegiance—brought to fulfillment by "fanatics"—Robespierre for instance—and finally tamed, reduced to the measure of ordinary societies by "practical men of action"—Cromwell, Bonaparte, Stalin. The "men of words" he finds are unusually gifted intellectuals filling the usual role of the intellectual in Western society, complaining against this harsh world, but not themselves at all suited for the rough work of actual revolution; and the "men of action" he again finds are essentially like men of action in all times, anxious to get the practical tasks of government carried out. The characteristic and critical factor in revolutionary mass leadership he finds to be the "fanatic" who is most often, Mr. Hoffer holds, the balked creative intellectual, the man who has not succeeded in impressing his fellow men with his depth and insight as thinker and artist. Marat the neglected scientist, Robespierre the dabbler in essay and verse at Arras, Lenin the ambitious philosophical thinker who would outdo Marx, or at least Plekhanov, Mussolini the would-be-intellectual, Hitler the man who failed as a painter, most of the Nazi crew of leaders, all fill neatly his category. Their fanaticism is nurtured on their sense of personal failure in the creative art they sought to excel in. Now in their revolutionary role they want to destroy a society that does not appreciate them. They are indeed idealists, but embittered, demonic, inhuman idealists, self-centered beyond the decencies of philosophy, *alienated* intellectuals unhappily placed in positions of power.

It should be noted here that revolutionists of all kinds and temperaments have over the last few centuries gained a good deal of sheer technical skills, in part at least by the study of past revolutions. Elizabeth Eisenstein has singled out Filippo Buonarroti, who began his lifework in the last days of the French Revolution during the Babeuf "conspiracy," as the first professional revolutionary. He is certainly a good choice, for he made a career of planning and preaching revolution, though he can hardly be said to have been a major factor in producing one. With Lenin, Trotsky, and even earlier—with some of the men of 1848 and 1870—the technical skills do help get results. But unless he is no more than a man of words and poses, the professional revolutionist is hardly a single psychological type.

There is, finally, the man who can hold crowds spellbound, the revolutionary orator. He may be listed as an idealist, because although part of his role is to egg the crowd on to acts of violence, he is even more typically the soother, the preacher, the ritual-maker, the man who holds the crowd together. In this role his words need hardly have any meaning at all, but commonly they can be analyzed out into pleasant aspirations and utterances. Much of Robespierre comes under this head, as do Patrick Henry, Vergniaud, Tseretelli. The type, of course, exists in all normal societies, and is usually esteemed. Zinoviev seems in the Russian Revolution to have borne some such role. Lenin realized how useful Zinoviev was as an orator and even as a kind of Petrograd boss, but he seems to have had a pretty complete contempt for his sense and intelligence.

v. *Summary*

To sum up, it should by now be clear that it takes almost as many kinds of men and women to make a revolution as to make a world. It is probable that, especially in their crisis periods, our revolutions threw up into positions of prominence and even of responsibility men of the kind who would in stable societies not attain similar positions. Notably, great revolutions would appear to put extreme idealists during the crisis periods in possession of power they do not ordinarily have. They would seem also to give scope for special talents, such as Marat had, for yellow journalism and muckraking of a very lively sort. They certainly create a number of empty places to fill, and give an opportunity to clever young men who may also be unscrupulous. They probably ensure a bit more public attention, for a while at least, to the chronic rebel and complainer, as well as to the lunatic fringe of peddlers of social and political nostrums.

But they do not re-create mankind, nor do they even make use of a completely new and hitherto suppressed set of men and women. In all four of our revolutions, even in the Russian Revolution, the rank and file was composed of quite ordinary men and women, probably a bit superior to their less active fellows in energy and willingness to experiment, and in the English, American, and French revolutions, even in their crisis periods, people of substantial property. These revolutionists were not in general afflicted with anything the psychiatrist could be called in about. They were certainly not riffraff, scoundrels, scum of the earth. They were above all *not* worms turning. Nor were their leaders by any means an inferior lot suddenly elevated to positions of power which they could not worthily occupy. There is no question that in the turmoil of revolutions a good many scoundrels rise to the top—though they can also rise to the top without benefit of revolution, as a glance at some of the phases of either the Grant or the Harding administrations should amply prove. But the level of ability, of ability not with moral overtones, but in a purely technical sense, the ability to handle men and to administer a complex social system, the level of ability suggested by names like Hampden, Pym, Cromwell, Washington, John Adams, Hamilton, Jefferson, Mirabeau, Talleyrand, Carnot, Cambon, Danton, Lenin, Trotsky, Stalin, is certainly very high.

All this by no means amounts to asserting the paradox that there are no real differences between revolutions and ordinary times. On the contrary, especially in their crisis periods, revolutions are like nothing else on earth. But you cannot altogether explain the differences between societies in revolution and societies in equilibrium by suggesting that a whole new crew operates during a revolution; by saying, if you dislike a particular revolution and all its works, that the scoundrels and the bums put it over on the good souls; or if you happen to like and approve a particular revolution, that the heroes and sages turned out the corrupt old gang. It just isn't as simple as all that. Since on the whole the evidence would seem to show that revolutionists are more or less a cross section of common humanity, an explanation for the undoubted fact that during certain phases of a revolution they behave in a way we should not expect such people to behave, must be sought in changes worked on them by the conditions they live under, by their revolutionary environment.

Chapter

5

THE RULE OF
THE MODERATES

1. The Problem of the Moderates

In the summer of 1792 Lafayette, with some of his officers, left the French Army and passed over to the Austrian lines. He was promptly put in prison by the Austrians, to whom he was a dangerous firebrand of revolution. Lafayette was, however, a good deal more fortunate than many of his fellow heroes of 1789 who elected to stay in France, and who were guillotined as dangerous reactionaries and counter-revolutionists. Fedor Linde, a moderate Socialist who in April, 1917, moved the Finnish Regiment to a mutinous demonstration against the pro-Ally and still more moderate Miliukov, was later sent to the front as a government commissar under Kerensky and there was lynched by mutinous soldiers who refused to obey his commands. In 1647 Denzil Holles, of whom we took note briefly back in 1629, as he was helping to hold down the Speaker in his chair, was with ten other Presbyterian members excluded from Parliament for "endeavoring to overthrow the rights and liberties of the subjects." He did indeed return briefly to his seat again in 1648, but was soon forced to flee to France to save his life. A famous phrase of the French moderate Vergniaud puts the thing neatly: "The revolution, like Saturn, devours its children."

The honeymoon was in these revolutions short; very soon after the old regime had fallen there began to be evident signs that the victors were not so unanimous about what was to be done to remake the country as had appeared in the first triumphant speeches and ceremonies. Those who had directly taken over the mechanism of government were in all four of our societies men of the kind usually called moderates. They represented the richer, better known, and higher placed of the old opposition to the government, and it is only to be expected that they should take over from that government. Indeed, as we have seen, their assumption of responsibility is almost a spontaneous act. So strong is this feeling that the moderates should take over power that it prevailed even in Russia in February, 1917. Not the socialists, but the mere "liberals" headed by Prince Lvov, became the provisional government.

The moderates, once in power, turned out to have less homogeneity and party discipline than they seemed to have when they were in opposition. They were faced with the difficult task of reforming existing institutions, or making a new constitution, and taking care at the same time of the ordinary work of governing. They were also confronted very soon with armed enemies, and found themselves engaged in a foreign or civil war, or in both together. They found against them an increasingly strong and intransigent group of radicals and extremists who insisted that the moderates were trying to stop the revolution, that they had betrayed it, that they were as bad as the rulers of the old regime—indeed, much worse, since they were traitors as well as fools and scoundrels. After a period, brief in Russia, longer in France and England, there came a show of force between moderates and extremists, a show of force in many ways quite like that earlier one between the old government and the revolutionists, and the moderates were beaten. They fled into exile, they were put into prison ultimately to face the scaffold, guillotine, or firing squad, or if they were lucky or obscure enough, they dropped out of sight and were forgotten. The extremists in their turn took power.

This process was not quite the same in the American Revolution, where it may be said that extremists like the

Independents, the Jacobins, and the Bolsheviks, did not attain undivided rule. Nevertheless, as we shall see, in America rather earlier in the revolutionary process a struggle between moderates and radicals had been fought out, and had ended with victory for the radicals. The fruit of that victory was the Declaration of Independence.

We may say then that in all our revolutions there is a tendency for power to go from Right to Center to Left, from the conservatives of the old regime to the moderates to the radicals or extremists. As power moves along this line, it gets more and more concentrated, more and more narrows its base in the country and among the people, since at each important crisis the defeated group has to drop out of politics. To put it in another way: after each crisis the victors tend to split into a more conservative wing holding power and a more radical one in opposition. Up to a certain stage, each crisis sees the radical opposition triumphant. The details of this process vary naturally from revolution to revolution. Its stages are not identical in length or in their time-sequence. In America power never got as far Left as it did in the other countries.

Finally, it must be insisted that the word "moderate" as here used of groups in these four specific revolutions has overtones not present when the word is used of politically stable societies. Both in methods and in aims our revolutionary moderates often behave quite immoderately. You can defend the position that the Presbyterians, not the Independents, the Gironde, not the Mountain, even perhaps the Mensheviks, not the Bolsheviks, were the extremists. Certainly the last three of each of these opposing factions came out in the end as defenders of order and authority. But in the jockeying of violent revolutionary politics the first three of each were at least maneuvered into a position where they were attacked from both Right and Left. Perhaps the term "compromisists," fastened on Mensheviks, Social Revolutionaries, Narodniks and the rest by the triumphant Bolsheviks, is an even better term than "moderate" for the reality we are in this chapter attempting to fix in words.

At any rate this struggle between moderates and extremists is a stage in our revolutions as definite as those we have studied in previous chapters, and by its very existence provides us with a useful if somewhat simple uniformity. Before we attempt to make refinements in this observation, before we try to discern uniformities in the conduct of moderates and extremists, we must review briefly the course of events during the rule of the moderates.

II. *Events During the Rule of the Moderates*

With the outbreak of the Civil War in the summer of 1642, Royalists and Parliamentarians stood opposed in arms. By the Battle of Marston Moor in 1644, and certainly by that of Naseby in 1645, the Royalist cause had become, in a military sense, hopeless. But almost from the first clear break with Charles, the Parliamentarians had won their revolution. The Royalists did but play more effectively the role played in America by the Loyalists, in France by the Royalists and clericals in the provinces, the *émigrés* abroad, in Russia by the numerous White Armies which opposed the Bolsheviks until 1921. We are not here so much interested in the Royalists as in the Parliamentarians. Within these latter there is from 1642 on an increasingly evident division between groups which we may call roughly moderates and extremists.

The division is not at first a simple one between two parties. At the extreme right of the Parliamentarians were a few moderate Episcopalians just touched with puritan notions, and usually also constitutional monarchists. Many of this group were on the whole indifferent to religious questions, felt that church matters would settle themselves decently if the political difficulties could be adjusted. Between these men and the moderate Royalists, who somewhat reluctantly chose to stand with their king, there was actually very little difference. Next came the great moderate party, Presbyterian in religion, puritan in ethics, monarchist at heart, but monarchist in a constitutional sense. The left wing of the Presbyterians, early disillusioned with the idea of monarchy by their hatred for Charles, merged easily with the main group of the extremists. These in the English Revolution are called the Independents, extreme Calvinists who insisted upon the independence of each separate congregation. Their notions of church government were substantially those well known in this country as Congregationalism. With them for most political purposes were other groups that subsequently made up the English nonconformists or dissenters—notably the Baptists. The New Model Army, through which these radicals made themselves an effective force in the revolution, contained individuals espousing almost every conceivable kind of evangelical religious belief, and a good many varieties of economic and social beliefs. But the group did work as a group, and its core was certainly Independent. To the left were other groups, Levellers, Diggers, Fifth Monarchy men, whom we shall consider in a later chapter.

Now the fact that Episcopalians, Presbyterians, and Independents are in the English Revolution respectively conservatives, moderates, and extremists, is a bit confusing to the modern reader. For the old-fashioned idealist, these seventeenth-century Englishmen are fighting over religious matters, fighting for ideals, and he finds it absurd to equate them with Frenchmen fighting for worldly liberty, equality, and fraternity, and shocking to compare them with Russians fighting for crude economic interests. On the other hand, the modern convert to the economic interpretation of history is likely to regard these religious differences as mere "ideologies," or pretexts for a quarrel which was really a simple economic one. To him, the Presbyterians were small gentry or bourgeois businessmen, the Independents petty bourgeois traders, artisans, and yeomen farmers who quarreled after they had disposed of the feudal upper classes. Both the idealist and the materialist are here clearly wrong. Politics, economics, church government, and theology are inextricably mingled in the minds and hearts of seventeenth-century Englishmen. Their conflicts are conflicts between human beings, not between the abstractions of the philosopher, the economist, or the sociologist. We must here observe the ways in which these conflicts worked out. From many points of view, it is profitable to regard these conflicts as exhibiting the sequence of domination first by conservatives, then by moderates, then by extremists. Naturally these conservatives, moderates, and extremists were not identical with similar groups in later revolutions. As compared with the men of 1789 or of 1917, they read different books, disputed over different ideas, just as they wore different clothes. Yet the course of their revolution does display a striking identity with our other revolutions in the relation between political organization and human temperaments. The Presbyterian "compromisists" were pushed aside by more determined if not more unscrupulously "extremist" men, just as were the Feuillants and Girondins in France and the Kadets and compromisist Socialist groups in Russia. In America, the career of John Dickinson, a moderate who refused to sign the Declaration of Independence, is revealing. Though he was never harmed or even imprisoned, he was bitterly attacked, and never attained political power again.

Under the leadership of the Westminster Assembly, a Presbyterian synod which began its meetings in the summer of 1643, that part of England under parliamentary control was brought under the famed Scottish Covenant. Crosses, images, crucifixes were torn down; the stained glass was removed from the churches; sermons were lengthened; and the liturgy simplified. Parliament became the supreme law of the land. But already there were signs that the Presbyterian rule was not to go unchallenged. Marston Moor was not a Presbyterian victory. It was won by Cromwell and his "Ironsides"; and these men were not good Presbyterians. They were Independents, and some were Anabaptists, Antinomians, and the like. It is said that someone complained to Cromwell because one of his officers was an Anabaptist, and received the reply, "Admit he be, shall that render him incapable to serve the public? Take heed of being too sharp . . . against those to whom you can object little but that they square not with you in every opinion concerning matters of religion."

When the New Model Army was constructed from the nucleus of Cromwell's Ironsides, and had won the Battle of Naseby, army and Parliament, Independent and Presbyterian, extremists and moderates, found themselves in opposition on various questions, notably on religious toleration and on what was to be done about Charles I. The Presbyterians wanted an established State Church, built on their own notions of church government and theology, with a minimum of toleration toward papists and prelatists on the right and the sects on the left. And they most certainly wanted a king, even if that king were Charles Stuart. The Independents wanted what they called toleration. They certainly didn't mean what a nineteenth-century Englishman or an American meant by religious toleration, and when they got into power they were very far from practicing toleration, even in the sense in which they had preached it. But at least while they were in opposition they agreed that religious belief was a personal matter and that the State should not seek to impose identical religious practices and organization on its citizens. As for the king, most of them by 1645 were sure Charles Stuart would never do. Cromwell was probably never a doctrinaire republican, but a great many of his men certainly were.

No single event marks exactly the transfer of power from the moderates to the extremists in England. The process had gone pretty far when Cornet Joyce of the army in June, 1646, seized the King at Holmby House as he was about to yield to the Parliament and consent to govern for three years as a Presbyterian king. It was almost completed when two months later Parliament at the dictation of the army reluctantly agreed to the exclusion of eleven of its own members, conspicuous leaders of the Presbyterian group. Charles took the occasion of the quarrel to attempt to further his own interests. His complicated intrigues ended in nothing better than a brief war between the Scottish Presbyterians and the Cromwellians, in which for a moment the moderates could look up hopefully. Cromwell defeated the Scots at Preston Pans in August, 1648, and his army was in undisputed control in Great Britain. After this the formal end of the moderates at Pride's Purge in December was unimportant. Colonel Pride and a few soldiers were stationed at the door of the House of Commons to turn back the unsuitable members as they came. Ninety-six Presbyterians were thus excluded, leaving a group of fifty or sixty regular voting members on whom the extremists could rely. The Long Parliament had become the Rump.

In America the conflict never took quite such clear lines. We may say that the conservatives were those Loyalists who never really complained about the imperial government—and who, like Jonathan Boucher, preached against the agitators—the moderates those merchants and prosperous landowners who in a sense began the whole movement by their agitation against the Stamp Act, and the radicals that by no means united group which finally put through the Declaration of Independence. There was thus a kind of three-way struggle going on among these groups in the ten years preceding the outbreak of hostilities with the British Army. In this struggle the radicals exhibited an extraordinary technical skill in the practical politics of revolution. As John Adams later wrote of the organizations which, starting with local committees of correspondence and committees of safety, worked up to the continental congresses: "What an engine! France imitated it and produced a revolution. . . . And all Europe was inclined to imitate it for the same revolutionary purpose."

The radicals really won their decisive victory by organizing as they did the first Continental Congress in 1774. Professor A. M. Schlesinger, Sr., admirably summarizes the work of this Congress.

> The radicals had achieved several important ends. They had reproduced on a national scale a type of organization and a species of tactics that in many parts of British America had enabled a determined minority to seize control of affairs . . . they had snatched from the merchant class the weapons which the latter had fashioned to advance their own selfish interests in former years, and had now reversed the weapons on them, in an attempt to secure ends desired solely by the radicals.

The taking of the Bastille on July 14, 1789, in France sealed the defeat of the most conservative group, the true Royalists. The victorious revolutionists did not long remain in harmony, and the process of transfer of power to the left began in a few months. In October of the same year the King and Queen were riotously brought back to Paris from Versailles in what are known as the October Days. These events sent into exile the leaders of the moderate conservatives, men like Mounier who greatly admired the

English Constitution, and wished France to have a bicameral legislature with a House of Lords and a House of Commons, and a real king. For the next few years a group of moderates centering about men like Mirabeau, Lafayette, and the Lameths, were opposed by a group of radicals centering around men—Pétion, Robespierre, Danton, Brissot—soon to be leaders of the rival republican groups of Gironde and Mountain, but at present more or less united against the moderates. The moderates succeeded in making the Constitution, and starting the new regime off. But war between France and the Central European powers of Austria and Prussia broke out, France was invaded and Paris threatened, certain provisions of the Constitution, notably those concerning religion and the monarchy, failed to work well, Louis himself was suspected of treason by many of his subjects, and in the general political turmoil the active and well-organized radicals overthrew the monarchy in the famous attack on the Tuileries Palace in Paris on August 10, 1792.

Avowed monarchists and such mild reformers and liberals as Lafayette were thus excluded from power, and France became a republic. But the final and critical defeat of the moderates in France is better placed on June 2, 1793. In matters of this sort, as in any splitting up of historical events into periods, there may be legitimate differences of interpretation. Conservatives, moderates, and radicals and extremists are not in any of our societies absolutely clear-cut and definite groups, nor is the transference of power from one to another very often a single event agreed upon by all to be such. You may feel that no moderate could have voted the end of the French monarchy. Nonetheless it would seem that the right wing of the republicans, known to history as the Girondins, and to their contemporaries as the Brissotins, were really moderates upon whom circumstances forced actions which were to them disagreeably radical and extreme. Notably they did not wish the death of the King. They were mostly prosperous bourgeois, lawyers, and intellectuals, and after the trial of the King in January, 1793, they became very sure that the revolution had gone far enough, that it ought to be stopped. Whatever their past, whatever their philosophical radicalism, they had now become moderates. By the early months of 1793 they had lost control of the Paris Jacobin Club and with it most of the other revolutionary clubs and the whole network of organizations which had helped the radicals achieve their ends in the early days of the revolution. They could not command the support of the hesitating and more or less neutral mass of deputies in the Convention who were called the Plain. Their enemies were better organized, more aggressive, and perhaps more unscrupulous. They were certainly more successful.

Just as with the Presbyterians in England, there came the demand that these now moderate leaders be excluded from the Convention and brought under arrest. In a test of strength in the Convention on June 2, 1793, the extremists took care to surround the meeting place of that body with sympathetic Parisian militiamen, back of whom assembled a large and hostile crowd. The Convention tried to stand on their representative dignity and to refuse to permit the arrest of the twenty-two members demanded by the radical Mountain. Headed by their president, they solemnly marched out to ensure that their position be respected as the embodiment of the will of the people. The deputies made the circuit of the gardens, finding an unyielding row of bayonets at every gate, and a "people" with a temporary will of its own. They returned indoors and voted the arrest of the twenty-two Girondins. The radical Mountain was now in undisputed command.

Events moved rather faster in Russia, but their sequence is almost identical with those in England and in France. The first provisional government headed nominally by Prince Lvov, really by Miliukov, was made up mostly of Kadets, the left wing of middle-class groups in the old duma, but no more than "progressives," "liberals," or "democrats" in Western political terminology. There were several representatives of more conservative groups, and only one Socialist, Kerensky. After a life of less than two months, this government broke down over the question of continuing an "imperialist" war on the side of the allies, with whom the United States was now associated. Miliukov was forced out for too great compliance with the wishes of the allies, and a number of Mensheviks and

Social-Revolutionaries accepted positions in the new government. In July Kerensky took the formal leadership after a crisis, and in September the Kadets finally withdrew altogether, leaving Kerensky at the head of a very shaky moderate Socialist government.

The Socialists who thus consented to co-operate with bourgeois governments in the prosecution of the war were christened by the Bolsheviks "compromisist." In the specific Russian situation, these Social-Revolutionaries, Trudoviks, Narodniks, Mensheviks, must be called moderates. They did not hope to introduce the dictatorship of the proletariat. They wanted to win the war, and they were willing to make use of parliamentary methods to secure social reforms. They had long been distrustful of the Kadets, but under the pressure of events they consented to co-operate with them. The Kadets themselves suffered the fate of the Puritan Episcopalians and the Feuillants; they were pushed out by their collaborators to the Left.

The Bolsheviks refused to take part in any of these governments. They insisted that the bourgeois revolution of February must sooner or later be followed by the proletarian revolution Marx had preached and predicted. Lenin, who returned from a Swiss exile in April to enjoy a few months of bourgeois freedom, decided that the proletarian revolution might be brought off in Russia. His party was by no means unanimously agreed, but his leadership kept the small band together, and the blunders of the compromisists, together with the heritage of defeat and disorganization, played into his hands. In July a premature rising of workers in Petrograd was apparently given local and reluctant leadership by some of the party, and its failure sent Lenin into hiding, and Trotsky and Lunacharsky to prison. The subsequent swing of the pendulum to the Right ended with the abortive attempt of General Kornilov to march on Petrograd, and in this whole process the Bolsheviks gradually acquired new courage and a new following. Lenin from hiding held a guiding hand. Trotsky was released and elected president of a Petrograd soviet now in Bolshevik control. Lenin, back secretly in Petrograd, presided at a final meeting of the party Central

Committee, and an insurrection was decided upon. In a masterly exhibition of revolutionary technique, a military revolution committee made sure of the Petrograd garrison, other groups contrived to hamstring the press and communications, and on the agreed day the Bolsheviks took over Petrograd with astonishingly little difficulty and almost no bloodshed. Even the siege of the Winter Palace, which forms the high point of the uprising, has a comic-opera touch. The October Revolution in Petrograd was almost as bloodless as Pride's Purge or the *journée* of June 2, 1793, the corresponding events in the English and French revolutions. In Moscow there was real fighting, but there, too, the Bolsheviks were successful within a week. Kerensky fled, and the rule of the moderates in Russia was over.

III. *Dual Sovereignty*

The Russian Revolution affords the neatest example of a uniformity that lies beyond the somewhat superficial uniformity of sequence of power from conservatives to moderates to extremists, from Right to Center to Left. This is at once an institution and a process; or better, a process that works through a very similar set of institutions. Theorists and historians of the Russian Revolution refer to it as the *dvoevlastie*, a word usually translated as dual power, but containing overtones that make it better translated, perhaps, as dual sovereignty. We must go briefly into the general situation to which this word refers.

The problem of sovereignty has long been in itself sufficient to keep hundreds of political philosophers busy and happy. In a normal Western society, it may well be difficult or impossible to locate any one person, or group of persons, who possesses the final, authoritative power to decide questions concerning what the society is to do. The pluralists would seem to be, from the point of view of description of social processes, quite right. Even the broader political policies of a modern state seem to be arrived at by so elaborately natural a process of adjusting the desires of conflicting groups, that to say a single and identifiable "sovereign" determines these policies is nonsense. And yet in a normal society, even in an open democratic society with division of powers, there is at least one co-ordinated chain of institutions through which conflicting groups do finally adjust their conflicts, for the moment at least, in action. That co-ordination may seem inefficient and irrational when academically analyzed, and it may well be so complicated that even the politicians who make it work do not understand it. For men are as often as not unaware of how they do things they do very successfully.

But it does work, and through it questions at issue are decided—or forgotten, which is also a kind of deciding. Those who do not like the decision may try to alter it by a very great variety of action, from agitation to conspiracy or sabotage. Socially powerful or numerous groups may under favoring conditions even go so far as to nullify for a time a given decision: the examples of the Eighteenth Amendment in the United States and of the desegregation of schools in the deep South will occur to everyone. For the most part, however, the decisions are carried out.

When another and conflicting chain of institutions pro-vides another and conflicting set of decisions, then you have a dual sovereignty. Within the same society, two sets of institutions, leaders, and laws demand obedience, not in one single respect, but in the whole interwoven series of actions which make up life for the average man. The resistance to desegregation in the South, the lawlessness of juvenile delinquency, the corruption of many sectors of American politics are by no means examples of dual sovereignty, merely of resistance to law. The conflict between state and federal governments over civil rights in a state like Alabama comes closer to being an instance of dual sovereignty. Were the White Citizens Councils, the Ku Klux Klan, the white trades-unions, and other groups, led by a revolutionary junta, to take over directly part of the *administration* of Alabama, we should have a kind of dual sovereignty, complicated, of course, by the federal structure of our politics; we should, as a matter of fact, have a state of affairs something like that in Russia in the summer of 1917, when the "legal" provisional government was challenged by the "illegal" soviets.

In *all* our revolutions, the legal government finds opposed to it, not merely hostile individuals and parties

—this any government finds—but a rival government, better organized, better staffed, better obeyed. This rival government is of course illegal, but not all of its leaders and followers are from the beginning consciously aiming to supplant the legal government. Very often they think of themselves as merely supplementing it, perhaps also as preserving it in a revolutionary course. Yet a rival government they are, and no mere critics or opponents. At a given revolutionary crisis they step naturally and easily into the place of the defeated government.

This process does indeed begin to work itself out in the old regimes before the first steps in revolution are taken. Puritans in England, Whigs in America, Third Estate in France, the Kadets and compromisist Socialists in Russia, all had organizations that demanded their allegiance and that enabled them to fight the old regime with revolution at least in the back of their minds. But the process is much more clear, more sharply edged at the stage we have now reached.

Once the first stage in revolution is over, the struggle that arises between moderates and extremists comes to be a struggle between two rival governmental machines. That of the moderates, the legal government, has inherited some of the prestige that goes with being established, some of the financial resources—actual or potential—of the old government, most of its liabilities, all of its institutions. Try to alter these latter as it may, it finds them annoyingly persistent, extremely difficult to blot out. The legal government is unpopular with many for the very reason that it is an obvious and responsible government and therefore has to shoulder some of the unpopularity of the government of the old regime.

The illegal government of the extremists, however, has to face no such difficulties. It has the prestige which recent events have given to attackers, to those who can claim to be in the forefront of the revolution. It has, as governments go, relatively few responsibilities. It does not have to try to use, if only temporarily, the worn-out machinery, the institutions of the old regime. It has, on the contrary, for the moment the great advantage of using the efficient machinery gradually constructed by the revolutionists, both moderates and extremists, from the time when they began under the old regime to emerge as a pressure group even, as in Russia, as an underground group of conspirators. Indeed, the final capture of this machinery—or this organization, if you prefer—seems to be what really determines the final victory of the extremists over the moderates, long before that final victory is apparent in events. Why the moderates do not keep control of the organization they have done so much to initiate and to mold is a question that permits of no simple answer. We may hope that some answer will emerge from a more detailed study of the fate of the moderates. We must first, however, see how well the foregoing analysis fits the facts in our four revolutions.

Charles and the Long Parliament were clearly dual sovereigns from the actual outbreak of hostilities in 1642 if not from the very first session of 1640. Once the Civil War was decided against Charles, Parliament, under the control of the moderates, found itself the legal government. But almost immediately it was confronted by the radical New Model Army, which very soon began to take the kind of action that in this world only a government can take. The fact that Charles was still on the scene and the existence of the Scottish Army complicated the situation in the three or four years before the execution of Charles in 1649, but the broad lines of the duel between the newly legal government of the Presbyterian moderates in Parliament and the illegal government of the extremist Independents in the New Model Army are clear.

In America this dual sovereignty is most obvious in the years before the final break in 1776. The lines between the legal and the illegal government were obscured, especially in a colony like Massachusetts, by the fact that town meetings and colonial legislatures were part of the legal government, but were often controlled by men active in the illegal government. Nonetheless, the machinery which culminated in the continental congresses—in themselves illegal bodies—was clearly used by revolutionists against constituted authority.

While the moderates in France, the Feuillants, or constitutional monarchists, still controlled the legislative body and the formal machinery of the centralized state, their increasingly republican opponents controlled the network of Jacobin societies which made up the frame of the other, or illegal, government. Through their control of these societies they worked into the control of many of the units of local government, and from this position of vantage were able to expel the Feuillant moderates and destroy the monarchy. The process was then repeated with the Girondin moderates controlling the legislative body and the Montagnard extremists controlling the important units of the Jacobin network and at least one exceedingly important local governmental unit—the Paris Commune. In the crisis of June 2, 1793, the illegal government again won out over the legal. For a moment in the earlier crisis of August 10, 1792, the legal and the illegal governments of Paris were actually sitting simultaneously in different rooms of the *hôtel de ville*.

In Russia the *dvoevlastie* is plain. The provisional government which emerged from the February Revolution had through its connection with the duma some claim to legitimacy. Though it absorbed more and more Socialists of various stripes in the next six months, thus exhibiting the leftward movement we have found in all our societies, it remained moderate and quite conscious of its legality.

On the other side the Bolsheviks and a few allied radical groups had by late summer obtained control of the network of soviets which was in part a heritage from the abortive revolution of 1905 and stood as an illegal government facing the legal one. Soviet means no more than "council" and had originally in Russia no more connotations than its English equivalent has for us. The soviets were local councils of trades-unionists, soldiers, sailors, peasants, and suitable intellectuals. They sprang up naturally enough with the dissolution of the Czarist power in 1917, all the more since memories of the rising of 1905, in which a St. Petersburg soviet had played a large part, were fresh in the minds of everyone. The Bolsheviks, wisely concentrating on the soviets while the attention of the compromisists was increasingly taken by participation in the legal government, were able to wrest control of key soviets in Petrograd, Moscow, and major industrial towns from the compromisists. There is here a curious detailed parallel with the French Revolution. The final insurrectionary victory of the Bolsheviks was achieved without complete control of the general network of soviets, just as that of the Montagnards was achieved without control of the whole network of Jacobin clubs. In each case control of the most important units of the illegal government was sufficient.

iv. *Weaknesses of the Moderates*

At this stage in revolution, then, the moderates in control of the formal machinery of government are confronted by the extremists, or if you prefer, merely by radical and determined opponents, in control of machinery devised for propaganda, pressure-group work, even insurrection, but now increasingly used as machinery of government. This stage ends with the triumph of the extremists and the merging of the dual sovereignty into a single one. We must now inquire into the reasons for the failure of the moderates in these revolutions to hold power.

There is first the paradox we have previously noted, that in the early stages of revolution the control of the machinery of government is in itself a source of weakness for those who hold such control. Little by little the moderates find themselves losing the credit they had gained as opponents of the old regime, and taking on more and more of the discredit innocently associated by the hopeful many with the status of heir to the old regime. Forced on the defensive, they make mistake after mistake, partly because they are so little used to being on the defensive. They are in a position from which only a superhuman wisdom could extricate them; and the moderates are among the most human of revolutionaries.

Faced with the opposition of more radical groups organized in the network we have called the illegal government, the moderates have broadly but three choices: they may try to suppress the illegal government; they may try to get control of it themselves; or they may let it alone. Actually their policy shifts around among these three policies, combining one with another; in these circumstances, the net effect is to produce a fourth policy, which amounts to a positive encouragement of their enemies in the illegal government.

In the revolutions we are studying the moderates are particularly handicapped in their efforts to suppress these enemy organizations. The revolutions were all made in the name of freedom, were all—even the Russian February Revolution—associated with what the Marxists call a bourgeois individualistic ideology. The moderates found themselves obliged to observe certain "rights" of their enemies —notably those of freedom of speech, of the press, of assembly. What is more, many if not most of the moderates sincerely believed in such rights, held that truth is great and will prevail. Had it not just prevailed against the tyranny of the old regime? Even when under pressure the moderate begins to try to suppress an extremist newspaper, forbid an extremist meeting, jail a few extremist leaders, his conscience troubles him. More important, any unsuppressed extremists raise a mighty howl. The moderates are betraying the revolution; they are using exactly the same methods the villainous tyrants of the old regime had used.

The Russian Revolution is here an excellent example. The Kadets and compromisists between February and October could not conveniently suppress Bolshevik propaganda, nor indeed any form of Bolshevik political activity. When they tried to do so after a premature Bolshevik rising, the street troubles in Petrograd known as the "July Days," they were met by protests from all sorts of people, including notably the Bolsheviks. This was despotism, this was Czarism of the worst sort. Had not the February Revolution brought political freedom, freedom of the press and association, to Russia forever? Kerensky mustn't make use of the kind of weapons the Czars had used. Stalin of course could later use methods worthy of Peter the Great or Ivan the Terrible, but that is only to say that the moderate, the "liberal" phase of the Russian Revolution was unquestionably over by the time Stalin took power. In 1917, however, even had Kerensky been the sort of man who could successfully organize repressive measures—and he plainly was not that sort of man—what we are bound to call public opinion would not in those days have permitted the execution of such measures. Much the same situation is to be found in France, where the Jacobins were permitted free speech and free association, and firmly and publicly insisted on their rights as free men to get ready for a dictatorship by suppressing the "enemies of the fatherland"—that is, what was left of royalists, non-juring priests, active conservatives.

Nor are the moderates more successful in their attempts to get—or rather to retain—control of the machinery which they and the extremists had jointly built up as a means of overthrowing the old regime. For this there seems to be no single preponderant reason. The moderates are, of course, occupied with a good deal of the work of actual governing, and they have less time for army committees or Jacobin clubs or soviet meetings. They feel themselves perhaps a trifle superior to such activity. They are temperamentally unfitted for the rougher and dirtier work of the politics of direct action. They have moral scruples. They are not quite the noble souls historical legend makes out the Girondin moderates in the French Revolution to have been; indeed many of them, like Brissot and Kerensky, have a good many of the gifts of the political manipulator. But they are in power, and they seem to set about quite naturally cultivating the sober virtues that go with power. Such virtues, however, make them inadequate leaders of militant revolutionary societies.

Whatever the explanation, the fact of the uniformity is clear. This particular failure of the moderates is well shown in the French Revolution. The Jacobin network of societies of "Friends of the Constitution" was in its inception hardly to the Left of Lafayette and his friends. When, however, it began to move further to the Left the Fayettists made a few feeble efforts to retain control, and then went off and founded their own society, the Feuillants. The Feuillants, however, could not spread with much success beyond narrow upper-class and intellectual Parisian circles. Later groups founded here and there throughout the country as "Friends of the Monarchy," or "Friends of Peace," tried to compete with the Jacobins, but with very little luck. If they gave bread to the poor, the Jacobins cried out that they were attempting bribery.

If they did nothing, the Jacobins complained that they lacked social conscience. Finally the Jacobins worked out a fairly systematic procedure. They would hire a few hoodlums—sometimes it was not necessary to hire them—to break up a meeting of the rival Friends of Peace, and would then send a deputation to the municipal authorities asking that the Friends of Peace be closed as a public nuisance. The authorities were either Jacobins themselves, or more afraid of the Jacobins than of the Friends of Peace, so that the matter received a suitable revolutionary solution.

Similarly the Presbyterians found themselves powerless to control the spread of Independency, not only in the army, but in local parishes. And in Russia the compromisists found the Bolsheviks formidable in all the important soviets. A detailed study of the Petrograd soviet from February to October will show how cleverly the party of Lenin took advantage of every mistake of its opponents, how successfully it burrowed from within, spreading its control from factory soviets on up until finally the city soviet was captured. Such a study will also show the compromisists gradually losing ground, in spite of the great oratorical gifts of leaders like Tseretelli, Chkheidze, and Kerensky.

There is, indeed, an almost organic weakness in the position of the moderates. They are placed between two groups, the disgruntled but not yet silenced conservatives and the confident, aggressive extremists. There are still freedom of speech and the other political rights, so that even conservatives have a voice. Now the moderates seem in all these revolutions to be following the slogan used so conspicuously for French politics of the *Cartel des Gauches* in 1924, a slogan that still gives difficulties to the noncommunist Left throughout the Western world today: "no enemies to the Left." They distrust the conservatives, against whom they have so recently risen; and they are reluctant to admit that the extremists, with whom they so recently stood united, can actually be their enemies. All the force of the ideas and sentiments with which the moderates entered the revolution give them a sort of twist toward the Left. Emotionally they cannot bear to think of themselves as falling behind in the revolutionary process.

Moreover, many of them hope to outbid the extremists for popular support, to beat them at their own game. But only in normal times can you trust in the nice smooth clichés of politics like "beat them at their own game." The moderates fail by this policy of "no enemies to the Left" to reconcile these enemies to the Left; and they make it quite impossible to rally to their support any of the not yet quite negligible conservatives. Then, after the moderates get thoroughly frightened about the threatening attitude of the extremists, they turn for help to the conservatives, and find there just aren't any on hand and available. They have emigrated, or retired to the country, hopeless and martyred in spirit. Needless to say, a martyred conservative is no longer a conservative, but only another maladjusted soul. This last turn of theirs toward the conservatives, however, finishes the moderates. Alone, unsupported in control of a government as yet by no means in assured and habitual control of a personnel, civil or military, they succumb easily to insurrection. It is significant that Pride's Purge, the French crisis of June 2, 1793, and the Petrograd October Revolution were all hardly more than *coups d'état*.

In the English, French, and Russian revolutions it is possible to distinguish one critical measure around which all these currents converge, a measure which, espoused by the moderates, cuts them off from support on the Right and leaves the radicals in a position to use this very measure against its authors. Such are the Root-and-Branch Bill in the English Revolution, the Civil Constitution of the Clergy in the French, and Order Number One in the Russian.

The Root-and-Branch Bill originated in a petition with 15,000 signatures presented to the House of Commons late in 1640, asking for the abolition of Episcopacy "with all its roots and branches." Naturally the moderate Episcopalians, from Hyde and Falkland to Digby, were against a measure which destroyed their Church; and just as naturally the Presbyterians were inclined to favor it. It is possible that politically minded moderates like Pym might have left the bill alone, but the refusal of the bishops to give up their seats in the House of Lords seems to have determined Pym to support the bill. This espousal made almost every thorough Episcopalian some kind of Royalist, and when the Civil War broke out in 1642 the Presbyterians were stranded on the extreme Right of the party groupings within the region controlled by the Parliamentarians. They could find no possible allies except to the Left. The Independents—and Cromwell had first actually introduced the Root-and-Branch Bill in the House—could now argue that presbyters were no better than bishops, that the reasons which held for the abolition of one held incontrovertibly for the abolition of the other. Later, when the moderates proved incapable of carrying the war to a successful conclusion, measures like the Self-Denying Ordinance and the creation of the New Model Army had to be accepted by a Presbyterian majority which was not by any means a commanding majority, and which had left itself with no possibility of conservative support.

The Civil Constitution of the Clergy emerged after months of discussion in the National Assembly as a charter for renewed Christianity in France. The moderates who put it through seem mostly to have been sincere men, bad Catholics in some ways, perhaps, but rather because they had absorbed some of the practical wordly spirit of the age than because they were outright anticlericals or "freethinkers." Yet their measure alienated the good Catholics and merely encouraged the violent freethinkers to try to root out the "vile superstitions" of Christianity altogether. The Civil Constitution in all innocence provided for the election of parish priests by the same local electoral bodies that chose lay officials for the new government positions, and for the election of bishops by the same departmental body that elected representatives to the Legislative Assembly. It scrapped all the historic dioceses of old France, and substituted nice, nearly uniform dioceses identical with the new *départements* into which France was governmentally divided. It did consent to "notify" the Pope of such elections.

Since the property of the Church as a corporation had been taken over to serve as security for the new paper money of the revolution, the *assignats*, the State was to support the expenses of the clergy under the new constitution. The election of priests and bishops by bodies to which Protestants, Jews, and avowed atheists were theoretically eligible was so completely uncanonical that no Pope could for a moment have considered accepting it. Although there was the usual diplomatic delay, the break between the Pope and the revolutionary government was inevitable, and with it a powerful and conservative group of Catholics was forced irreconcilably into opposition. The new Constitutional Church was hardly more acceptable to the real radicals than the old Roman Catholic Church, and as the critical days of the Terror drew nearer the moderates found themselves saddled with the protection of a church which returned them no important support.

Order Number One emerged from no such long debate as did the Root-and-Branch Bill and the Civil Constitution of the Clergy. Indeed, it is not quite fair to list it as a definite measure sponsored by the moderates, though the soviet leader most prominent in the group which prepared it was the moderate N. D. Sokolov, and the compromisists energetically promulgated it. The Order emerged in the very last days of the February Revolution from the headquarters of the Petrograd soviet. It was addressed to the army, and in addition to the usual revolutionary measures toward a standing army of the old regime—abolition of salutes, social and political equality of privates with officers, and so on—it provided for elected company and battalion committees which were to have entire charge of arms, above all of those of officers; and it ordered that every military unit obey the soviets in political matters. The military committee of the duma might be obeyed in military matters, provided the soviet did not object in a specific case. The Order was devised primarily with the Petrograd garrison in mind, but its main provisions were rapidly taken up at the front. This order at once convinced the conservatives that there was nothing to be hoped for from the revolution, and put even the more liberal officers in a state of mind to welcome later attempts at a conservative *coup d'état*. It made the subsequent task of the moderates in bringing Russia back to military efficiency for the war on Germany more difficult than ever. And it by no means served to reconcile the soldiers themselves with the continuation of the war. Most of the popularity of Order Number One eventually redounded to the credit of the Bolsheviks; most of its unpopularity came back on the compromisists. This is the typical fate of the moderates in these revolutions.

Again, the moderates are in all our societies confronted sooner or later with the task of fighting a war; and they prove poor war leaders. In England the fighting broke out in 1642, and before the first Civil War was over Cromwell and the Independents had made themselves indispensable, and were on the threshold of power. Foreign war in France broke out in the spring of 1792, and a few months later the monarchy had fallen; the war went very badly in the spring of 1793, and in June the moderate Girondins, who had on the French side been the most eager for war, were turned out by the Montagnards. The Russian Revolution was born in the midst of a disastrous war, and the Russian moderates never had a chance at peaceful administration. The fact is clear. The moderates cannot seem to succeed in war. The reasons why are less clear. No doubt the commitment of the moderates to protect the liberties of the individual is a factor. You cannot organize an army if you take Liberty, Equality, and Fraternity at all seriously.

Modern wars seem to carry with them the necessity for organizing civil government along military lines, for the exercise of strong, centralized governmental authority in which the liberty of the individual is far from a matter of first concern, in which there is very little debate, very little of the government by discussion so prized by the moderates, very little compromise and moderation. War, said Madison, is the mother of executive aggrandizement, and even here in America our wars have borne him out. But in the midst of a revolution the executive that gets aggrandized is not the moderate executive. The Reigns of Terror in France and in Russia are in part explicable as the concentration of power in a government of national defense made necessary by the fact of war. This is by no means a complete explanation of the Reigns of Terror. But certainly the necessity for a strong centralized government to run the war is one of the reasons why the moderates failed. They simply could not provide the discipline, the enthusiasm, the unpondered loyalty necessary to fight a war, and they went out.

v. *Summary*

To the kindly souls who for the most part wrote the history from which we get our notions of modern revolutions, this failure of the moderates was a great tragedy. The moderates appear as good men worsted by circumstances and unscrupulous opponents. They seem to be idealists crushed by a harsh world, but thereby sure of the resurrection history holds out to the just. The gentle Falkland and the scholarly Condorcet—the latter in his political and ethical *ideas* an immoderate—smile down upon us from the only heaven to which mere mortals hold the key. It is true that not even foreign historians have as yet made a heaven for Miliukov or Kerensky. Their failure, for one thing, is still too stark; and for another, the Russian moderates are still without honor in their own country.

Perhaps most of the moderates would be morally better or at least more normal men than their extremist opponents. Yet, leaders and led together, they make a motley lot, by no means easily catalogued by Marxist or by psychologist. And the traditional notion that they were idealists and that they failed because in the rough give-and-take the idealist must always fail is here peculiarly misleading. It is more accurate to risk the paradox: they failed because they were in so many respects what is usually called realists; that is, some of them were reasonably well adapted to a common-sense world.

Pym and Mirabeau, who died peacefully before the defeat of the moderates was evident, still enjoy reputations as skilled politicians, as sensible moderates. Over most of the others there hangs something of the kind of reputation most definite and clear with Kerensky. The eloquent compromisist leader seems to us a man of words, an orator who could move crowds but could not guide them, an impractical and incompetent person in the field of action. The Gironde seems much the same, as also the lesser Presbyterian leaders like Holles. It seems emptily paradoxical to list these people as realists. Yet realists of a kind they were. They used grand words and phrases grandly as a consolation and a joy to their listeners and to themselves. But they did not believe in them as the radicals believed in them; they did not intend to try to pursue them to their logical conclusions in action. They were, in short, using words in the way most men in normal societies, including such realistic politicians as Gladstone, use them. They would not seem realists to a hard-headed horse trader. But within the limits which tradition and ritual have set for the work of such people as they—part priest, part administrator, part actor, part teacher—they were good quiet practitioners.

But the times were turned topsy-turvy, and as the crisis of the revolution approached, only the man with a touch—or more—of fanatic idealism in him, or at least with the ability to act the part of such a fanatic, could attain to leadership. The normal social roles of realism and idealism are reversed in the acute phases of a revolution. We shall return to this topic in our next chapter. Here we need only note that the outward evidences of the approach of this kind of crisis appear as a heightened form of class antagonism. The moderates by definition are not great haters, are not endowed with the effective blindness which keeps men like Robespierre and Lenin undistracted in their rise to power. In normal times, ordinary men are not capable of feeling for groups of their fellow men hatred as intense, continuous, and uncomfortable as that preached by the extremists in revolution. Such hatred is a heroic emotion, and heroic emotions are exhausting. The poor may hate the rich, the Protestant the Catholic, the bourgeois the noble, the Southerner the Yankee, and so on. But this hate is normally in human beings a routine and consoling hate, a part of life, like food, drink, and loving, integrated with an existence as alien to the possibility of revolution as that of a vegetable.

The moderates, then, do not really believe in the big words they have to use. They do not really believe a heavenly perfection is suddenly coming to men on earth. They are all for compromise, common sense, toleration, comfort. In a normal society, these desires are part of their strength and give them their hold over their fellows, who share at least their desire for comfort. But in these three revolutions large numbers of men were for the moment lifted by desire and emotion to a point where they seemed to despise even comfort. The moderates could not deal politically with such men; they could not take the first steps which are necessary if such men are to be understood. The moderates were cut off from the immoderates by a gap neither philosophy nor common sense could fill. There is an adage that in the kingdom of the blind the one-eyed man is king. In one of his subtler short stories, "The Kingdom of the Blind," H. G. Wells exposed the weakness of this apothegm. In the heat of a violent revolution, its weakness is perhaps even more apparent than in the imaginary Andean valley of Wells's tale. The moderates we have been dealing with were all very human and very fallible; but even had they been as wise as the heroes of Plutarch, as wise as Washington, it would seem that they must have failed. For we are here in a land fabulous but real, where the wisdom and common sense of the moderate are not wisdom and common sense, but folly.

THE ACCESSION OF THE EXTREMISTS

1. *The Coup d'État*

The struggle between the moderates and the extremists, which begins almost as soon as the dramatic overthrow of the old regime is effected, is marked by a series of exciting episodes: here street fighting, there a forced seizure of property, almost everywhere heated debates, attempted repressions, a steady stream of violent propaganda. Tempers are strained to the breaking point over matters that in a stable society are capable of an almost automatic solution. There is an almost universal state of tension. The fever is working its way to a crisis. As with many fevers, its progress is in detail jerky, with now an apparent improvement and then a sudden jump ahead. But the cumulative effect is unmistakable. With the final overthrow of the moderates the revolution may be said to have entered its crisis stage.

Before we attempt to describe the behavior of men in societies in such a crisis, we shall have to go a bit further into the process by which the extremists acceded to power. In a sense, such an analysis will be but pointing out in reverse what we have already said of the moderates: the reasons why the extremists succeeded are but the other side of the reasons why the moderates failed. Where the moderates were weak, the extremists were strong. The actual steps by which the extremists rise to power are, however, too important to be left with this general statement. We must parallel our analysis of moderate weaknesses with an analysis of extremist strengths.

The extremists win out because they secure control of the illegal government and turn it in a decisive *coup d'état* against the legal government. The problem of the dual sovereignty is solved by the revolutionary acts in which the Independents, the Jacobins, and the Bolsheviks seized power. But the moderates had once shared with them the control of the organizations which they had turned against the government. The key to the success of the extremists lies in their monopoly of control over these organizations— New Model Army and Independent churches, Jacobin clubs, and soviets.

They obtain this monopoly by ousting, usually in a series of conflicts, any and all *active and effective* opponents from these organizations. The discipline, single-mindedness, and centralization of authority which mark the rule of the triumphant extremists are first developed and brought to perfection in the revolutionary groups of the illegal government. The characteristics which were formed in the growth of the illegal government remain those of the radicals after the illegal government becomes the legal. Indeed, many of these useful characteristics were first molded even further back in the days of the old regime, when the extremists were very small concentrated groups subject to the full "tyranny" of the government.

The Independents gained discipline and devotion from a long series of persecutions which began under Elizabeth, whose famed love of tolerance was not extended to Catholics or Brownists. The French radicals were not so badly treated under the old regime as their descendants and historians like to think, but the censorship, the Bastille, and the *lettres de cachet* were real enough, even if they rarely fell to the lot of the rank and file of the enlightened. As for Russia, its extremists were molded in the most melodramatic traditions of oppression, were backed by almost a century of secret organization, plotting, oaths, and martyrdom. We shall see later that the great Russian Revolution is indeed over; but many of the authoritarian features of the extremist period have clearly survived in the Russia of today. One of the reasons for that survival is the very great strength of the Communist authoritarian discipline, forged by years of underground conspiracy and control from above and within.

II. *Organization of the Extremists*

The first thing likely to strike an observer of the successful extremists in the English, French, and Russian revolutions, and indeed, the not quite so radical patriots who put through the American Revolution, is their fewness in numbers. The membership of the formal organizations which did the work of beating the moderates was never more than a small minority of the total population. Their active membership was of course always smaller than the membership on the books. It is not easy to get exact figures, either for membership or for populations, but the following figures are not erroneous enough to be misleading. The New Model Army was created at a membership of 22,000, and was not more than 40,000 in its most obstreperous days. The population of England was somewhere between three and five million. The Jacobins at the most generous estimate numbered in their struggle with the moderates about 500,000. The population of France was probably over rather than under twenty million. The Communist party in Russia has always prided itself on its numerical smallness; this is no bloated bourgeois party, full of indifferent members who cast a lazy vote, or don't even vote at all. Figures again are uncertain, but it seems likely that at no time during the active revolution—say up to Stalin's final acquisition of power by the expulsion of the "Rightist opposition" in 1929—did the Communist party number even 1 per cent of a population of well over one hundred million. In America the difficulty of even approximate figures is greater, since the patriots were not organized into a single body. It is clearly not fair to take the relatively small continental armies as exactly measuring the strength of the patriot—or Whig—group. Nevertheless, the best authorities are agreed that if you count out avowed Loyalists and the very numerous indifferent or neutral, cultivating their own gardens throughout the war, the group which actively engineered, supported, and fought the American Revolution is a minority, probably not more than 10 per cent of the population.

It is easy to remark that though the facts clearly show that these revolutionary groups are very small minorities indeed, all politically active groups are minorities, and that in these revolutions the radicals in some way "represented" or "carried out" what the soul, will, genius, of their nations demanded. This may well be so in terms familiar to the metaphysician, but the relation involved is one which at present we cannot pretend to be able to study by the methods we have laid down in this book. Perhaps the Jacobins were the agents of the general will of the French people; but the general will is a metaphysical concept the relation of which with tangible Jacobins we cannot possibly measure here.

Trotsky in one of his less realistic moods had a fine time reconciling the fewness of the Bolsheviks in 1917 with the largeness of Russia, and with the various groups clearly hostile to the Bolsheviks. "The Bolsheviks," he wrote, in a fine anticipation of George Orwell's 1984, "took the people as preceding history had created them, and as they were called to achieve the Revolution. The Bolsheviks saw it as their mission to stand at the head of this people. *Those against the insurrection were 'everybody'—except the Bolsheviks. But the Bolsheviks were the people.*" Trotsky wasn't quite metaphysician—or psychologist—enough to insist that the Bolsheviks were forcing the Russian people to be free.

In fact, neither revolutionists of the Right nor of the Left have in the twentieth century quite dared to take a consistently Nietzschean position in this matter of the relation between their own elect few and their own masses; that is, they have not dared to say that the elect should be masters in the full connotation of that term and the rest should be slaves in the full connotation of that term. Lenin seems often on the edge of this Nietzschean position, and Hitler in *Mein Kampf* falls over into it not infrequently. But the official position of the Communist, Nazi, and Fascist parties was that the party, the elect, the minority in power, is really a trustee, a shepherd of the people, ruling to improve the people's lot; and Communism to this day holds out the promise that eventually—in a long "eventually," after world capitalism is beaten—the distinction between leaders and led, between party and people, between brain workers and manual workers, will vanish in the classless society.

In all our societies these radicals were very conscious, and usually very proud, of their small numbers. They felt definitely set off from their countrymen, consecrated to a cause which their countrymen were certainly not consciously and actively equal to. Some of the radicals may have satisfied themselves that they really represented the better selves of their fellow countrymen, that they were the reality of which the others were the potentiality. But here and now they were very sure that they were superior to the inert and flabby many. The English saints of the seventeenth century, the elect of a God more exclusive than any poor worldly king, made no attempt to conceal their contempt for the damned masses—and dukes and earls were of course masses for these determined Puritans. The Jacobins inherited from the Enlightenment a belief in the natural goodness or the natural reasonableness of the common man, and this belief put a limit to their expressed scorn for their fellows. But the scorn is there, and the Jacobin was almost as loftily consecrated as was the Independent. The Bolsheviks were brought up to believe that dialectical materialism works through an elite of the laboring classes aided by intellectuals, and that the peasants in particular were incapable of working out their own salvation. The Bolsheviks therefore took their fewness naturally enough, and their superiority as well.

There is also a good deal of evidence that as the revolutions go on, a very large number of people just drop out of active politics, make no attempt to register their votes. Now it may be that most of these people again are at heart in sympathy with the active radicals; but on the whole it looks as if most of them were cowed conservatives or moderates, men and women not anxious for martyrdom, but quite incapable of the mental and moral as well as physical strain of being a devoted extremist in the crisis of a revolution. We have very clear evidence of this dropping out of the ordinary man in *two* of our revolutions, and we may reasonably assume that it is one of the uniformities we are seeking.

In Russia, the February Revolution brought in universal suffrage as a matter of course. Russia had at last caught up with the West. At the first elections almost everybody, men and women alike, took the opportunity to vote in various local elections. But very shortly there set in a noticeable decline in the total number of votes cast. In the June, 1917, elections for the Moscow district dumas the Social-Revolutionary groups received 58 per cent of the votes; in the September elections the Bolsheviks received 52 per cent. A clear gain for the Bolsheviks by democratic methods? Not at all. In June the Social-Revolutionaries got 375,000 votes out of 647,000 cast; in September the Bolsheviks got 198,000 out of 381,000 cast. In three months half the electorate dropped out. Trotsky himself has a simple explanation for this: "many small-town people who, in the vapor of the first illusions, had joined the Compromisers fell back soon after into political non-existence." The same story is graphically recorded in French municipal and national elections between the rosy days of 1789, days of almost universal suffrage in practice, and 1793, when in some cases less than a tenth of the qualified voters actually voted. The "people" did not vote for Bolsheviks or Jacobins, and it seems more than likely that if most Englishmen could have voted at all in 1648, they would not have voted for Independents, Levellers, Diggers, Fifth Monarchy Men, or Millenarians. It seems likely also that a full referendum or plebiscite on the American Declaration of Independence in 1776 would have been pretty close. The great numbers of qualified voters just don't vote; in Trotsky's compact phrase, they are politically nonexistent.

Their political nonexistence is not achieved without a good deal of help from the extremists. The elections are supposedly free and open, but the extremists are not hindered by any beliefs in freedom they may have expressed in other days. They soon take steps familiar in this country through the history of groups like the Ku Klux Klan and

Tammany Hall. They beat up well-known aristocrats and suchlike class enemies, they start riots at polling places or in electoral assemblies, they break windows and start street fights, they howl down moderate candidates, they bring to bear good journalists, skilled at libel and innuendo, and in a hundred ways which any realistic student of politics can uncover with a little study, they make it very difficult for ordinary, peaceful, humdrum men and women to go to the polls and cast their votes for the moderates to whom ordinary, peaceful, humdrum men and women seem attracted. Not that terrorism alone scares off the ordinary man. Mere laziness, an inability to give to political affairs the ceaseless attention revolutions demand, is also instrumental in keeping the man in the street from expressing himself. He gets fed up with the constant meetings, the deputations, the papers, the elections of dogcatchers, general inspectors, presidents, the committees, the rituals, the ceaseless moil and toil of self-government on a more than Athenian basis. At any rate he quits, and the extremists have the field to themselves.

Their fewness is indeed one of the great sources of the extremists' strength. Great numbers are almost as unwieldy in politics as on the battlefield. In the politics of revolutions what counts is the ability to move swiftly, to make clear and final decisions, to push through to a goal without regard for injured human dispositions. For such a purpose the active political group must be small. You cannot otherwise obtain the single-mindedness and devotion, the energy and the discipline, necessary to defeat the moderates. You cannot maintain the fever of fanaticism in large numbers of people long enough to secure the ultimate victory. The masses do not make revolutions. They may be enlisted for some impressive pageantry once the active few have won the revolution. Our twentieth-century revolutions, both of the Right and the Left, have achieved apparent miracles of mass participation. But the impressive demonstrations the camera has recorded in Germany, Italy, Russia and China ought not to deceive the careful student of politics. Neither Communist, Nazi, nor Fascist victory over the moderates was achieved by the participation of the many; all were achieved by small, disciplined, principled, fanatical bodies.

Nor at this stage of revolution do the victorious radicals dare make use of the plebiscite. They cannot risk anything like a free election. Only later, when the crisis is followed by a convalescence, by a return to normal ways, does the plebiscite stage arrive, if it ever does. This interval may not be a very long one, and in the case of Rightist revolutions may be very brief, since the full fury of the Ideal rarely inspires the men of the Right. But certainly for the revolutions we are here studying, the generalization holds: the honest plebiscite is absent from the struggle between extremists and moderates, and is not used by the extremists even after their accession to power. This still holds true in Russia and in her satellites.

The extremists are not only few; they are fanatically devoted to their cause. Their awareness of being few seems correlated with the intensity of their fanaticism. One feeds upon and strengthens the other. With their objects, with the content of their dreams of a better world, we shall concern ourselves later. For those who think that only in the service of a personal God can feelings properly defined as "fanatical" be aroused, our application of the word to Jacobins and Bolsheviks may seem illegitimate. But this is surely an undue narrowing of a clear and useful word. Bolsheviks and Jacobins were as convinced as any Calvinist that they alone were right, that what they proposed was the only possible course. All of our revolutionary radicals displayed a willingness to work hard, to sacrifice their peace and security, to submit to discipline, to submerge their personalities in the group. They were all aware of the spiritual difficulties of keeping "always at the height of revolutionary circumstances," as the Jacobins used to put it; but to a surprising extent they overcame these difficulties and maintained on this earth an *esprit de corps,* an active moral union, that is far beyond the powers of ordinary men in ordinary circumstances to attain and to maintain.

And they are disciplined. Partly, as we have explained, this is an inheritance from their oppressed past. It correlates with their fewness and with their fanatical strength. The New Model Army is an excellent example. It defeated the hapazard aggregations which the ordinary recruiting methods of the Royalists opposed to it; it defeated the cream of the opposing forces, the cavalry recruited from faithful country gentlemen and their dependents. The New Model was recruited from ardent Puritans, vouched for by men who knew them; and it was submitted to a brief but effective course of training incomparably more severe than any that had yet been used in English military history. The result was a fine army—and a compact body of hard revolutionists who could cut through the best intentions and the best rhetoric of the moderates. The discipline of the Jacobins was not military, but it was very rigorous, and indeed resembled the kind of discipline which a militant religious body imposes on its members. The Jacobins were always scrutinizing their own membership, submitting to the ordeal of an *épuration,* literally a "purification," better, a "purge." The slightest deviation from the established order of the day might bring a warning and possible expulsion. With the Spartan ways of the Russian Communist party in the early days of the Soviet state most of us are familiar; it is a point on which all reporters, kindly and unkindly, are agreed.

The extremists put their disciplined skill into the realization of the revolutionary ends. There has been worked out in the last few hundred years an elaborate technique of revolutionary action, of which the Russian, Chinese, and Cuban Communists were the latest heirs. A good deal has been written about this technique, which is in part simply the technique of any successful pressure group: propaganda, electioneering, lobbying, parading, street fighting, guerrilla warfare, Gandhian non-violent violence, delegation making, direct pressure on magistrates, sporadic terrorism of the tar-and-feather or castor-oil variety and other techniques in various combinations. Jacobins, Communists, and Sons of Liberty did a notably good job at this sort of thing. But it is rather surprising to note how many of these techniques can be found in England, and especially in London, as early as the seventeenth century. In this respect, as in many others, the English Revolution is clearly of a modern type. Here is a bit that might have come from the French Revolution: during the debate on the Militia Order, a crowd of apprentices "came into the House of Commons and kept the door open, and their hats on . . . and called out as they stood, 'Vote, vote,' and in this arrogant posture stood until the votes passed." One suspects that these apprentices did not march in spontaneously. This is the kind of thing that takes organization.

Finally, the extremists follow their leaders with a devotion and a unanimity not to be found among the moderates. Theories of democratic equality, which crop up at the start of all our revolutions, prove no obstacle to the development among the extremists of something very like the "Führer" principle we associate with Fascist movements. Here it is the moderates who live up to their theories, and in the early stages of the revolutions it is not uncommon to find complaints that So-and-so is arrogating to himself powers, a personal leadership, no good man would want to possess. Mirabeau and Kerensky, to take neat examples, were accused by moderates and extremists alike of aiming at a personal dictatorship. Yet Robespierre and Lenin followed in their footsteps almost literally and for them only the cheering could be heard—at least in the homeland. This magnifying of the principle of leadership runs right through the organization, from the subalterns up to the great national heroes—Cromwell, Robespierre, Lenin.

On the whole, this leadership is effective, and especially so at the very top. Now if they are seen as full and rounded human beings, there are unquestionably differences among the men who make up the general staffs of the extremists. The psychologist and the novelist, indeed the historian as well, could not lump them all together. Yet they have in common one aspect which is of great importance to the sociologist; they combine, in varying degrees, very high ideals and a complete contempt for the inhibitions and principles which serve most other men as ideals. They present a strange variant of Plato's pleasant scheme: they are not philosopher-kings but philosopher-killers. They have the realistic, the practical touch very few of the moderate leaders had, and yet they have also enough of the prophet's fire to hold followers who expect the New

Jerusalem around the next corner. They are practical men unfettered by common sense, Machiavellians in the service of the Beautiful and the Good.

A bit from Lenin's life will make the point clear. At a secret meeting of the Central Committee of the Bolshevik party just before the October Revolution, Lenin was urging insurrection on the more tender-minded of his colleagues, who thought that the Bolsheviks ought to respect the will of the majority of Russians, which was clearly against them. "We are inclined to consider the systematic preparation of an uprising as something in the nature of a political sin," said he. "To wait for the Constituent Assembly, which will clearly not be with us, is senseless." There is the practical Lenin, unworried by a democratic dogma that stands in his way. After the October Revolution he wrote in *Pravda* of "the crisis which has arisen as a result of the lack of correspondence between the elections to the Constituent Assembly and the will of the people and the interest of the toiling and exploited classes." Here the will of the people is somehow at bottom the will of the minority party of Bolsheviks. We are back again in the midst of democratic dogma. Parallel cases could readily be drawn from Robespierre, Cromwell, and even, one fears, from Jefferson.

Hypocrisy? To those of little imagination or experience of the world, such acts must always seem hypocritical. But, on a less heroic scale, they are far too much a part of normal human action to deserve so opprobrious a label. The Robespierre who, as an enlightened young man, had held capital punishment wrong did not hypocritically send his enemies to the guillotine. He had convinced himself that his enemies were scarcely men at all; they were sinners, corrupt souls, agents of a worse-than-Satan, and their removal from this earth wasn't really capital punishment in the conventional sense at all. You could still treat ordinary criminals in full accord with the most humanitarian principles of jurisprudence. Most of us make this sort of compromise with ourselves often enough in daily life. But with us comfort, convenience, habit, even common sense, determine the limits of compromise. For the revolutionary extremist such limits are off; in the delirium, in the crisis, there is an extraordinary reversal of the roles played in normal times by the real and the ideal. Here briefly and at last the blind—or the seer—is king; plain earthly seeing, the kind that concerns the oculist, is for once of very little use. The seers have just enough of it to keep their positions of leadership. Cromwell, indeed, had a good deal of what seems an English sense of the contingent, and Lenin was certainly no academic idealist. Robespierre is in some ways the most unadulterated seer of the lot.

Yet all of them, including even Robespierre, were what the world calls men of action. They could and did get things done, were administrators and executives, ran organizations for which tradition and routine had not yet been able to build up much that worked automatically. If they have left behind them a reputation for unusual ruthlessness, this may be in part a reflection of the ill repute terrorism has for most of us. And the ruthlessness, in the proper service of the ideal, went while they were alive into the making of their leadership. Cromwell gained credit among the Saints for his Irish massacres. The guillotine in France was for a few months the "holy guillotine." Trotsky, early in his famous rallying of the Bolshevik troops in the Civil War, ordered shot the commander, commissar, and one soldier out of ten in a Petrograd workers' regiment that had fled the enemy, and to the dismay of gentler colleagues showed no hesitation about continuing the policy of discipline through bloodshed. Trotsky became briefly a savior and a hero. We are a long way from Order Number One!

For most men, there is a gap between their deeds and their professions, between what they are and what they would like to be, between what they are and what they think they are. Normally, however, they manage to keep the gap small enough, or turn their attention away from one side of it or the other, so that they are not unduly troubled by it. For the leaders of the extremists in times of revolution the gap looks to an outside observer enormous, bigger than it ever is in normal times. A few men, like Fouché, seem to have been terrorists to save their own skins. But, in general, only a sincere extremist in a revolution can kill men because he loves man, attain peace through violence, and free men by enslaving them. Such contrasts in action would paralyze a conventionally practical leader, but the extremist seems quite undisturbed by it. Where the ordinary man would be troubled by something like a split personality, where his conscience or his sense of reality, or both, would be haunted, the extremist goes boldly ahead. Wide though the gap between the real and the ideal is in the crisis period, he can cross it at his own convenience. He has, for the moment, the best of both worlds. He can manipulate with equal skill the concrete and complex human beings on committees, deputations, bureaus, ministries, all the unsettling problems of administration, and yet use gracefully and convincingly the abstract, indispensable, haunting words which have in revolutions such magic power over large groups of men.

It is this last gift that seems to lie all but wholly beyond the capacity of the most ambitious hypocrite. The great leaders of the Terrors are fitted for their task by a genuine vocation, a vocation which in ordinary times would exclude them from political power. Their belief in the Absolute is not assumed, and is as real as their ability to handle the contingent. And for once the Absolute is practical politics. F. W. Maitland has a passage, suggested by Coleridge, which puts the point neatly:

> Coleridge has remarked how, in times of great political excitement, the terms in which political theories are expressed become, not more and more practical, but more and more abstract and impractical. It is in such times that men clothe their theories in universal terms. . . . The absolute spirit is abroad. Relative or partial good seems a poor ideal. It is not of these, or those men that we speak, of this nation or that age, but of Man.

III. *Fitness of the Extremists*

The transition from opposition to power is not a sudden one for the extremists. The whole point about the *dvoevlastie*, the dual sovereignty, is that it is not a struggle between government and opposition, between ins and outs, but between two governments within the same state, an irregular civil war. Under the old regime perhaps no more than a pressure group, the revolutionists' organization gradually takes over, in the confusion of the first stages of actual revolution, governmental powers which are never thereafter wholly subordinated to the provisional government, the almost legal heir of the old regime. The process is especially clear in Russia, though it is substantially uniform in all our revolutions.

Practically all the soviets, even in the market towns, did administrative work from the very beginning. Trotsky, here in his role of historian, gives some good succinct examples:

> The soviet in Saratov was compelled to interfere in economic conflicts, to arrest manufacturers, confiscate the tramway belonging to Belgians, introduce workers' control, and organize production in the abandoned factories. . . . In the Urals the soviets frequently instituted courts of justice for the trial of citizens, created their own militia in several factories, paying for its equipment out of the factory cash-box, organized a workers' inspection which assembled raw materials and fuel for the factories, superintended the sale of manufactured goods and established a wage-scale.

Obviously, in parts of Russia the slogan "All power to the Soviets" had become a bit superfluous even before the October Revolution.

In France the "Societies of Friends of the Constitution," at their formation in 1789 hardly more than pressure groups, or possibly French variants of the Yankee caucus, had by june 2, 1793, taken over a good many functions normally carried out by governmental bodies. When the "constituted authorities," as the Jacobins respectfully called governing councils and legislatures, failed to do what the Jacobins wanted, the Jacobins went ahead and did it themselves. Notably the whole repressive legislation on the non-juring (Catholic) clergy was anticipated in practice by the Jacobin clubs in the provinces.

The clubs were organized like parliamentary bodies, with elaborate rules on debating, with committees, officers, minutes, and indeed all the apparatus of a proper legislature. Sometimes a club would overawe or persuade municipal or departmental officers into an approved Jacobin policy; sometimes, failing in this, a club would almost openly pass laws and decrees. Those of the members who protested against this shocking interference with authorities chosen by popular election—and many did protest on just such grounds—were thereby ticketed as moderates, and were lucky if they avoided the guillotine later.

That the men who made the American Revolution were by no means unexercised in the art of actual governing has long been a commonplace of proud Anglo-Saxon writers on both sides of the Atlantic. What we must note here is that that preparation had by no means been wholly of the conventional legal sort. Not only in town meeting and colonial legislatures, but in caucuses, committees, and congresses that bear a close parallel with soviets and Jacobin clubs, the American radicals were schooled to take over the government from the agents of the Crown. We shall see in the next chapter that they did not hesitate to use terroristic means to preserve, as they had used them to attain, that power.

In England the situation is complicated by the fact that though the illegal organization headed up in the New Model Army, the various Independent congregations were also in their way agents of the extremists in their drive to power. The army itself, of course, began very soon after Naseby to interfere in politics in a way no conventional army does; and the first explusion of Presbyterians from Parliament was initiated and carried through by army resolutions and an army committee. But the Independents, and especially the Independent clergy, had much earlier taken a hand in matters very terrestrial indeed. As Professor Grierson has said, "It is not what Laud did that Baxter [a Puritan divine] seems to complain of, so much as what he would not allow them, the parish pastors, to do, viz., to exercise a moral discipline co-extensive with the parish." And by a moral discipline a Puritan meant something co-extensive with the whole of human life.

The extremists are not, then, politically innocent or inexperienced; they have had a long experience of oppression, and a briefer, but very intensive, training in actual government before they come to full power. To call either leaders or rank and file inexperienced, "pure theorists," and "metaphysicians," as has long been the habit especially among political writers in English, is misleading. Neither their aims nor their methods are those that good Victorians like Bagehot or Maine could approve or sympathize with. They are certainly heaven-storming idealists, scornful of compromise. But they are not academic theorists totally unadapted to action. *On the contrary, they are admirably adapted, almost in the sense a biologist gives to adaptation, to the special, the unique environment of the crisis.* That is why they succeed.

The actual overthrow of the moderates is usually a very neat job, an excellent example of the skill of the revolutionary leaders and the close adaptation of the revolutionary organizations to their functions. It is, as we have seen, by no means a great popular uprising. The crowds whose confused milling about makes an exact account of the taking of the Bastille or the February Revolution in Petrograd impossible for the historian, do not interfere with the professional dispatch with which Pride's Purge, the purge of the Girondins, and the October Revolution were put through. In France the extremists reached power in two of these *coups d'état*. The first, the overthrow of the monarchy on August 10, 1792, was achieved through an elaborate but never confused collaboration of various organs of the illegal government—Jacobin and other political clubs, the *fédérés*, local militia from all over France assembled in Paris to celebrate the anniversary of the fall of the Bastille, and the ward organizations out of which the revolutionary Parisian Commune was made. Almost the same elements were integrated ten months later for the easier task of bullying the Convention into giving up the Girondins. Danton, Marat, possibly Robespierre, and certainly a number of less famous but very skilled secondary leaders formed a general staff which engineered both of these *coups*.

The October Revolution was elaborately prepared, and

has been clearly described in Trotsky's own *History of the Russian Revolution*. We need not here go into details of this preparation. But a quotation from Trotsky will show how the details were taken care of:

> The typographical workers through their union, called to the attention of the Committee [the Military-Revolution Committee in Petrograd, the general staff of the October Revolution] an increase in Black Hundred [reactionary] leaflets and brochures. It was decided that in all suspicious cases the printers' union should come for instructions to the Military-Revolution Committee. This control was the most effective of all possible forms of control over the printed agitation of the counter-revolution.

Naturally; printed agitation has to have printers as well as legal freedom of the press. Perón in Argentina used a very similar technique to get rid of the independent newspaper *La Prensa*. In a dozen such ways the moderates were hamstrung in the last few days before the Bolshevik insurrection. There was no nonsense about a general strike; there was simply a co-ordinated series of seizures of centers of military and police power, press, post and telegraph, banks, and ministries.

The dramatic seizure of Charles I by Cornet Joyce on June 3, 1647, at Holmby House is perhaps the first assumption of sovereign power by the New Model. When Charles asked Joyce whence he had his commission to remove him, Joyce is said to have replied, pointing to his soldiers drawn up on the lawn. "There is my commission." The reply will serve in all our revolutions. Once the extremists are in power, there is no more finicky regard for the liberties of the individual or for the forms of legality. The extremists, after clamoring for liberty and toleration while they were in opposition, turn very authoritarian when they reach power. There is no need for us to sigh over this, or grow indignant, or talk of hypocrisy. We are attempting to discern uniformities in the behavior of men during certain revolutions in specific social systems, and this seems to be one of the uniformities.

It was but a bare six months [writes Gardiner] since the Independent leaders [Cromwell and Vane] who now permitted some hundreds of sufferers to be excluded for conscience's sake from the University of Oxford, had been striving to lay the foundations of a broad system of toleration in *The Heads of the Proposals* and had even taken into consideration a scheme for extending that toleration to the Roman Catholic priesthood itself.

Later under the Rump a strict censorship of the press was instituted, and the various canons and tastes of Puritanism enforced as far as possible by government policy. Similarly in France and Russia the new government clamped down at once on its enemies and began to build up the machinery of the coming Terror. Where, as in France and Russia, the army had lost its discipline under active attempts to introduce Liberty, Equality, and Fraternity, discipline was reintroduced with a good deal of firmness. Mr. Chamberlin describes the Russian situation:

The Bolshevik military authorities now began to talk about the harmful and disruptive influence of army committees very much as Kornilov, Denikin, and the old army officers had spoken in 1917; and strict obedience to the orders of the officers gradually became embedded in the discipline of the Red Army.

The Heads of Proposals and *The Agreement of the People,* radical platforms adopted by the army under Leveller influence, had proposed something very close to what came to be conventional nineteenth-century democracy—equal electoral districts, frequent parliaments, specific limitations on the executive power, even universal manhood suffrage. Cromwell seems never to have been in any sense a doctrinaire rebel, and indeed probably had many of the sentiments about authority and tradition one would expect from a country gentleman. If he suffered at all in mind about the situation, it was probably because the good old parliamentary institutions could not be restored. Certainly the last thing that could be done was to hold an open and free election on any conceivable franchise. The so-called Parliament of Saints which met in 1653 after the dissolution of the Rump was hardly more than a council sent up from trustworthy Independent groups and chosen by caucus methods.

Similarly in France, the victors of June 2nd did not dare go to the people. As a gesture they promulgated the so-called Constitution of 1793, based on universal suffrage, bill of rights, and the rest of the paraphernalia of democracy, but they took good care to go no further than printing it. It was never put into effect.

The Bolsheviks had for months attacked the Provisional government for not calling a constituent assembly. Such an assembly was finally chosen by universal suffrage just before the Bolshevik *coup*. In it the Bolsheviks were in a clear minority. Lenin dissolved this constituent assembly in January, 1918, with a light heart, but many of his followers, in spite of their Marxist training, were really hurt by such a defiance of democratic sentiments and traditions. Many good Jacobins were also worried by the fact of their new dictatorship.

Theory came to provide a salve to wounded consciences —no mean or unimportant function in any society. The theory of revolutionary dictatorship is very nearly identical in all three of our revolutions. Liberty for everyone, liberty full, free, and fair, is of course the ultimate goal. But such liberty at present would mean that men corrupted by the bad old ways would be able to realize their wicked plans, restore the bad old institutions, and frustrate the good men. On reflection, the extremist continues, it is clear that we must distinguish between liberty for those who deserve it, and liberty for those who don't, which latter is, of course, false liberty, pseudo-liberty, license or anarchy. God had given liberty to the Saints—true liberty, which is obedience to Him—but he clearly did not give liberty to sinners. You repress papists as you would repress devils. To argue that such sinners ought to be left alone would have seemed to seventeenth-century English Puritans as absurd as it would to us to suggest that yellow-fever-bearing mosquitoes be left alone. Robespierre himself phrased it with classic neatness: the revolutionary government, he said, was the despotism of liberty against tyranny. For Marx, the dictatorship of the proletariat is a necessary transitional stage, in which the last vestiges of capitalistic methods and capitalistic mentality are wiped out. Ruthless use of force will be necessary in this period —unfortunately of indeterminate length. Once a capitalist, always a capitalist, apparently. But when men are finally brothers, then the freedom of the classless society will finally begin.

Solaced by the knowledge that they are serving Liberty —in the high, true sense of the word—by a rigorous application of what to the unbelievers seems tyranny, the extremists go ahead to consolidate their power through institutions. Before we attempt a brief, generalized description of these institutions, we may note another uniformity. With the triumph of the extremists as we have defined them, the process of transfer of power from Right to Left ceases. The extremists are not indeed exempt from the difficulty other triumphant groups had faced from the very beginning of the revolutionary process. They develop internal conflicts, tend to split up into groups too hostile among themselves for co-operation. But these groups cannot usually be neatly ranged from Right to Left; and their dissension is ended quickly and without even the turmoil and confusion of a *coup d'état*. The dissensions have by now become so subtly doctrinal, so remote from the masses of the population, that they can be centered on a few leaders. And they are settled by the banishment or "judicial murder"—as it seems to the defeated partisans—of some of these leaders. What began with large-scale popular uprisings has now come to the dramatic intimacy of a courtroom.

France is here the clearest case. The victorious Montagnards of June 2nd divided into three major factions, that of which Robespierre stands as the head, that of Danton, and that of Hébert. There were, of course, subfactions, wheels within wheels, and had Marat not been already assassinated in the summer of 1793, there might have been still further complications. Robespierre, eventually victorious, rationalized the situation as a conflict between the true revolutionaries on one hand and the ultra-revolutionaries (Hébert) and the citra-revolutionaries (Danton) on the

other. He was, to himself, the golden and virtuous mean
between proletarian vice and bourgeois corruption. The
actual situation is almost unbelievably complicated, and
only the narrative historian with plenty of space to command can disentangle it. Contemporary French historians,
Communist or at least Marxist in inspiration, have long
sought for the true, the devoted core of real revolutionists,
proto-Communists. Such have been found in the Hébertists, the *Enragés,* the *bras nus,* or just in *les militants* of
the Parisian little people. Most of these groups are real
enough; but the best word for them is that old, non-Marxist word, "factions." Both Dantonists and Hébertists, "traitors" and "anarchists," were condemned before the Revolutionary Tribunal, and went to the guillotine in two large
and rather miscellaneous batches. For the next few
months, the "faction of Robespierre" was in complete control of France.

The victorious Independents in England in 1649 found
themselves facing an astonishing variety of sects which
had been carried along in the general good work for the
cause of complete toleration of all Dissenters. We shall in a
moment have a word to say about the doctrinal aspect of
these groups. Meantime we may note that not only did
Cromwell continue to keep down papists, prelatists, and
Presbyterians, but he and his officers saw to it that Fifth
Monarchy Men, Diggers, Levellers, Millenarians, Quakers,
and the rest were not allowed to try out their wilder
schemes in practice. The Diggers could dig no more in this
earth. The old tactics of "no enemy to the Left," which
had held ever since the beginning of the revolution, were
now definitely abandoned. As G. M. Trevelyan has written,
"All revolutionists, the moment they undertake the actual
responsibilities, become in some sort conservatives. Robespierre guillotined the Anarchists. The first administrative act of the [English] Regicides was to silence the
Levellers." There are, then, if you like, those more extreme
than the group we have called the extremists. But such
men are of the lunatic fringe. They are the impractical
people erroneously thought by some conservatives to be
typical revolutionists. They definitely do not succeed in
attaining power.

The Russian situation is still somewhat obscured in respect to the opposition to official Bolshevism after October, 1917, and this obscurity seems in some ways thicker than ever today. Nevertheless it is clear that even while Lenin was alive, and especially in the year or so after the October Revolution, there were a good many stresses and strains within the Bolshevik party. Lenin and his followers suppressed opposing groups even when they claimed to be more "revolutionary" than the Leninists. There was no nonsense about "no enemies to the Left." Thanks to the excellent discipline of the Bolshevik party and to the particularly pressing nature of the war against the Whites and the Allies, these quarrels were not as public as they had been in England and in France. But after Lenin's death these struggles came out in the open —or as near the open as possible in Russia. Trotsky the "ultra" and Bukharin the "citra" fell before the orthodox Stalin as Danton and Hébert had fallen before the orthodox Robespierre. The Russian trials and confessions of the later 1930's and the accompanying Terror of the Yezhov period seem to belong to a different phase of revolution, or rather, are internal difficulties of a specific society that has gone through one cycle of revolution. In spite of certain superficial analogies, they do not seem to be a part of the uniformity we are here discussing. We shall later return to them.

These little opposition factions are inextricably woven in with various eccentric groups which are not completely stilled until the height of the Terror—if even then. They represent, as we have seen, the lunatic fringes common to any complex civilization, and they are especially active and vocal in the early stages of our revolutions, and during the struggle between moderates and extremists. They are less important in the actual course of these revolutions than conservative historians, and conservatives generally, like to make out. But they are interesting variations in the main body of revolutionary orthodoxy, and they illuminate in many ways the general history of heresy and heretics.

"Never did the human mind attain such magnificent height of self-assertiveness as in England about the year 1650," wrote Lytton Strachey. And certainly what we now think of as almost a racially founded British love for the middle-of-the-road is not very evident in these years. Strachey ironically lists the possibility of becoming a Behmenist, a Bidellian, a Coppinist, a Salmonist, a Dipper, a Traskite, a Tyronist, a Philadelphian, Christadelphian, or Seventh Day Baptist, omitting the subject he was actually writing on, Ludovic Muggleton, leader of the Muggletonians. The terms mean almost as little to us today as do those with which John Goodwin is referred to in the third volume of *Gangraena*: "a monotonous sectary, a compound of Socinianism, Arminianism, Libertinism, Antinomianism, Independency, Popery and Skepticism." As early as 1647 John Hare published a pamphlet, *Plain English to our Wilful Bearers of Normanism*, in which he attacked the institution of private property without being very clear about what might take its place. Chamberlen, in his *Poor Man's Advocate*, urged the nationalization of all Crown and Church possessions, the resumption of all common lands that had been enclosed. This land was to be called the national stock, and was to be administered for the benefit of the poor.

In comparison with the wealth of imagination the English put into the effort to bring heaven to earth, the other two extremist revolutions seem poverty-stricken. Perhaps the old Anglo-Saxon belief that the French lack imaginative depth is valid, but surely this cannot be brought up against the Russians. Perhaps the answer is simply that as sources of imaginative inspiration neither the Enlightenment of the eighteenth-century *philosophes* nor the dialectic materialism of the Marxist can hold a candle to the King James version of the Bible. Yet France was by no means unproductive on the side of the lunatic fringe. The *Enragés*, the *bras nus*, the followers of Babeuf, have, as we have noted, been variously hailed as proto-Marxists; they were certainly firm social, economic, and political egalitarians. Then there was the incredible little circle around Catherine Théot, "Mother of God"—with Robespierre designated at least as one of the manifestations of God. It does indeed seem likely that republican professors in France are right, and that much of this was stirred up by Robespierre's enemies to make him seem ridiculous; for even at the crisis period of revolutions some men retain a sense of humor. Yet the fact remains that Catherine Théot and her circle existed.

In Russia the completeness and quickness of the Bolshevik victory probably explains the relative lack of rival Utopias. It is true that from 1918 to 1921 the Bolsheviks were forced to fight off Whites and Allies on a dozen fronts, and that in a region like the Ukraine, for instance, you can find everything from Czarist rulers through mild *narodniks* and partisan or guerrilla rulers to pure Reds. But there is a dog-eat-dog cruelty in the Russian Revolution that seems to exclude the mild delusions of an Everard or a Catherine Théot.

iv. *The Machinery of Dictatorship*

The dictatorship of the extremists is embodied in governmental forms as a rough-and-ready centralization. In detail these forms vary in our different societies, but the Commonwealth in England, the *gouvernement révolutionnaire* in France, and the Bolshevik dictatorship during the period of "war communism" in Russia all display uniformities of the kind the systematist in biology or zoölogy would not hesitate to catalogue as uniformities. Notably the making of final decisions in a wide range of matters is taken away from local and secondary authorities, especially if those authorities have been "democratically" elected, and is concentrated on a few persons in the national capital. Though names like Cromwell, Robespierre, and Lenin stand out as those of rulers, and although these men did exercise unquestioned power in many ways, the characteristic form of this supreme authority is that of a committee. The government of the Terror is a dictatorship in commission.

This centralized executive commission—Army Council or Council of State, Committee of Public Safety, the All-Russian Central Executive Committee (Vtsik)—rests on a supine if talkative legislative body—Rump, Convention, All-Russian Congress of Soviets—and gets its orders carried out by an extemporized bureaucracy, largely recruited from party workers, and from that club-sect-pressure-group we have seen as the body of the extremist group. The old law courts cannot work, at least in their traditional manner. They are therefore supplemented by extraordinary courts, revolutionary tribunals, or are wholly transformed by new appointments and by special jurisdictions. Finally, a special sort of revolutionary police appears. The Russian Cheka is familiar to everyone with the slightest knowledge of recent history. Its continuation under different names (Ogpu, NKVD, MVD) is evidence, not so much that Russia is in continual revolution, as that Soviet Russia remains in many ways like Czarist Russia, which also had secret police. In France the *comité de sûreté générale* and the *comités révolutionnaires* fulfilled these police functions; in the English Revolution they were carried out very effectively by the new Independent parish clergy, aided by various *ad hoc* committees in the army. But in England the whole fabric of governmental centralization was rudimentary and simple—Cromwell's own anomalous dictatorship, the new Council of State, annually elected by the Rump, in which legislative, administrative, and judicial powers were as thoroughly combined as ever in the Tudor and Stuart Star Chamber, the curious experiment of the Major Generals in 1655-56. The fact of the centralization in England is, however, unquestionable. Even the sacred functions of that holiest guardian of English local liberties, the Justice of the Peace, were under attack all during the domination of the extremists.

These extemporized dictatorships were faced not only with the ordinary problems of government, but with civil and foreign war, and with at least a certain number of actual reform measures which they had to try to put through. Notably in the French and Russian revolutions, the new government had to administer what, to avoid dispute as to the meaning of Socialism, we may call measures of economic planning—fixed prices and wages, managed currency, food rationing, and so on. We need not here bother with the problem as to whether in France these were purely war measures or not. The point is that the government found itself obliged to try to administer them. In Russia, of course, there were conscious efforts to embody Marxist Socialism in working institutions.

But these were all very rough-and-ready forms of dictatorship. The governments of the Terror were on the whole much less efficient, less effectively absolute than many peacetime governments with nowhere near their reputation for arbitrariness and bloodshed. The present Russian government is infinitely more efficiently centralized than was Lenin's; Napoleon's than Robespierre's. Indeed, one of the reasons why the governments of the Terror seem so tyrannical and hard to bear, even retrospectively, is precisely that they were so inefficient. They got their big tasks done —saved England, France, and Russia from dissolution or conquest, but they did it very messily and, in detail, very badly. The actual administrators were usually inexperienced, were often petty fanatics, often incompetent blowhards who had risen to prominence in politics of the New Model Army, in the clubs or the party. They were under tremendous pressure from above to get results. They were frequently in charge of operations very close to the heart of the revolution as an economic movement—confiscation of Royalist estates and clerical livings in England, disposition of the confiscated lands of clergy and *émigrés* in France, nationalization of land and factories in Russia—which gave them grand opportunities for graft. They had to work with a population many if not most of whom were distrustful or hostile. Small wonder then that these reigns of terror stand out rather for irregular acts of violence, that their full history is a matter of incredible complexity. Nothing is more illuminating in the study of these revolutions than the study of local history. Here you see the Terror as it really was, no steady and efficient rule from above, as in an army or in Sparta, but a state of suspense and fear, a dissolution of the sober little uniformities of provincial life. Much depends on the accidents of personality—a sensible squire, a moderate and able local revolutionary or two, and a given town or village may go through a revolution fairly serenely. In others, terror may rule as bitterly as in the capital.

This inefficiency of the governments of the crisis period comes out clearly in their attempts to regulate and control the economic life of the State. This whole matter has probably very little to do with the general problem of what is now known as "economic planning." Again we must emphasize that we are concerned only with the anatomies of certain specific revolutions. Suffice it to say that in France in 1793-94 and in Russia in 1918-21 armies were fed and supplied with munitions, and some civilians kept alive at any rate, under a pretty absolute state control of economic activity. The French *maximum* meant of course price and wage fixing, and the Russian war communism was an even more complete form of central planning. Yet in France violation of the *maximum* was as frequent as bootlegging used to be in this country, and the detailed history of the *maximum* seen as part of local history would certainly provide some amusing bits. In Russia illegal trading in the war years was again very like our bootlegging. The famous Sukharevka Market in Moscow was occasionally raided but on the whole winked at by Lenin's government. All city dwellers who could possibly do so made trips to the country to bargain with peasants for forbidden food supplies. Here again the intimate little details of daily life are fascinating, and call for the full talents of the social historian.

There seems to be a pretty unanimous admission by historians, even when they are hostile to revolutions in general, that during the crisis period ordinary crimes of violence are rare. There may be plenty of cruelty and corruption among these new administrators and judges, the new regime may be very far from ensuring peace and order, but conventional robbers, cutthroats, kidnapers, and their like are not very active. Your good stupid Tory has a simple explanation: they've all got government jobs. We can, however, hardly accept this as a blanket explanation. It seems likely that the ordinary criminals are for the moment pretty well cowed by the general crusade against ordinary vice and crime which is a part of the crisis period and to which we are coming shortly. Petty thieves and in several instances even prostitutes were summarily disposed of by what amounts to lynch law during the French Revolution, and similar instances can be found in England and Russia. One need not accept it as a general suggestion that you can always cow criminals by lynching; here, as throughout this book, we are studying a particular set of events, seeking some rough uniformities, and making no attempt at general conclusions in any such field as criminology. It may be that in the general tension, in the extraordinary widening of public concerns until privacy is almost impossible, so private a thing as ordinary crime is difficult. The criminal is disturbed, not only by fear of being lynched, but by an indefinable general fear which he shares with ordinary citizens. For fear needs no object, and in the Terror often has none. It must be remembered that this crisis period is brief—a few months, a few years at the most. At any rate, again a simple uniformity stands out: a considerable lessening in the number of ordinary crimes is to be noted during the crisis period. Mr. Chamberlin notes that Moscow in 1918-19 was a very safe place to live in—if you could get enough to eat and keep warm.

There is usually a short period between the overthrow of the moderates and the full impact of the Terror. The machinery of the Terror, for one thing, hastily assembled though it is, cannot be assembled overnight. Though the earlier history of the revolution has had its share of violence, there has been an interlude or so of apparent peace at times during the struggle between the moderates and the extremists. The pressure of foreign enemies and their *émigré* allies is not immediately at its strongest. Yet as the weeks go on the forces that make for the Terror come into full operation.

We have in this chapter briefly described the rise of the extremists, and have attempted to analyze the reasons for their victory. We have taken them to the point where they have disposed of all important conflicting groups, and have consolidated their position by installing a centralized system of government. For the next few months, or for a year or so, the extremists can be as extreme as they like. No one dare challenge them. We have come to that crisis in the fever of revolution men commonly call the Reign of Terror. This very important subject must be treated in a separate chapter.

7

REIGNS OF TERROR
AND VIRTUE

---

1. Pervasiveness of the Terror

"August 8, 1775. Riflemen took a man in New Milford, Connecticut, a most incorrigible Tory, who called them d—d rebels, etc., and made him walk before them to Litchfield, which is twenty miles, and carry one of his own geese all the way in his hand. When they arrived there, they tarred him, and made him pluck his goose, and then bestowed the feathers on him, drummed him out of the company, and obliged him to kneel down and thank them for their lenity." On October 3, 1775, the New York Sons of Liberty "in solemn Congress assembled" took a vote of thanks "to Mr. Jacob Vredenburgh, barber, for his firm, spirited, and patriotic conduct in refusing to complete an operation vulgarly called *shaving*, which he had begun on the face of Captain John Croser, commander . . . of one of his Majesty's transports. . . . It is to be wished that all gentlemen of the razor will follow this wise, prudent, interesting example." We cite deliberately these examples from the United States, for while it is true that the final victory of the extremists in this country did not quite follow the pattern of our other three revolutions, there is more than a touch of the reign of terror and virtue, as there is more than a touch of social revolution, in our revered revolution.

The undignified little details are important, for they help bring home to us the pervasiveness of the Reign of Terror. There is not only the melodrama of the block, the guillotine, and the firing squad, not only the heightened struggle for power among the great of the new order, not only the tension of foreign and civil war, there is also the tragicomedy of thousands of little lives invaded by heroic concerns which are ordinarily not theirs at all. The Terror touches great and small with the obsessive power of a fashion; it holds men as little of the common weal ever holds them, unless they are professionally devoted to the study or practice of politics. During the Terror, politics becomes as real, as pressing, as unavoidable for John Jones or Jacques Dupont or Ivan Ivanovich as food and drink, wife or mistress, his job and the weather. Political indifference, that mainstay of the modern state, becomes impossible for even the most selfish, the most unworldly.

This participation in the common thing, in the drama of the revolutionary state, means different things to those we may call outsiders and those we may call insiders. The opposition is purely one of convenience. No doubt there are insensible gradations from the ardent revolutionary extremist—the admirably drawn Evariste Gamelin of Anatole France's *The Gods Are Athirst*, for instance—through the neutral and colorless Center to skulking and repressed antirevolutionaries. But in broad lines the division between the many outside the revolutionary cult and the small active band of orthodox believers in the new dispensation is worth making. Let us look first at the Terror as it affects the life of the outsider.

II. *The Terror and the Outsider*

This ordinary outsider is not the actively hostile person, the *émigré* in fact or, as the French actually put it, the *émigré d'esprit*, the *émigré* who has quit spiritually if not in the flesh. He is not the disgruntled moderate. He is simply the man who makes up the bulk of modern societies, the man who on the whole accepts what others do in politics, the man who fairly soon gets on the band wagon. Especially in its crisis period, the revolution is awfully hard on this outsider. It may provide him with a certain

number of spectacles in the form of various celebrations of
the new revolutionary cults—processions, trees of liberty,
festivals of reason, and so on. He hardly had even these in
austere Puritan England. But certainly in the French Revolution there are many indications that the outsiders got
very tired of this, that in the long run they found the old
Catholic ceremonials more to their liking. On the other
hand, there can be no doubt that our modern revolutionists
are much better stage managers than their predecessors;
and of course our patterns of revolution are not neatly
identical. In Russia, notably, something of the atmosphere
of the Terror has survived in the comparatively mild post-
Stalin regimes.

The revolutionary mania for renaming seems also to
tend to confuse and annoy the outsider. The English
confined their efforts largely to the names of persons,
where they achieved some remarkable results. We are all
familiar with Praise God Barebone, and Put-Thy-Trust-in-
Christ-and-Flee-Fornication Williams is no doubt more
than a legend. The Puritans of course drew chiefly from
the Bible and from evangelical abstractions—Faith, Pru-
dence, Charity, and so on.

The French drew from the virtuous days of Roman re-
publicanism, from the abstractions of the Enlightenment,
and from their own leaders and martyrs. François-Noël
Babeuf, the forerunner of Socialism, renamed himself
Gracchus Babeuf. Claude Henri, Comte de St. Simon, kept
his Christian names, but dropped the compromising contact with a saint, and became Claude Henri Bonhomme.
The unfortunate Leroys (Kings) found it well to change to
Laloys (Laws) or something equally patriotic. One faithful
Jacobin had his child republicanly baptized Libre Consti-
tution Leturc. The French, however, did not stop with
persons. Corrupt street names were changed, the Place
Louis XV becoming Place de la Révolution, the rue de la
Couronne becoming rue de la Nation. Place names under-
went wholesale and inconvenient changes. Most of the
Saints were dropped. Lyons, having sinned against the
revolution by siding with the Federalists, on being taken
by troops of the Convention was rechristened Commune
Affranchie (Freed Town). Le Havre became Havre-
Marat. In the conventional greeting of one's fellows, *mon-*

sieur became *citoyen.* For a while the word *"roi"* was under a taboo as definite as the kind the anthropologist studies, and was actually cut out of classic authors like Racine. There was an attempt, possibly serious, possibly journalistic, to change *"reine abeille"* into *"abeille pondeuse"*—"queen bee" into "laying bee."

In their determination to uproot everything of the contaminated past, the French revolutionists decided to revolutionize the calendar. So they made twelve new months, and named them, in poetic French, after the glorious works of Nature—*germinal,* the month of buds, *fructidor,* the month of ripening, *brumaire,* the month of mists. Although the French boasted the universality of their revolutionary aims and principles, they were apparently undisturbed by the narrow limitation of their new calendar to French climatic conditions. The calendar is, of course, most inappropriate to Australia.

The Russians, in addition to their fondness for personal revolutionary *noms de guerre,* have been particularly addicted to changing place names, and unlike the French, they keep changing them. Catherine the Great, in particular, had put herself on the map as successfully as did Alexander the Great, but she has vanished altogether from Soviet Russia. Ekaterinodar became Krasnodar; Ekaterinburg, Sverdlovsk; and Ekaterinoslav, Dnepropetrovsk. Stalin, at his height memorialized even more effectively in place names than Catherine, has now vanished from the map. Stalingrad, once Tsaritsyn, is now Volgograd; Stalin Peak, highest point in the USSR, is now Mt. Communism. From long Socialist tradition, "comrade" took the place occupied by "citizen" in the French Revolution. Children, too, were given names as suitable to the day as were Praise God and Libre Constitution to their day. Vladilen or Vladlen, a telescoping of Vladimir and Lenin, is one of the most shockingly unconventional to an old Russian.

This renaming is clearly one of the uniformities we can list for all our revolutions. Even the moderate American Revolution indulged in some renaming. Boston saw King Street and Queen Street give way to names like Federal and State, thoroughly suited to the new regime; but for some reason or other the tainted name of Hanover Street survived. The American name for a certain harmful fly is the Hessian fly, a name given it in revolutionary days. A kind of cousin of that fly is still known in parts of the South as the Abe Lincoln bug, which is a reminder of the fact that what we call the Civil War was essentially an abortive revolution.

There is no need to worry much over an explanation of this rage for renaming. Change a name and you change the thing. It's all very simple. We are here, however, interested rather in the effect of all this renaming on the outsider, and we can be reasonably sure that it affords an example of the kind of thing that begins to wear on him. The revolution in names is petty enough. But for John Jones life is an accumulation of petty matters; and John is not built to support a very complete set of changes in the trivial details of which his habits are made. Witness Rip Van Winkle.

There is also, of course, the strain of living under the kind of government we have in the last chapter described as the government of the Terror. Even the humblest person, the person most indifferent to politics, can never tell when the lightning is going to strike him or his household, when he may be haled into court as a class enemy or a counterrevolutionary. Detailed study of this constant threat, this omnipresence of the government, cannot be attempted here. It appears at its clearest in the recrudescence of Terror in Russia in the 1930's, the period of trials and purges. We may, however, take up briefly two phases which particularly affect the outsider.

First, as we shall see shortly from the point of view of the insider, all these revolutions have at their crises a quality unmistakably puritanical or ascetic or, to use an overworked word, idealistic. There is a serious attempt by those in authority to eradicate the minor vices, as well as what some might feel inclined to call the major pleasures. With what the Saints in England tried to do in the seventeenth century most Americans are familiar, if only from repercussions in New England. But Americans, who have always exaggerated the French capacity for the pleasures of the senses, are perhaps not so aware of the fact that in '93 and '94 there was an earnest attempt to clean up Paris, to shut up brothels, gaming houses, to eliminate actual drunkenness. Virtue was the order of the day. You couldn't even be lazy. Some Jacobin would be sure to report you to the club, with the suggestion that the best place to cure you of unrepublican laziness was the army. The puritanism of the Bolsheviks may seem even more paradoxical, but it most certainly existed, and we shall return shortly to its consideration.

Now there is no doubt that in the better world toward which we all in some measure aspire, drinking, whoring, gambling, laziness, boastfulness, and a whole lot of things we all condemn, will simply not exist. But it seems equally undeniable that here and now on this earth, and for some generations back, a fairly large number of human beings have been and are addicted to one or more of these pursuits, regarding them—not always consciously with the intellect—as necessary compensations for dullness or other inadequacies in their daily lives. We must again remind ourselves that we are not dealing with moral questions, not praising or condemning, but trying to arrange facts in a useful order. It seems then that the following uniformity is clear: the extremists' attempt to enforce a life without the ordinary vices within a fairly short time puts a strain on the outsider very hard for him, or her, to bear.

Not only is the outsider denied access to what he probably regards as legitimate amusement; the new authorities will not even leave him to himself. Revolutions are very hard indeed on privacy. Gorki once wrote that "Lenin was a man who prevented people from leading their accustomed lives as no one before him was able to do." And as people have a certain inertia in the direction of leading their "accustomed lives," we can perhaps understand better why Stalin rather than Trotsky proved to be Lenin's successor—and Krushchev Stalin's. In the crisis period the revolution comes to hound John Jones in whatever he does. In a revolution even the conventional backbiting, gossip and hatreds of ordinary social life are intensified beyond endurance. The Jacobins, especially in the provinces, were eager to pick up any bit of gossip that would show a reform was needed. Citizen A should keep his dog tied up, citizen B should be made to marry the girl, citizen C should be admonished against outbursts of temper, rich citizen D should be made to give his consent to the marriage of his daughter to a poor but honest Jacobin youth in good standing with the club. One expects this sort of thing from one's own family and friends, but not, even in the totalitarian state, from the government. The Germans have a consoling proverb: "The soup is never eaten as hot as it's cooked." But certainly in the crisis period of revolutions there is an effort to force it steaming down the throat of the ordinary citizen. In the long run, he can't stand it, and his cooks learn their lesson and allow it to cool off a bit. When that happens, however, the crisis of the revolution is over.

Shut out from his ordinary pleasures and vices, constrained to fight for, or at least to cheer long, loud, and conspicuously for the revolutionary state in its struggle with foreign and civil foes, exposed to privation and suffering from scarcity attendant on war and the inevitable inefficiencies of the new government, urged to the "height of revolutionary circumstances" on every hand, in press, theater, pulpit, rostrum, mass demonstration, above all inescapably caught in the common and very exhausting nervous excitement which marks the crisis period, John Jones, even Ivan Ivanovich, sooner or later finds these strains insupportable, and gets ready to welcome anyone who can put an end to them.

Perhaps no *one* of these strains would be in itself unbearable, though it does seem likely that there is a kind of saturation point in large-scale, obsessive political propaganda after which such propaganda actually backfires. We may hope to learn more in this respect from the experience of contemporary dictatorships. People may yet tire of Mao, and even of Castro.

III. *The Terror and the Insider: The Religious Parallel*

To the insider, to the true believer, the revolution appears as a very different thing in this crisis period, though one may guess that for some of the less ardent insiders much of what has been said about the outsiders begins, after a while, to apply pretty well. The revolution begins to take too much out of him, and he begins to have his hesitations and his doubts, to be bored with the endless ceremonies, deputations, committees, Stakhanovite competitions, tribunals, militia work, and the other chores necessary to achieve the reign of virtue on earth. He, too, becomes an outsider. But the true faithful stay to the end, to the block, the guillotine, the firing squad, or exile.

Now this insider, it would seem, finds in his devoted service to the revolution most of the psychological satisfactions commonly supplied by what we call religion. This analogy with religion has been frequently made. It has been applied, not only to the English Revolution where its fitness is undisputed, but also to the French and Russian revolutions. Since both Jacobins and Bolsheviks were violently hostile to Christianity and boasted themselves atheists or at least deists, this analogy has given a great deal of offense both to Christians and to their enemies. For the Marxist in particular the assertion that his behavior has similarities with the behavior of men under the acknowledged influence of religion is most irritating. Nor is the Marxist wholly unjustified in his anger, for the glib phrase, "Oh, the Communists are just another fanatical sect," is frequently thrown out by shallow conservatives as at once a reproach and a dismissal. Actually, to judge from past experience, it would seem that large numbers of men can be brought to do certain very important things of the kind the Communists want to have done only under the influence of what we call religion; that is, some pattern of more or less similar—and necessarily strong—sentiments, moral aspirations, cosmic beliefs and ritualistic practices. Marxism as a religion has already got a great deal done; Marxism as a "scientific theory" alone would hardly have got beyond the covers of *Das Kapital* and the learned journals.

But the dispute sketched above is endless, and we are not rash enough to suppose we can settle it. Those who use the term "religion" in this connection seem to us to be trying to describe a phenomenon of the world of sense-experience, one that needs to be integrated with other phenomena of revolutions. It is certainly true, however, that this use apparently arouses in many persons emotions unfavorable to the continued objective study of the subject. Anyone who could suggest a neutral term as effectively pointing to the same phenomena as does the term "religion" would be performing a great service for sociology. No such term at present existing, we shall have to continue to use the word "religion." We must insist that this word does not refer necessarily and exclusively to a formally theistic cult like Christianity; and above all, that it does not necessarily imply belief in the "supernatural." We take it that in the present analysis the important thing about a religious belief is that under its influence men work very hard and excitedly in common to achieve here or somewhere an ideal, a pattern of life not at the moment universally—or even largely—achieved. Religion attempts to close in favor of human hopes the gap between what men are and what men would like to be; at least in its youthful, fresh, and active phase, it will not for a moment admit that such a gap can long exist.

To discern the element of religious belief and aspiration in the behavior of the ardent extremist is not to deny him economic motives. Indeed, at this stage some of the most acute phases of the struggle among classes are to be noticed, and make one of the uniformities we can clearly consider established. Whatever the place of economic class struggles in the days just before the revolution—and in our four revolutions it takes varied forms by no means adequately summed up in phrases such as "feudal nobility," "middle class," and "proletariat"—once the revolution gets going these class struggles have at least one phase common in all four societies. The property of many, if not most, of those openly and stubbornly identified with the beaten parties is confiscated for the benefit of the successful parties, usually identified as "the people." Furthermore, as the different moderate groups are defeated their property, too, is commonly confiscated in the same way.

In the English Revolution the Royalists lost a large part of their property, mostly in land; and though lay Presbyterians were not as a rule subjected to confiscation of property unless they were actively on the wrong side in politics, there was a great deal of easing Presbyterians and other unacceptable ecclesiastics out of their livings. Laurence Washington, a clergyman, the father of the John of Virginia, and a direct ancestor of George, was "plundered" (deprived of his living) as the phrase went in 1643, because he was reputed to have said that the parliamentary army had more papists in it than there were around the King. We need hardly be reminded that Loyalist property was confiscated during the American Revolution. Indeed J. F. Jameson concluded that in a quiet way —quiet at least for revolutions—the American Revolution effected in its whole course a very sensible democratization, or spreading into smaller units, of ownership of property in this country. Both in France and in Russia the revolutions saw the confiscation primarily of land, but even in France to some extent also of capital, and their redistribution. We need not go into detail here on these agrarian problems. Sufficient to state that many of those who came to the top in the crisis period, both leaders and followers, had good reason to hope that by staying on top their economic status would be consistently better than it had been. This is true regardless of what theories and ideals, laissez-faire or Socialism, were appealed to as guiding the new distribution.

But though we must recognize the economic motive, as we recognize the drive to political and military centralization to repel attacks from within and without, our picture is incomplete until we consider those elements unavoidably called religious. Partly because the economic and political elements are in their conventional sense familiar to most people nowadays, partly because these religious—or at any rate, psychological—elements appear to be among the most important variables in the situation, we are emphasizing them here. They seem to be among the most important variables because their presence in an acute form gives a different and much more pervasive tone to the political and economic elements of struggle, which frequently occur by themselves in very similar form and even somewhat similar intensity in situations we do not commonly label revolutionary. It is also true that in the growth of Wesleyan Methodism in eighteenth-century England, for instance, in times not to be called revolutionary, one finds actively religious behavior among large numbers of people, behavior in many ways like that we are going to analyze in our revolutionary insider. But Wesleyanism was politically conservative on the whole, and not directed against a given social and political system. The whole point, indeed, of the three revolutions we are about to analyze is that religious enthusiasms, organization, ritual, and ideas appear inextricably bound up with economic and political aims, with a program to change *things, institutions, laws,* not just to convert *people*.

The insiders in all three of our complete revolutions, and indeed to a certain extent in the fourth, the American Revolution, seem to have wished to put into life here on earth some of the order, the discipline, the contempt for the easy vices, which the Calvinists sought to put there. Indeed our first revolution, the English, is commonly labeled the Calvinist or Puritan Revolution. Here we may expect a protest from the Communists, an indignant assertion that Marx put such Christian weaknesses as a desire to subdue flesh well behind him, that his followers are all for an abundance of food and drink, and the other good things of this world for everybody. We shall return to that question in a moment. In the meantime we can begin to see some lurking ascetic tendency in Communism if we reflect on how indignant good Communists would be over the slogan "wine, women, and song for everybody."

That the Puritans were in some sense puritanical we may take in stride as a reasonable assumption, in spite of the tendency of our times to worry over semantics. Not even contemporary American undebunkers can persuade us that the Puritans were fine lusty libertines. As for the Jacobins, their legislation and above all their somewhat informal administration in 1793-94 had striking analogies with the kind of things the English Puritans tried to put over. The Jacobins were in principle against gambling, drunkenness, sexual irregularities of all sorts, ostentatious display of poverty, idleness, thieving, and of course in general all sorts of crimes. In practice they felt at liberty to enforce abstention from these vices and to insist with force on the carrying out of positive acts of virtue—such as selling goods always at the legal fixed maximum price, even if a little bootlegging seemed quite safe, attending celebrations in honor of the Supreme Being, expressing in public the opinion that William Pitt was a corrupt villain and the English nation a lot of pathetic slaves. Such a system of action they sought to enforce by making each man his own detective, God's own private spy, much as was said to have been done in Calvin's own Geneva.

Those who chiefly did the prying were the members of the local clubs, urged on by the local leaders, just as with the Puritans it was the parish clergy, aided by the active elders of the Church, who saw to it that the sheep were properly shepherded. The most undignified matters, apparently the most insignificant also, might under these conditions set a parish or a community on end. The first dissension in the English Separatist Church at Amsterdam, we are told, arose not over any point of doctrine or ritual, but over the lace on Mrs. Francis Johnson's sleeve. One could find dozens of parallels for this in the behavior of the Jacobins. There was the lively debate in a little club in Normandy over the question whether the local physician wasn't making his professional calls on aristocrats too long, his calls on patriots too short. And the great row at Bourgoin when the secretary announced that he wasn't going to wear the red Liberty cap because it didn't become him. This shocking display of vanity overcoming patriotism unleashed the full fury of the virtuous republicans of Bourgoin, and the secretary was lucky to escape with his life.

The other-wordliness of the Russian revolutionists affords a problem more apparent than important, or even real. It is quite true that "philosophically" modern Communism is based on materialism, that it insists men must be happy here on earth, enjoying the good things of this earth. But surely it is most important if you wish to understand the problems of men in society to find out what men do, how they behave, as well as what they say on paper or in the pulpit that they are doing, or want to do, or ought to do. It is also quite true that Communists, fellow travelers, and the brethren of the Left in general in this country tend to be extremely indignant when their behavior is analyzed as we propose to analyze it. Here, as so often, indignation is not refutation.

That the old Bolshevik leaders were almost all ascetics is perhaps a commonplace. Lenin was notably austere and contemptuous of ordinary comfort, and at the height of his power his apartments in the Kremlin were of barracklike

simplicity. Some of Lenin's sayings sound like the bourgeois Calvinists as analyzed by Max Weber: "Carry out
an accurate and honest account of money, manage economically, don't loaf, don't steal, maintain the strictest discipline in labor." Indeed, the general tone among the high
command of Bolshevism was in those early years that of a
consecrated and almost monastic group. In a Russia where
men were starving or freezing it was for one thing pretty
impolitic for leaders to look too sleek and well-fed. But just
as the pressure of the war is not a complete explanation for
the Terror, so neither necessity nor policy explains the
asceticism of the Bolsheviks. They felt, as the Puritans had
felt, that the ordinary vices and weaknesses of human
beings are disgusting, that the good life cannot be led until
these weaknesses are eliminated. Early the Bolsheviks prohibited the national drink, vodka, and almost all the first
soviets took steps against prostitution, gambling, night life,
and so on. Theoretically the Bolsheviks thought women
should be free, for instance, free from the shocking limitations bourgeois laws had put upon them: hence the notable freedom allowed at the height of the revolution in
Russia as to marriage, divorce, abortion, and other phases
of family and sex relationships. But the Bolsheviks did not
intend by this that women were to be free to behave as
they were sure they secretly behaved—or wanted to behave—in dissolute old bourgeois society. On the contrary,
they expected their women to behave as they would behave in the classless society—and that is a pretty strict
canon.

Even in the 1930's, when apparently the crisis stage was
over in Russia, there were numerous survivals of the intense asceticism of the true Communist party members of
the crisis period. In their innocent book on Soviet Russia,
the innocent Webbs declared that there was no asceticism
in Russia, of course, and then went on and explained how
the Komsomols (Communist Youth) were encouraged to
take the pledge—not for any silly evangelical reasons,
heavens, no, but because drinking anything alcoholic is "a
breach of the rule requiring maintenance of perfect health."
Petting, too, was very definitely discouraged as unworthy

of the Communist Youth, especially when it is done in public. "Nothing pornographic is allowed in literature or in any form of art. There is less public sex appeal in evidence in Russia than in any Western land." Since the Webbs wrote this, the Russians seem to have relaxed a bit in their public restraints, at least in official entertainment of foreigners. But it is still true that the Russian press has no equivalent of our "cheesecake." To the spiritual heirs of the Webbs, Russia can even today seem devoted to the cultivation of the simpler virtues.

The Russians of old being notoriously dirty about their public places—almost as dirty as we Americans are—the new regime has made it a point of discipline that no litter, papers, and suchlike truck be left in public parks, streets, and stations. Indeed, membership in the Communist party itself, always a very select and disciplined minority, demanded for years, and to a certain extent still demands, the exercise of a great deal of self-restraint, a willingness to live simply, to work hard, to conform to very high standards of personal morality. As usual in such circumstances, and as we have already noted for the Puritans and the Jacobins, self-restraint was apparently not enough, and there grew up in Russia all sorts of official and unofficial methods of spying, prying, checking-up on the actions of individuals, and controlling them by Terrorist methods. The Cheka or secret police, become the NKVD, served the Stalinite revival of terror in 1936-39 quite as faithfully as if this Terror had been the fresh, religiously inspired Terror of the crisis period. Finally, of course, the vast difference in personality between the worldly—and earthy—Khrushchev and the dedicated, austere, puritanical Lenin was symbolic of the end of the reign of virtue in Russia. And the present regime has given no indication of a desire to return to the earlier, more ascetic phase.

Now groups thoroughly disciplined into lives almost as unnaturally ascetic as those our Puritans, Jacobins, and Bolsheviks sought to impose have existed for relatively long periods. The Spartans contrived to support an almost heroic Communism for several centuries. But this discipline is of slow growth, intimately tied up with the kind of behavior in men that changes with geological slowness. A revolution cannot manufacture this kind of discipline overnight, and perhaps the violence—and here is meant rather spiritual violence than mere bloodshed—of the Terror is in some sense an overcompensation for the inability of the extremists to carry their ordinary brothers along with them. The Terror is a desperate overshooting of the mark. Again, the existence in individuals of a certain amount of inclination to meddle with their neighbor's private affairs is probably a useful thing, part of what cements societies together. But here, too, the ardent revolutionists overshoot the mark and make life unbearable for their neighbors.

There are traces of this kind of organized asceticism, this crusade against the customary vices, even in the American Revolution, where the crisis stage was never so intense as in our other revolutions. There were many restrictive measures justified chiefly as necessary to the efficient prosecution of the war against George III. There were others quite as obviously dictated by the traditions of middle-class Protestant ethics which had long been established in the Middle Colonies and in New England. But here and there one encounters the true accent of revolutionary idealism. Here is a passage worthy of Robespierre:

> Titles are the offspring of monarchical and arbitrary governments. . . . Let us leave the titles of excellency and honorable to the abandoned servants of a tyrant King . . . while we satisfy ourselves with beholding our senators, governors, and generals rich in real excellence and honor.

Again we find a neat illustration from the pen of a Connecticut patriot writing in July, 1775:

> Wednesday evening last, a number of ladies and gentlemen collected at a place called East Farms, in Connecticut, where they had a needless entertainment, and made themselves extremely merry with a good glass of wine. Such entertainments and diversions can hardly be justified upon any occasion; but at such a day as this, when everything around us has a threatening aspect, they ought to be discoun-

tenanced, and every good man should use his influence to suppress them.

Our orthodox and successful extremists, then, are crusaders, fanatics, ascetics, men who seek to bring heaven to earth. No doubt many of them are hypocrites, career-seekers masquerading as believers, no doubt many of them climb on the band wagon for selfish motives. Yet it is most unrealistic to hold that men may not be allowed to reconcile their interests with their ideas. Many an ardent and sincere follower of Robespierre, many a seeker after Calvinist truth, was able, with the best of conscience, to buy lands confiscated from the unrepublican or the ungodly. Our extremists are also, as the intimate details of their daily lives should convince us, for the most part quite ordinary people, with the loves and hatreds, aspirations and doubts, hopes and fears, of ordinary people. Once the crisis period is over, they will, save for the few born martyrs, cease to be crusaders, fanatics, ascetics. Their revolutionary beliefs will be softly cushioned in a comfortable ritual, will be a consolation and a habit rather than a constant prick of the ideal. But now, in the crisis period, they are in what we may call the active phase of a religion. Let us briefly take up some of the striking characteristics of this phase in our three societies.

Calvinism, Jacobinism, Marxism, are all rigidly deterministic. All believe that what happens here below is foreordained, predestined to follow a course which no mere human being can alter, least of all those who oppose respectively Calvinism, Jacobinism, or Marxism. In fact, the more priest and prelate storm and rage, the more certain is the Calvinists' victory. The acts of aristocrats, traitors, Pitts and Cobourgs can but make the triumph of the French Republic greater. The harder the Rockefellers and the Morgans work, the more capitalistic their behavior, the sooner will come the inevitable, glorious, and final uprising of the proletariat. God for the Calvinist, nature and reason for the Jacobin, dialectical or scientific materialism for the Marxist, provide comforting assurance that the believer is on the side that *must* win. Obviously the belief that you can't lose will in most—not all—cases make you a better fighter.

Those whom God, nature, or science has chosen are quite willing to advertise the fact of this choice, and, indeed, display an inconsistency which is purely logical, and not at all of the emotions, in that they seem very anxious to help the inevitable come about. Rigid determinists are also usually ardent proselyters, presumably on the grounds that they are instruments of the inevitable, the means through which the inevitable realizes itself. They do not, however, seem to behave as if they held that resistance to their proselyting, refusal of unbelievers to accept their message, were also determined, inevitable, and even pardonable.

At any rate, our revolutionists all sought to spread the gospel of their revolution. What we now call "nationalism" is certainly present as an element in all these revolutionary gospels. But at least in the earlier years, and during the crisis of a revolution, crude notions of national expansion do not prevail. The fortunate people to whom the gospel has been revealed wish to spread it properly abroad. In the Messianic fervor of the crisis period, aggressive nationalism is not on the surface. This nationalism doubtless helps drive the revolutionists on, and in the period of reaction it emerges into the light, barely if at all disguised as the "destiny" of a chosen people and its leader. The Jacobins announced they were bringing the blessings of freedom to all the people of the earth, and such is the power of imagination that some men still think of Napoleon as agent of the new freedom. The Bolsheviks are still present to our generation as great apostles of a world-wide revolution; but today, in contrast to 1918, it has become a commonplace even among Western conservatives to assert that what Stalin sought was to spread abroad rather Russian imperialism than world Communism. It is still doctrine among orthodox Communists that Communism is the wave of the future.

The Calvinists as Christians, of course, were ardent proselyters. But the victorious English Independents were also capable of mixing their religious with political propaganda, were anxious to win the world over to their superior form of society. Cromwell's famous collaborator, Admiral Blake, used to spread the gospel in foreign lands. Thanks to the example of England, Blake said, "All kingdoms will annihilate tyranny and become republics." England had done so already. France was following in her wake; and as the natural gravity of the Spaniards rendered them somewhat slower, he gave them ten years. All Europe is shortly to be republican—and this in the 1650's! Those who today boast or bemoan that soon the Western world will be all Communist, or all free enterprise democracy, might ponder a while the circumstances of this remark of Blake's.

A good deal of ink and oratory has been expended over this effort of the extremists to propagate their faiths among the nations. Conservatives in other nations are naturally very suspicious. Moscow must be at the bottom of every liberal or radical movement; there is an organized international plot to establish the world-rule of atheistic Jacobinism and destroy Christianity. Probably in most cases these fears and suspicions are much exaggerated. The revolutionists in the crisis period are usually too poor, and too occupied at home, to devote more than a small part of their energies to these foreign missions. There are, moreover, in the other countries usually enough disgruntled natives to form a solid nucleus for revolutionary action. The importation into these countries of English, French, or Russian phrases and other revolutionary fashions is the most natural thing in the world. Here once more the extremes of *conspiracy* or *spontaneity* are quite simply false analyses; reality is a confusing medley of both.

At any rate, there is no doubt about the fact of the uniformity. Even in the seventeenth century, when the world was so much larger, so much slower to cross, the English Revolution spread itself abroad. Edward Sexby at Bordeaux proposed to the French radicals a republican constitution which was to be called *L'Accord du Peuple*—an adaptation of the English Agreement of the People—and was obliged in consequence to flee the town. In Holland at the news of trouble in England, "the people began to take sides for one or the other of the parties and with such fervor that in many cases they came to blows." This sounds a lot like the behavior of Federalists and Republicans in the United States in the 1790's, when the French Revolution provided most of the dramatic material of

American politics. But the point need not be labored. Similar examples from the Russian Revolution will occur to everyone.

The religious parallel may be pushed a bit further. Our revolutionists are convinced that they are the elect, destined to carry out the will of God, nature, or science. That feeling was particularly strong among the Russian Communists, where in pure logic it should be less strong than among the Calvinists, believers in a personal God. The opponents of these revolutionists are not just political enemies, not just mistaken men, grafters, logrollers, or damned fools; they are sinners, and must not merely be beaten—they must be wiped out. Hence the justification of the guillotine and the firing squad. For our revolutionists display that vigorous intolerance which in the logic of the emotions, as well as in that of the intellect, follows perfectly on the conviction of being absolutely, eternally, monopolistically right. If there is but one truth, and you have that truth completely, toleration of differences means an encouragement to error, crime, evil, sin. Indeed, toleration in this sense is harmful to the tolerated, as well as very trying on the tolerator. As Bellarmine said, it is a positive benefit to obstinate heretics to kill them because the longer they live the more damnation they heap upon themselves.

These revolutionary faiths are very interesting in their eschatologies, their notions of final ends like heaven and hell. The English Revolution was dominated by some of the wilder as well as by the more conventional of Christian eschatologies. The Millenarians expected the second coming year after year. The rule of the Saints was just around the corner. The Jacobins had a much less concrete notion of heaven, and this heaven was to be definitely here on earth—the Republic of Virtue which we have seen as Robespierre's ideal. After the dictatorship of the revolutionary government, this perfect republic was to appear, and Liberty, Equality, Fraternity, would be more than a slogan. To hardened Americans a republic doesn't sound at all like a heaven, but we must believe that it was very different for the earnest Jacobin of 1794. The Russian heaven is the classless society, to be attained after the purgatory of the dictatorship of the proletariat has slowly put an end to the worldly miseries of the class struggle. The specific content of life in the classless society is somewhat vaguely described by most Communists. There will be competition, one gathers, for Marx after all started from a Hegelian base, but no struggle and certainly no struggle over economic goods. Competition will be on a lofty plane, as among artists or English public schoolboys at play. At any rate, as in a more robust heaven, the Old German Valhalla, the heroes will fight all day, but at night their wounds will heal.

All of these faiths were incorporated in social groups, and hence had rituals. The present writer has elsewhere described at some length the Jacobin ritual, a strange hodgepodge of Catholic, Protestant, classical and other elements, with republican creeds, republican baptisms and prayers, even with a revolutionary sign of the cross in the name of *Marat, Lepeletier, la liberté ou la mort.* Communist ritual is less crudely imitative, and perhaps less rich. But it is just as definite, as you will find in talking to an initiated Communist. The French revolutionists had their saints and martyrs, especially the murdered Marat: the apotheosis of Lenin, clearly begun in his lifetime, has become a cult centered around his tomb in Moscow. Lenin is perhaps, like Jeremy Bentham preserved in University College, London, a purely secularist saint; but a saint he is. Smaller groups, like the Communist Youth, are brought up in an atmosphere of ritual, and are in this respect more like some of the social activities of our Protestant churches than like comparatively secular groups such as the Boy Scouts.

Religious symbolism goes along with this ritual, and was especially developed in France. During the Terror, one met symbolic devices everywhere: the eye of surveillance, seeking out the enemies of the Republic; the triangle of Liberty, Equality, Fraternity; the Phrygian cap of liberty, the *bonnet rouge;* the carpenter's level, symbolizing equality; any kind of mound, which served as symbol for the beneficent Mountain, the party that had carried out the revolution to its logical end. Most of these and many other symbols are to be found in the elaborate pageant of the

20th Prairial at Paris, when Robespierre personally supervised the festival of the Supreme Being. The Russians, aided by modern poster technique, have made a similar, if less pedantic, use of symbols to hold the people together in a Communist society.

Perhaps the most important uniformity in our four revolutions is that as gospels, as forms of religion, they are all universalist in aspiration and nationalist, exclusive, in ultimate fact. They end up with a God meant indeed for all mankind, but brought to mankind, usually a not altogether willing mankind, by a Chosen People. We Americans can see all this most clearly in our contemporaries, the Russian Communists. But to many outsiders, especially if they take the phrase "the American century" seriously, we too are nationalists spreading a gospel born of revolution long ago in the eighteenth century. Manifest Destiny is by no means the palest of the gods.

Yet beyond this uniformity there is a much deeper one, which helps explain the more obvious and paradoxical uniformity of nationalistic universalism born of revolution. These four revolutions show a progressively increasing hostility to organized Christianity, and particularly to the more ecumenical forms of organized Christianity. There is a secular touch even to the seventeenth-century English Revolution, and an overwhelming preponderance of emphasis on the individual conscience over against the corporate Church and its traditions; the French and even the American revolutions are full in the tide of eighteenth-century secularism; the Russian Revolution is proudly materialistic.

Now this progressive repudiation of traditional Christianity has not, as the traditional Christian is perhaps too readily inclined to feel, been inspired by devilish and corrupt men who want to shut out the finer things from human life. Many of these revolutionaries have indeed been full of pride, and many other sins. But their heaven has been very close indeed to the Christian heaven, their ethics close to Christian ethics, indeed the ethics of all the higher religions. Marxist "materialism" is really pretty abstract, even elevated; it is hardly grosser, hardly nearer common sense, than the materialism of the physicist.

What separates these revolutionaries from traditional Christianity is most obviously their insistence on having their heaven here, now, on earth, their impatient intent to conquer evil once and for all. Christianity in its traditional forms has long since, not by any means given up the moral struggle, but given up its chiliastic hopes—the hopes it too had when it was young and revolutionary, the hopes of the immediate Second Coming of Christ. By distinguishing between this world and the next world, the natural and the supernatural or divine, Christianity can bridge the gap between what men are and have and what men want to be and want to have. This gap your revolutionary knows well enough. He proposes, however, not to bridge it, but to fill it in or leap over it. He often ends, where the mystic begins, by persuading himself the gap isn't really there.

Even if you assume, as the positivist, the materialist, does, that man is an animal and nothing more, a part of nature—and that nature is all there is—it seems reasonably clear that man is unique in nature and among animals in being able to conceive a future. At any rate, no other animal seems able to plan, to think. Other animals can be frustrated, but not, apparently, by the failure of their ideas and symbolically stated plans to work out. Plenty of positivist philosophers can indeed console themselves with this world as they see it. But not large masses of men. Here is where Voltaire's impertinent and rather patronizing remark comes in: if God did not exist, it would be necessary to invent him.

And that is just what our revolutionaries have done. But they have had to invent abstract gods, tribal gods, jealous gods. Their new faiths have not the maturity of the old. They have not, despite their aspirations, the universalism of the old. They have not for the weary and the disappointed the consoling power of the old. They have not yet gained the power of successful syncretism, the wisdom of the ages. They are still, in short, revolutionary faiths, more effective as goads or prods than as pacifiers. This is notably true of the newest of them, Marxist Communism. The Russian leadership may well have grave difficulty in removing the revolutionary sting from their now much less chiliastic faith in a new heaven on earth.

IV. *Explanations of the Terror*

In the crisis periods of all four of our revolutions we may distinguish the same set of variables, differently combined and mixed with all sorts of contingent factors to produce the specific situations the narrative historian of these revolutions tends to regard as unique. There are no doubt a very great number of these variables, but for the purposes of a first approximation we may here distinguish seven. These seem not to be related one to another in any important one-way casual relationship. They seem, indeed, more or less like the independent variables of the mathematician, though it is inconceivable that they should be strictly independent. The temptation to single out one of them as the "cause" of the Terror is, like the temptation to find a hero or a villain in any situation, hard to resist. And each one of them has a history, goes back at least to the last generation or two of the old regime.

They are all woven together in a complicated pattern of reality; but without all of them—and this is the important point—you would not have a Reign of Terror, would not have a full crisis in the revolution. The problem of their possible independence need not worry us. Temperature and pressure are independent variables in the mathematical formulation of the laws of thermodynamics; but ice can form at 0° centigrade only if the pressure is negligibly small. We have already stressed this point, perhaps beyond the bounds of good writing. But the old notion of simple, linear, one-way causation is so rooted in our habits of thought, is indeed so useful to us in daily life, that we almost instinctively demand an explanation of a complex situation like the Terror which will enable us to isolate a villain-cause—or a hero-cause.

First, there is what we may call the habit of violence, the paradoxical situation of a people conditioned to expect the unexpected. The more violent and terroristic periods of our revolutions come only after a series of troubles have prepared the way. Not until after several years of civil war in England did the Independents carry out their rigorous measures against the habitual ways of "Merrie England."

The Terror in France in a formal sense does not begin until late in 1793; sporadic outbreaks like the Great Fear in 1789 and the September Massacres of 1792 simply help to establish the mood necessary for a Terror. Even in Russia, where events were telescoped together in a shorter period than in any of our other revolutions, organized violence under the patronage of the government does not clearly appear until the autumn of 1918, a year and a half after the outbreak against the Czar. A telegram from Petrovsky to all soviets is quoted by Mr. Chamberlin, who sees in this the signal for organized Terror. "Last of all, the rear of our armies must be finally cleared of all White Guardism and all scoundrelly conspirators against the power of the working class and the poorest peasants. Not the least wavering, not the least indecision in the application of mass terror."

This telegram brings forward a second and most important variable—the pressure of a foreign and civil war. War necessities help explain the rapid centralization of the government of the Terror, the hostility to dissenters within the group—they now seem deserters—the widespread excitement which our generation knows well enough by the cant term "war psychosis." Both in France and in Russia there is a rough correlation between the military situation of the revolutionary armies and the violence of the Terror; as the danger of defeat grows, so does the number of victims of revolutionary tribunals. There is, however, a certain lag, and the Terror continues after the worst of the military danger is over. We may again recall that in England the Irish and the Scots fulfilled the function of the foreign enemy, even though Great Britain kept relatively free of the continent during the whole period of her Puritan Revolution. And both in America and in England the crisis period was accompanied by a formal war, largely a civil war. No sensible person would wish to deny the important place these wars have in the total situation we have called the crisis period.

Third, there is the newness of the machinery of this centralized government. The extremists are certainly not— and we have already emphasized this point—altogether without experience in handling men, though they have

dealt with *revolutionists,* not with *all men.* Their long apprenticeship in the cause of the revolution has been a
political training of a sort. And in many ways their new
network of institutions is able to use some of the routine
channels used by the old government. This is especially
true in local government. Nevertheless, it is certainly true
that the institutions of the Terror are in a sense new, that
they do not work smoothly, that those charged with ad-
ministering them, even if they are not politically inexperienced, are administratively inexperienced. The machinery
of the Terror works in fits and starts, and frequently jams
badly. Conflicts between administrators arise, and are
settled in no routine manner, but by violence. Each failure
of the machine annoys those who are trying to run it, and
impels them to a new and sudden decision, to another act
of violence. This in turn further jams the machinery. It is
our old friend the vicious circle.

Fourth, this is also a time of acute economic crisis—not
merely what we now call a depression, but a definite short-
age of the necessities of life. Again it must be recalled that
the Terror does not come at once, in the very beginning of
the revolution, but is preceded by a time of troubles very
disrupting to the ordinary processes of production. Capital
gets frightened and begins to leave the country. Businessmen hesitate to undertake new enterprises or to continue
on the same basis with the old. Peasant difficulties lessen
agricultural production. Then comes the war with its demand for men and munitions. The ensuing dictatorship of
the victorious extremists is in part an economic dictatorship, a supervision of the whole economic life of the country, controlled currency, price fixing, food rationing, a kind
of socialism of the fact long before Marx. The difficulty of
distributing inadequate supplies further tries the temper of
administrators, adds to the opportunities of denunciators
and spies, serves to maintain and sharpen the peculiar
excitement, the universal jumpiness of the Terror. It adds
to the tenseness of the class struggles which we have already discerned in our study of the old regimes.

In one form or another our fifth variable, class struggles,
clearly appears in the crisis of all our revolutions. The
hatred of Puritan for Cavalier, of Jacobin for aristocrats,

Federalists, and other enemies of the Republic of Virtue, the hatred of Bolsheviks for Whites, Kadets, and compromisists, of American Whigs for Tories, was in itself an elaborate compound. One element in this compound was probably about what the Marxist means when he talks about the class struggle. At any rate, by the time of the Terror the different antagonistic groups within the society have polarized into the orthodox revolutionists in power and the somewhat mixed bloc of their enemies. Heightened like all other tensions and conflicts by the course of the revolution, these class antagonisms now take on a sharpness they normally possess only in the writings and speeches of intellectuals and agitators. The party spirit, which is in one element probably but one form of the antagonism between classes, here seizes upon the most trivial symbols to make men aware of their irreconcilable differences. Thus the Jacobins adopted the term "sans-culottes" as a rallying cry to emphasize the class struggle. The *culottes* are the knee breeches of the silk-stockinged gentlemen of the old regime, and those without *culottes* presumably wore the long trousers of the common man, the workingman. The Russian Revolution was filled with the slogans of the class struggle in the narrow Marxist sense. Now, though there was much more than class struggles in our revolutions, and though these struggles are not quite so simply determined as many believers in the economic interpretation of history sometimes make out, it would be very foolish to deny the importance of one of the variables in the Terror—those antagonisms between groups or "classes" largely held together by economic interests and by a common social and intellectual heritage, a common way of life, which our generation knows as the class struggle.

Our sixth variable is even more obviously than the others an abstraction, a presumably useful way of gathering together a great number of concrete facts. It is not logically on an exact level with our other variables, and would not fit into a nice series of philosophical categories. This is a variable based on observation of the behavior of the relatively small group of leaders formed during the revolution and now in control of the government of the Terror.

Much of their behavior is affected, like the behavior of their followers and fellow citizens, by the other variables in our list, and no doubt by much that has escaped us. But some very important elements in their behavior depend on the fact that they are leaders, that they have gone through a certain apprenticeship in revolutionary tactics, that they have been selected, almost in a Darwinian sense, for their ability to manipulate an extremist revolutionary group. This does not mean that they are necessarily or even usually "impractical" men, "theoreticians," "metaphysicians," or any other of the names simple critics like Taine invented for them. It does mean that they are not formed for compromise, for the dull expedients of politics in unexcited, relatively stable societies. It does mean that they are formed to push on to extremes, to use their special influence to heighten the already high tension of life in society. Like all politicians, they have learned the skills necessary for success in their trade; they have come to feel their trade is something like a game, as indeed it is; but they are reckless players, apt to play to the gallery, and always trying to annihilate the opposing side. Moreover, they are at least as jealous of one another as, to use another comparison, actors, and each one must always try for the center of the stage. What in more ordinary times has been lately no more than a conventional struggle for power among politicians is thus in the crisis period of revolutions stepped up to a murderous intensity.

Finally, there is the variable we have dwelt upon at length in an earlier part of this chapter. This is the element of religious faith shared by Independents, Jacobins, Bolsheviks. We need not here repeat what we have just written about the religious aspect of the Reigns of Terror. But it is this element that makes the Reigns of Terror also Reigns of Virtue, heroic attempts to close once for all the gap between human nature and human aspirations. This is but one of the variables, but it is a very important one. Religious aims and emotions help to differentiate the crises of our revolutions from ordinary military or economic crises, and to give to the Reigns of Terror and Virtue their extraordinary mixture of spiritual fury, of exaltation, of devotion and self-sacrifice, of cruelty, madness, and high-grade humbug.

Now all these elements are in constant interaction one with another, a change in one affecting complex corresponding changes in all the others, and hence in the total situation. We must not think of them in terms of horse and cart, or chicken and egg, or of one billiard ball hitting another. It is instead as complicated and mad a chase as we conceive that of the molecules in a physico-chemical system. Thus the stresses and strains of the early stages of our revolutions make it easier to work the nation into war —witness the war-provoking Girondins in France—and the war itself increases the stresses, accustoms people to violence and suspense. War makes for economic scarcity and economic scarcity sharpens the class struggle, and so on in a merry round robin. All these effects, up to the end of the crisis period, are cumulative. Each old habit sloughed off, each definite break with the past at once invites others and increases the strain upon everybody, or nearly everybody, in the social system.

For it would seem to be an observable fact of human behavior that large numbers of men can stand only so much interference with the routines and rituals of their daily existence. It would also seem that most men cannot long stand the strain of prolonged effort to live in accordance with very high ideals. The outsider in the crisis period is pushed to the limit of his endurance by interference with some of his most prized and intimate routines; the insider is held to a pitch of spiritual effort and excitement beyond his powers of endurance. For both sorts of men there would seem to be a limit to their social action as real as the limit a chemist finds for a chemical reaction. Human beings can go only so far and so long under the stimulus of an ideal. Social systems composed of human beings can endure for but a limited time the concerted attempt to bring heaven to earth which we call the Reign of Terror and Virtue. Thermidor comes as naturally to societies in revolution as an ebbing tide, as calm after a storm, as convalescence after fever, as the snapping-back of a stretched elastic band. Such figures of speech, taken from established uniformities in the physical world, seem to impose themselves. Perhaps, in spite of the efforts of philosophers, theologians, moralists, political theorists, social scientists, and a good many other inspired thinkers in the last two thousand years, social systems are still in many respects almost as perversely unaffected by revolutionary good intentions as tides or rubber bands.

8

THERMIDOR

---

1. *Universality of the Thermidorean Reaction*

As we have had to note in earlier attempts to fit our four revolutions into our conceptual scheme, this fitting cannot be done with finicky exactness. It is quite impossible to say that the crisis of a given revolution ended at 4:03 P.M. on August 6th of a given year. France does indeed furnish us with an instance almost as precise as this. The end of the crisis in France may be dated from the fall of Robespierre on July 27, 1794, or on the ninth Thermidor, year II of the poetic new French calendar. The ensuing slow and uneven return to quieter, less heroic times has long been known to French historians as the Thermidorean reaction. The Marxists, or rather, the Trotskyites and other anti-Stalinist heretics, have often applied the word to the Russian Revolution, so that we may adopt it, as we did "old regime," as a term in general acceptance. All our revolutions had their Thermidors, though in no two were the sequence of events, the time-schedules, the ups and downs of daily life, anything like identical.

In terms of our conceptual scheme, we shall have to call Thermidor a convalescence from the fever of revolution, even though "convalescence" suggests something nice, and seems therefore to be a way of praising the Thermidorean reaction. We can but repeat previous assertions that no such eulogistic sense is here intended. We continue to try to discover first approximations of uniformities in phenomena we mean neither to praise nor to blame, neither to cherish nor to damn.

In England the beginning of the Thermidorean period, the convalescence, is not to be put with any preciseness. The year or so following the execution of Charles I represents the height of the crisis in England, and as long as the Rump sat some strong flavor of revolution remained. Perhaps the best date for the English Thermidor is Cromwell's dissolution of the Rump on April 20, 1653, when the great general made some celebrated and un-English remarks about the resemblance between the parliamentary mace and a jester's staff. With Cromwell installed as Protector under the "instrument of Government" of 1653—the English actually did indulge themselves for once in a written constitution—Thermidor may be said to be well on its way. In 1657 Cromwell became Lord Protector, half a king at least, and with the restoration of the Stuarts in 1660 the great English Revolution may be said to have ended.

The fall of Robespierre in France had been brought about largely by a conspiracy among outwardly orthodox Jacobin deputies to the Convention, many of whom were involved in war profiteering, parliamentary corruption, stock speculation and other activities unworthy of citizens of the Republic of Virtue. Fear of the "Incorruptible" Robespierre seems to have been one of the main reasons for their action. They were successful, not unaided by Robespierre's lack of political wisdom. The Thermidoreans themselves had apparently not intended to end the Terror; the guillotining of Robespierre was just another in a long list of revolutionary guillotinings to which they had now become well accustomed. But for once public opinion got to work, and Frenchmen made it clear that they were through with the "tigers athirst for blood." The reaction continued at a fairly steady rate for some years, both under the declining Convention and the new government of the Directory. There were definite relapses, as one might expect in a convalescence. Especially in the summer of 1799, after French defeats abroad, there was a striking revival of Jacobinism. The clubs reopened, and the good old slogans resounded once more in public halls, in cafés, and on street corners. A few months later Napoleon Bonaparte had achieved his *coup d'état* of the 18th Brumaire, and the French convalescence was nearly over. The actual restoration of the Bourbons in 1814 is hardly a part of the course of revolution in France. It was rather an accident, a consequence of such purely personal factors as Napoleon's megalomaniac insistence on fighting all Europe to the bitter end in 1813-14, Talleyrand's knack for calling the turn, the difficulties in the way of succession for Napoleon's son by Marie Louise, and the pious intentions of Alexander I of Russia. Thermidor in Russia has been complicated and prolonged. We may perhaps regard the period of war communism, 1917-21, as the first main crisis of the Russian Revolution. With the New Economic Policy of 1921 began Russia's Thermidor. Lenin's death and the subsequent rivalry between Stalin and Trotsky led up to a second crisis, or rather relapse during convalescence, which we may date at the more acute periods of violent enforcement of the first Five Year Plan. But as many an observer has noted, this secondary crisis lacked the hopeful idealism of the first, lacked its improvisations and its adventures, lacked its active foreign and White Guard enemies, and looks from even our brief historical perspective much like characteristic acts of the "tyrants" who came to power during other Thermidors—the Cromwellian settlement of Ireland, for instance, or the Napoleonic enforcement of the Continental System. But the whole question of how far Russia has in mid-twentieth century returned to normal—Russian normal—will require a section in itself.

II. *Amnesty and Repression*

Politically the most striking uniformity to be noted in the period of convalescence is the ultimate establishment of a "tyrant" in something like the old Greek sense of the word, an unconstitutional ruler brought to power by revolution. This uniformity has been frequently noted: Cromwell, Bonaparte, Stalin, all seem to confirm it. Indeed, in the Federalist period in the United States there were Jeffersonians ungrateful enough to suggest that

Washington was a perfectly good example of the tyrant born of revolution. There is nothing very puzzling about the phenomenon. After a revolution has undergone the crisis and the accompanying centralization of power, some strong leader must handle that centralized power when the mad religious energy of the crisis period has burned itself out. Dictatorships and revolutions are inevitably closely associated, because revolutions to a certain extent break down, or at least weaken, laws, customs, habits, beliefs which bind men together in society; and when laws, customs, habits, beliefs tie men together insufficiently, force must be used to remedy that insufficiency. Military force is for short terms the most efficient kind of force available for social and political uses, and military force demands a hierarchy of obedience culminating in a generalissimo. As Ferrero has put it, when the "silken threads" of habit, tradition, legality are broken, men must be held together in society by the "iron chains" of dictatorship. All this, however, is pretty much a commonplace of our times.

The rule of one man does not come immediately with the Thermidorean reaction. Even Cromwell, the earliest-established of the three, did not become uncontested ruler with the dissolution of the Rump. The reaction to the crisis is at first slow and uncertain. The habit of violence is by now thoroughly established. There is left from the crisis a tendency to dramatic steps and whole-hog measures. Even sober and peace-loving men have moments of excited relapses to the jitters of the Terror. Seen in this light, the Moscow purges and trials of the 1930's are no indication that the Russian Revolution has had an unusually long life, that it fails to fit our pattern. These melodramatic displays are no more than the expected aftermath of revolution in a land and among peoples relatively backward in economic and political structure. As time goes on, the pressures the Terror applied to ordinary men are relaxed: the special tribunals give place to more regular ones, the revolutionary police are absorbed into the regular police—which are not necessarily the equivalent of London bobbies; they may be agents of the NKVD—and the block, guillotine or firing squad are reserved for the more dramatic criminals. It is not, of course, that political life shortly assumes the idyllic stability some of our own contemporaries like to describe as the Rule of Law, and which, one suspects, was never quite as nice as appears in their books—not even in staid nineteenth-century England, or in the thirteenth century in which St. Thomas Aquinas lived so pleasantly. The taste and habit of political violence live on in *coups d'état*, in purges, in well-staged trials. But John Jones, Jacques Dupont, Ivan Ivanovich, the man in the street, is no longer included in the cast—he is now left to his normal role of spectator or supernumerary.

Gradually, too, the politically proscribed are amnestied, and come back; sometimes to be caught up again in the scramble of competitive politics; sometimes to become part of that staff of modern life, the bureaucracy; sometimes to live quietly as private citizens. The process is naturally the reverse of the process in which these men and women had been driven out. They go from Right to Left, and come back from Left to Right—first the almost pure radicals, then the moderates, then moderate conservatives, until the final restoration brings back remnants of the old gang. Such at least was the process in France and in England. After 1653, the Presbyterians took heart and began to emerge into politics, followed by the more moderate Episcopalians and Royalists, until in 1660 the Stuarts and their courtiers returned. In France the succession was very exact and ratified by formal bills of amnesty: first the Girondins —those who had survived—came back, while tears were shed over, and monuments erected to, the innocent victims of the bloodthirsty tiger Robespierre; then the Feuillants, the Lafayette-Lameths; then the out-and-out Royalists and suchlike *émigrés*, whom Napoleon, however, was able to control fairly well; then finally, in 1814, the Bourbons themselves.

So far the Romanovs have not returned to Russia, and hardly anyone now seriously expects them to be restored. We must not ask our revolutions to make too neat a picture. It is clear, however, that save for the final monarchical restoration, the process we have outlined above has been going on irregularly, much less neatly than in France, in Soviet Russia. Even the aristocrats can go back if they make the proper submission and get the proper publicity

—which was true of Napoleonic France. Even the now sainted Gorki was what in France would be called a *rallié*, a man who rallied to the Communist regime only after the worst of the initial Terror was safely over. On the other hand, almost all the old Bolsheviks, the men who ruled Russia in the period of crisis, have by now been liquidated. It is a commonplace in Western editorials to refer to both Stalin and Khrushchev as successors to the Czars.

The personnel of government in the Thermidorean period and in the new-old regime that finally emerges from the revolution is likely to be varied in origin. Napoleon was served by old aristocrats of the *noblesse d'épée*, by bureaucrats trained in the old regime, by Fayettists, by Girondins and even by a few once-violent Jacobins. Of men like Albemarle, Shaftesbury, and Downing, who stood high in the government of Charles II after his restoration, it has been written: "They were of the same school as Blake and Vane; they represented the most solid political attainments of the Cromwellian party." Downing's career is an especially good example of how men of ability and a certain moral elasticity can traverse revolutions. He was graduated from Harvard in 1642, and went to England at the happy moment of Puritan supremacy. He soon rose high in the ranks of the Cromwellians, devoting his talents especially to diplomacy. He contrived to turn his coat at just the right time, and was accepted in the service of the new king. It is from this early and somewhat atypical Harvard man that Downing Street in London takes its name. Even in Russia, though by now old Bolsheviks are almost completely weeded out of the very highest councils, there are undoubtedly many of them, their fires well banked, in the great new bureaucracy. But the Russian is still a bureaucracy without fully recognized inheritable property rights, which is still another reason, probably, for the recurrent Terror of 1936-39. The Russian convalescence has been a troubled one.

The new governing classes in all our societies are then a very miscellaneous lot, with very little in common as regards social origins, education, and earlier party affiliations. They have in common a certain adaptability. They have survived a rigorous if somewhat arbitrary selection

They seem, after the heroes of the Terror, tame and unen-
terprising in many ways. But they usually do a pretty good
job in getting institutions, laws, routines, all the necessary
standard ways of doing things, once more working.

Along with amnesty to former moderates there goes on a
reverse process of repression and persecution of unrepent-
ant revolutionists of all sorts. The further the reaction
moves to the Right, the wider its definition of revolutionists to be duly restrained as suitable reaction against the
horrors of the Reign of Terror. The Thermidoreans themselves were by no means unwilling to apply terroristic
methods in the proper direction. The White Terrors are as
real as the Red. Even in England, the well-known Claren-
don Code of the Restoration conforms closely enough to
the general pattern of repression later carried out in
France and in Russia. The clever and unprincipled extremist is almost always able to weather the White Terror—
witness Fouché again. It is only the convinced and persistent extremists who suffer.

As for the more active and violent leaders of the original
Terror, they are of course eliminated, either by exile or by
death. They are now declared to have been fanatics, villains, bloodthirsty tyrants, scoundrels. They become very
convenient scapegoats, explanations of the difficulties the
new regime has getting things settled. If there is one very
dramatic scapegoat, and he is already dead, so much the
better. Cromwell's body was dug up after the Stuart Restoration and hanged at Tyburn, along with Ireton's and
Bradshaw's. He became a tyrant, an ogre, a blasphemer,
and so remained on the whole until in the nineteenth century Carlyle started the rehabilitation which has made him
a hero. Except for a small sect led by the late Albert
Mathiez, Robespierre has never recovered the status of
hero. The Thermidoreans made Robespierre a prime
scapegoat, the leader of the gang of terrorists, a vain and
capricious tyrant, a bloody villain. Lenin, of course, died a
saint, but fortunately for Stalin, Trotsky made a grand
scapegoat.

The lift of the ideal has gone by now, though the grand
phrases are still there, frozen in ritual. The new ruling
class settles down to do as good a job as it can. But it

clearly intends also to enjoy life, to possess the privileges and wealth a ruling class has hitherto always had. This new ruling class is certainly not going to try to achieve Liberty, Equality, Fraternity for everyone in the society. It is quite content with the stratification which has worked itself out during the revolution. It will settle its own internal conflicts as far as it can, in the traditional way of ruling classes. There will be none of the dangerous direct appeals to the people, no risks of great popular uprisings. We have already noted how as the crisis period approaches the people come less and less into active politics, how the extremists reach power through what is no more than a *coup d'état*. With the Thermidoreans this process continues, until the political changes, the transfers of power during this period—and they are numerous, and by no means altogether regular and orderly—are hardly more than palace revolutions. When all is quiet and safe the victors will risk a plebiscite. Appearances have to be kept up, and a certain number of stereotypes about the will of the people have by now got fairly well established in the mind of John Jones. Hence, of course, the "democracy" of Stalin's constitution of 1936.

John Jones may well be somewhat tired of political turmoil. But he is certainly not in the Thermidorean period in a generally prosperous condition. One of the most striking uniformities we can discern in this period is that, notably in France and Russia, but to a certain extent also in the England of the 1650's and the America of the Articles of Confederation, there was more widespread economic suffering, especially among the poorest classes, than during the Terror, or during the last years of the old regime. When the Thermidoreans in France abandoned price fixing and food rationing, prices rocketed, paper money went on its classic decline, and the poor were left in a very bad way. There seems to be a general agreement that there was more actual suffering in France in the winters of 1795 and 1796 than at any other time in the revolutionary era. Yet save for a few pathetic bread riots at Paris and in some of the large cities, riots easily put down by the government, nothing happened. Similarly in Russia, there seems to be no doubt that the liquidation of the *kulaks* and the great famine during the first Five Year Plan brought a greater toll of death and misery than even the period of war communism. Possibly the explanation of the failure of this suffering to produce a rising is that suffering is not in itself a spur to effective revolt; perhaps it is merely that the new ruling class in Thermidor can and does use force with an effectiveness the old ruling class did not command; perhaps it is also that by Thermidor the great mass of people neither rich nor poor, not at any rate quite on the margin of existence, is worn out, exhausted, fed up with the experiences of the crusade for the Republic of Virtue. At any rate, the lack of any *effective* rising of those who suffer most during these Thermidors is a serious challenge to those who hold that suffering and deprivation among the many is a kind of master-cause of revolution in our world.

The lift of the ideal has also gone out of the wars the revolutionists have been waging to spread their gospel. It is doubtless true that these wars were never wholly devoted to the spreading of this gospel, and certainly the catchwords of the gospel continue to be used long after the heroic period of the crisis. But aggressive nationalism gradually supplants the missionary spirit, a Messianic crusade gradually becomes clearly a war of conquest. Cromwell turned English energies to the reconquest of Ireland and then to the re-establishment of English prestige abroad. The seizure of Jamaica is a little thing if compared with Napoleon's conquests, but it is cut from the same sociological pattern. With Sexby and Blake in earlier years, patriotism had taken the form of wishing to make all Europe republican; by the middle of the decade of the fifties, English patriotism had returned to more normal channels. That under the Directory and Napoleon, French nationalism conformed to the pattern we have sketched above should be clear even to the idolaters of Napoleon.

In Russia in the early days of the revolution nationalism in the aggressive sense was virtuously abandoned according to the best tenets of Marx; in the purely cultural sense nationalism became the prized basis of soviet federalism. To many admirers of the Russian Revolution it will not be at all clear that Russia has also conformed to our pattern, has fitted in with the uniformity by which Messianic revolutionary proselyting in other lands becomes the aggressive nationalism with which we are familiar. The skeptical can only reply that the boasted federal equality of the national groups within the Soviet Union has not proved incompatible with practical domination by the Great Russians, though unquestionably the Soviet government has been in most respects more "liberal" toward the other national groups than was Czarist Russia, and more successful in integrating them into the larger unity of the U.S.S.R. Even within the old U.S.S.R., however, it was found necessary to suppress the Volga Germans and certain autonomous groups in the Caucasus after the German armies were driven out in 1943-44.

More important for our purposes is the clear reappearance of ordinary nationalism in Stalin's Russia. In the late 1930's, an observer friendly to Russia might explain away the obvious signs of reviving nationalism—the rehabilitation of the old historic Czarist heroes, the return to traditional balance-of-power politics, and the like—as purely defensive measures against the threat of Hitler. But since 1939 only a very case-hardened fellow traveler can doubt that Marxist Russia is at least as ardently, as simply, and as aggressively nationalistic as ever was Czarist Russia. That stupidly conservative journalists in the West relish saying so does not, unfortunately, alter the truth of this statement.

III. Return of the Church

The position of the recognized religions of the old regimes is one of the very best indicators of the nature and extent of these Thermidorean reactions. We saw in the last chapter that the extremists had developed what we had to call a religion of their own, an active, crusading, intolerant faith that sent its devotees storming the gates of heaven on earth. Naturally enough during their supremacy the extremists persecuted the old established faiths, Catholic and Protestant alike. The English Independents persecuted papists, prelatists, and Presbyterians with a zeal perhaps diminishing in that order. In France the Catholic Church had been long a target for the *philosophes*. The victorious Jacobins were not altogether of one mind either as to the treatment of the Catholic Church or as to just what sort of substitute might be desirable. Cults of Reason, of the Fatherland, of the Supreme Being, all had their advocates. Most of them could agree on banning the non-juring Catholics who were loyal to the Pope. At the height of the Terror the most violent "dechristianizers" had their way in some regions, destroying or defacing churches, guillotining or banishing priests, staging burlesques of Catholic ceremonials. Fouché at Nevers caused to be inscribed over the gate of the cemetery the confident assertion: *Death is an eternal Sleep*.

The Bolsheviks were brought up in a hatred for the Greek Orthodox Church at least as violent as that which the Jacobins felt for the Roman Catholic. They had a firm belief, nourished by much repetition, that religion is "the opium of the people." They thought of themselves as men of science and hence atheists. Once in power the Bolsheviks began an active campaign against the churches, though especially in the early days of war communism they had a good deal else to do, and left the clergy to struggle along by itself. There were the usual acts of violence against persons of the clergy and against the church buildings, shutting of the monasteries, and so on. Priests were of course classed in the nonproductive group, and suffered more than other men from lack of food during the great scarcity. Yet one gets the impression that in Russia sheer terrorism directed against organized Christianity was not quite as intense as it had been in France. The Bolsheviks had a great belief in the power of proper education, and planned from the first a state monopoly which should ensure the young against exposure to the danger of infection with Christian notions. For adults the government trusted in antireligious propaganda, in museums exposing the fakes and horrors of the old religion, and in the general spread of enlightenment and desire for the good things of this world. The "League of the Militant Godless" was formed with government support, the presses and the artists got to work on posters, the newspapers went enthusiastically into this relatively safe pursuit, and for a while in the 1920's foreign observers might not unreasonably report that Christianity in Russia seemed well on the way to extinction.

It is very difficult indeed to get trustworthy information on the present status of organized Christianity in Russia. On this subject, even more than on most subjects, the Iron Curtain is difficult to penetrate. But it does seem definitely established that now after some fifty years of Bolshevik supremacy Christianity has not been wiped out in Russia, is not even wholly limited to older people brought up before the revolution. During World War II, it seems clear, the Russian government was quite willing to find help in maintaining morale through what was left of Orthodox Christianity. Even in the 1930's, there were signs that the Church was making its peace with Communism. Nowadays there clearly are younger Orthodox priests who, if not party members, are acceptable Russian Communists. It remains true that Communism, like Jacobinism before it, takes very seriously its anti-Christian mission. It may be that in a generation or two Christianity really will be wiped out in Russia, though hardly, one believes, in many of the present Russian satellites such as Poland and Hungary. It is perhaps more likely that in Russia, as in France, Christianity and militant anti-Christian "materialism" will continue to exist side by side in uneasy mutual toleration. Meanwhile, it is clear that "root-and-branch" has not yet worked even in Russia. It is still possible to attend the services of the Eastern Orthodox Church in the land of the successful Marxist revolution. The Politburo may not attend; but neither did most cabinet officers of the Third French Republic attend Mass—officially. Official Communism may yet be as piously materialist, positivist, and anti-clerical as official French Radical-Socialism has been in our times—and as oddly willing to put up with Christians they have given up trying to eliminate entirely. At this time, however, it looks as though the best the Russian church can hope for is survival as a minority cult. The Bolsheviks seems to have succeeded more completely in suppressing the old religion than the Jacobins before them. We must repeat that our uniformities are not identities.

In France the reconciliation of the Thermidoreans and

the old church went on so rapidly that within less than a decade from the "dechristianizing" movement of the Terror Napoleon could sign a Concordat with the Pope which officially re-established Roman Catholicism as the State Church of France. During the worst of the Terror, Catholics in France had had to hold their services in secret, in spite of the fact that freedom of worship was guaranteed by law. With the fall of Robespierre they began to risk public services in the buildings still spared them. As more and more moderates were amnestied, the government became more and more friendly, and the last four years of the eighteenth century saw France with complete religious freedom and with almost complete separation of Church and State. Napoleon and many of the new ruling class felt the need of winning the Catholics over completely, and the formal Concordat was negotiated. The re-established Catholic Church was not, however, in exactly the same legal position as under the old regime, when it had been the sole recognized faith. Protestants and Jews were by the new laws given equal status with the Catholics.

Organized Christianity does not enter in the same way into the American Revolution. In England, however, there is a striking similarity to the broad lines of development in France and Russia. The established faith of the old regime was the Church of England, in many ways, liturgically, theologically, governmentally, not very far removed from the Catholic tradition. The new revolutionary faith was Calvinism in its various forms, of which the Independent finally triumphed. Under Independent rule the Anglican worship, and indeed rival forms of Calvinist worship, were kept down. On paper, at least, this religious persecution was even more violent than that in France and in Russia. The disputants in the pamphlet warfare among the sects were learned men with abundant vocabularies and firm convictions. On the other hand, save in Ireland, there was rather less violence and bloodshed in immediately religious quarrels during the English Revolution than in those of France and Russia. With the repressing of the more radical sects, and especially the Quakers, the swing back begins in England. In the later years of Cromwell, Presbyterians and even Anglicans reasserted themselves in public life and carried on their religious services in virtual freedom. When Charles II came back the Church of England was re-established in very nearly its old prestige and privileges, and the cycle took its usual form with the persecution of the sects that had made the revolution. It was, however, a half-hearted persecution, and the dissenters survived to become nonconformists and nowadays, free churchmen— a significant progression from a dyslogistic to a eulogistic term.

IV. *The Search for Pleasure*

The full flavor of the Thermidorean reaction is reserved for the social historian. In the dress, amusements, in the petty details of the daily lives of ordinary men and women, the full extent of the popular abandonment of the Republic of Virtue becomes clear. So marked is this letdown that even the historian feels it, and most nineteenth-century liberal historians hardly concealed their disgust and disappointment when they came to record the indecent pleasures of the English Restoration or of the French Directory. The austerities of the good life according to Calvin or Robespierre seemed a noble standard, a goal toward which men might struggle with a heroism that adorns a work of history. The doings of a society in which a Nell Gwyn or a Teresia de Cabarrus were apparently the most important actors could hardly be edifying to anybody, and could be made instructive only with the addition of proper sermonizing. Scandal writers, romantic biographers, and other purveyors to a corrupt public taste have of course fallen with delight on the ripe tidbits of the Thermidors, but the high-minded men who write serious history have passed by these periods holding their hands to their noses. From one source or another, however, we can find what we need to know about the social history of our societies in this particular phase of revolution. We shall try to avoid being shocked or titillated, and to see how the obvious moral looseness of the Thermidorean reactions fits in with the uniformities we have been working out. But first for a brief review of the facts.

Within a few days of the guillotining of Robespierre and

his more conspicuous followers Parisians began to indulge publicly and with gusto in a whole series of pleasures denied them during the tension of the Terror. Politicians may have thought that "Terror will not cease to be the order of the day until the last enemies of the Republic have perished," but ordinary men and women for once imposed their obvious wants and needs directly on the politicians. One gets the impression that few phenomena in the course of the French Revolution were more genuinely "popular" and "spontaneous" than the revulsion from the restraints of the Terror. The people of Paris took Robespierre's death as a signal that the lid was off.

Dance halls were opened up all over Paris, prostitutes began operating "with their former audacity" (to quote a police report), well-dressed prosperous young men most unrepublicanly drunk began running about and cracking dour, virtuous republicans over the head. These young men were the famous *jeunesse dorée*, a gilded youth with no illusions about a Republic of Virtue, and which would nowadays certainly be labeled Fascist at once. Both male and female costume had during the crisis period tended toward sobriety, the women being wrapped in flowing Roman robes and in more than Roman virtue. Now all was changed. The men's clothes became extremely foppish, with tight trousers, elaborate waistcoats, and stocks that mounted beyond the chin. The women's dressmakers were still classically inspired, but with a sure erotic sense they concentrated their efforts on the skillful revealing of the breasts. The *costume directoire* is an excellent symbol of the period.

With the abandonment of price fixing and in the inflation which followed, a class of newly rich speculators, war profiteers, and clever politicians arose. Parliamentary scandals do indeed crop up in earlier periods of the revolutions, even in the crisis period. Corruption can be pretty well proved for certain members of the English Long Parliament and the French Convention even in their great days. But in these earlier periods exposure was followed by swift and sure punishment. Now, in Thermidor, no one seems to care very much and certainly nothing is done. There is gossip, and in some quarters indignation. But mostly politicians who grafted successfully were admired, as they later were to be in the United States.

Still jittery over the Terror, fearing its return, uncertain of their wealth and position, often quite uneducated in the patrician arts, the Thermidoreans spent their money freely and vulgarly. They gambled, they raced horses and fought cocks, they were mad about dancing. All this they did noisily and with little regard for the traditional decencies of the eighteenth century. In these short years the real basis for the romantic taste of nineteenth-century France was laid. The ladies of the period are famous for their gaiety and abandon. Their leader was Teresia de Cabarrus, once mistress of the corrupt representative Tallien, and now his wife. She was universally known, in a phrase that displays the cynicism of the age, as "Our Lady of Thermidor."

All of us know the age of Charles II as an extreme reaction from the rule of the Saints. Restoration Comedy has, especially since Victorian times, been a symbol for naughtiness, for the kind of play no nice person could witness without blushing. Nell Gwyn has, in the national memory, ruled in triumph over a court life in which vice was as aristocratic as the most virtuous commoner could wish and suspect it to be. As a matter of fact, the Puritan code of manners and morals was never perfectly established, even in the years immediately following the death of Charles I. The less public pleasures were always possible, and prohibitions against horse racing, bear baiting, Christmas and other heathen festivals were subject to the same kind of nullification the Eighteenth Amendment received in this country. The very harshness of some of the Puritan prohibitions was in itself an indication that the Puritans were having a hard time getting all Englishmen to behave in such a way that they would not "stink in the nostrils of the just."

Yet the Puritan rule was in fact harsh and rigid enough to give non-Puritans plenty of grievances, and in its main lines the Thermidorean reaction was as real in England as it was to be in France. There was not in England the same mixture of *parvenus* and tired and lucky aristocrats as in France, and esthetically speaking the reaction in England was on a much higher level than that in France. But in the frank return to the pleasures of the senses, to gambling, drinking, dancing, open love-making, to a light and cynical literature, to a frank joy in clothes and other vanities, the two countries present a very close parallel. Nor was the English Restoration altogether without a lushness of taste which chaster souls find offensive. Especially in female costume the contrast to the sobrieties of the early period is very striking. The ladies wore dresses of riotous and often conflicting colors, put on towering lace headdresses, fantastic patches and generous cosmetics on their faces, wore and displayed elaborately brocaded petticoats.

We need hardly labor this point about the loosening of moral restraints in the Thermidorean period in England and in France. We shall have to be more careful in establishing the facts about any such loosening of moral restraints in Soviet Russia. Yet before the threat of war helped bring on new austerities, there were in Russia real signs of a return to the simpler pleasures of the flesh. There seems to have been no Nell Gwyn, no Mme. de Cabarrus, in Russia. But again we must not expect our uniformities to be suspiciously exact. In its broad lines, the Russian Thermidor runs as true to form morally and socially as we have seen it does politically.

In the first place, Thermidor in Russia began in Lenin's own lifetime, with the coming of the New Economic Policy in 1921. Private property and private trading were once more permitted in Russia. The new class of entrepreneurs who rose out of this situation, the Nepmen, remind one forcibly of the similar class of profiteers who rose in France out of the abandonment of price fixing after the fall of Robespierre. They were never quite sure of their status, and they carried over into their legal activities during the NEP a good many of the habits they had acquired in their bootlegging days under the Terror. As a class, they were "exceptionally vulgar, profiteering, crude, and noisy." In the next few years prostitution, gambling, and other un-Marxist pleasures returned so obviously to Moscow and Leningrad that only the most convinced of fellow travelers were unable to see them. Most sympathetic foreigners in Russia since 1917 have perhaps been prevented from what we may hopefully call the normal use of their eyesight less by the activities of Communist officials entrusted with the task of guiding foreigners than by their own strong religious conviction that all must be well in the Marxist heaven. Yet until the Five Year Plan was initiated, the return of the bourgeois vices was so obvious, especially in the middle twenties, that even foreign Communists noticed the fact.

Stalin's apparent return to Communism in 1928-29 is really no more significant than Napoleon's apparent repudiation of the corruptness and moral looseness of the Directory once he had achieved secure power by the *coup d'état* of the 18th Brumaire. There seems to be in all our societies a certain reaction to the Thermidorean reaction, notably in this matter of the public pursuit of pleasure. Men in great numbers can no more devote themselves heroically and permanently to sin than to holiness. The thousand dance halls said to have been opened up in Paris immediately after the Terror could have kept going profitably only if most of the population of Paris wanted to dance most of the time. And in spite of Anglo-Saxon ideas to the contrary, Parisians are really not built that way.

What happens in the years following the crisis of the Terror is a kind of seesaw between moral restraint and moral looseness, at the end of which a kind of equilibrium is arrived at in which most men and women behave in respect to such matters as gambling, drinking, lovemaking, the adornment of their persons, and the use of leisure, about the way their grandfathers and grandmothers had behaved. If we look at Stalin's Russia before the war and ask ourselves how far there seemed to be opportunity for the old Adam and the old Eve to come out in the lives of Russians we shall get a more accurate measure of the reality of Thermidor in Russia than we could get from any amount of Marxist or anti-Marxist theorizing.

Eugene Lyons tells with malicious delight the story of the bafflement and anger of a correspondent of the New York *Freiheit,* a Communist paper, when he was excluded from a government reception in Russia in the 1930's because he did not have a dinner jacket. Dinner jackets a part of the dictatorship of the proletariat! Nothing could be more absurd, illogical, and wholly natural. The dinner jacket satisfies a number of human needs—the anthropologist could analyze most of them for you—and there seems to be no evidence that any of our revolutions had much long-run effect on these needs. A commissar needed a dinner jacket at least as much as a Congressman or a D.A.R. lecturer.

Detail after detail might be brought forward to show how the dictatorship of the proletariat in prewar Russia was by no means the dictatorship of virtue we have seen prevailing in the crisis periods of our revolutions. Jazz, for instance, was long prohibited in Russia. Jazz was clearly the product of a decadent bourgeois civilization, an indecent way of stimulating what no good Marxist would want, or need, to have stimulated, one of the protean forms of "opium for the people" in capitalistic countries. Communists would dance from sheer joy to innocent, springlike music. In the late twenties, however, the fox trot and similar dances began to seep into Communist Russia, and until the present crisis brought renewed and strengthened hostility to the West, American dance music was played almost as frequently and as badly in Russia as in the rest of Europe.

No one dramatic event like the fall of Robespierre can be used to date Thermidor in Russia. But a whole series of little matters of daily life combine to make an impressive case for the reality of the Russian reaction. A youth leader appeared at a national youth congress in a necktie, a step which when first taken must have been as shocking as would be in this country the appearance of a Commencement speaker in overalls. A fashion show was held in Moscow, and mannequins actually paraded, gliding and smiling with conventional lack of abandon, almost as if they were poor little wage-slaves in Paris or New York. Lipsticks and other cosmetics began to appear even in the shops patronized by working girls. Stories of crime, "human interest" stories, began to appear in the pages of newspapers hitherto superior to such capitalistic drivel, and hitherto consecrated to the pure heights of politics. Movies were made in which are to be seen recognizable human beings, insignificant, comic, stupid, jealous, even Russian, rather than bloodless abstractions representing Capitalism, the Landlord, Communism, the Proletariat, Man in Revolt.

The Bolsheviks had been very superior about the family. It was an institution of the old regime, interwoven with all sorts of religious elements, inevitably conservative in its social action. The family was a stuffy little nest breeding selfishness, jealousy, love of property, indifference toward the great needs of society. The family kept the young indoctrinated with the stupidities of the old. The Bolsheviks would break up the family, encourage divorce, educate the children to the true selflessness of Communism, get them used to collective enterprises and collective social life, get rid of the influence of the Church in family relations. Stalin began a continuing process of restoring the old family virtues. Movies, plays and novels emphasized respect for parents, family ties, bourgeois virtues and bourgeois tastes. Divorce, once about as easy and inexpensive as it could possibly be, was made more expensive and more difficult. More important, the government encouraged the spread of a sentiment that marriage is a serious and permanent affair, something made in heaven as heaven now seems understood in Russia. Abortion, which the old Bolsheviks proudly made as legal and as easy as appendectomy in America, and almost as frequent, has now been forbidden by law save where it can be certified as necessary to preserve the woman's life. And underlying these various measures, and much more important as a general indication of what is going on in Russia than any one of them, is an atmosphere we should almost call Victorian. The recent and current rulers of Russia seem to be trying deliberately to cultivate the kind of sentiments characteristic of societies in equilibrium—the domestic affections, simple patriotism, love of work and routine, obedience to those in power, dislike for individual eccentricities, in short, what Pareto called the "persistent aggregates." Khrushchev was obviously still hostile to "modern" art as something at bottom contrary to what the many really want, or what is really good for them.

Pursuing these ends, Stalin long since decreed that Marxist debunking of Russian history was to cease, that Russians were once more to learn of the glories of the

Russian past. The Byzantine missionaries who brought Christianity to Russia were no longer to be painted as fools and villains, agents of what was clearly capitalistic imperialism, abject persons like contemporary missionaries bringing Bible, rum, and syphilis to the South Seas. On the contrary, Christianity in Russia was to be seen as an essential step in preparing the barbarous Slavs for higher things. Peter the Great and Catherine were no longer to be made cruel despots. They, too, were great architects of Russia's destiny, without whom millions of other Slavs and Asiatics might not now enjoy the blessings of Communism.

A nice specific example of the return of Russia to the sad ways of capitalism is the apparent growth of that horror of a competitive individualistic economy, advertising. Of course the Soviet government has always used its full control of modern mass media for propaganda, but now, even under socialism, the particular form of propaganda we call advertising has begun to appear. Consumer goods are advertised on billboards, radio and television, and in newspapers and magazines—even on match covers—not yet as insistently and as vulgarly as in the United States, but still advertised in a way that would shock an Old Bolshevik were any left alive.

v. *Russia: Permanent Revolution?*

Yet it is still difficult for many of us to dismiss the Russian Revolution as really finished, or even as finished as were our other revolutions at a comparable interval of time after their beginning. In Russia, as we have just seen, there certainly were after 1921 many signs of the Thermidorean reaction. But there has been no formal restoration of the old regime. That fact in itself is not really significant, for none of the other restorations really restored the old regimes just as they had been before the revolution. *Toute restoration*, says the French aphorism, *est révolution.*

To put the matter most simply, it looks to an outsider as if in Russia something like the Reign of Terror and Virtue, especially in the sense of continuous pressure on the individual to participate in the common thing, to be always "at the height of revolutionary circumstances," has been recurrent. The horrors of enforced collectivization in the countryside in the early thirties, the trials, confessions, and purges in the years 1936-39, set off by the assassination of Kirov, war austerity, the latter phases of Stalin's personal rule, the continuation, even under Khrushchev's return to Russian normality, of the great cultural split between Russia and the West—all this adds up to something that does indeed seem like "permanent revolution."

First, a warning we have often repeated in the course of this study. We must not expect our revolutions to be identical. The uniformities we are seeking to find in our revolutions ought not to turn out to be identities, or we should indeed be suspected of being false to the traditions of scientific method. Second, another warning we have frequently made. We must not fall into the error of assuming one-way causation. If the anatomy of the Russian Revolution is not identical with that of our others, we must not assume that there is one single variable in the Russian situation—the hero or the villain variable—that explains everything. Here as always in complicated social situations, there are many variables at work. Messrs. F. Beck and W. Godin in their book on *Russian Purge and the Extraction of Confession* seek to account for that recurrence of Terror in 1936-39 they call, after the head of the secret police at the time, the "Yezhov period." They record no less than fifteen "theories" to account for this recurrence of Terror in Russia, which claimed more victims, probably, than did the Terror of 1918-21. In all of them they find at least some grain of truth.

One of their theories may give us a start in explaining why Russia seems still not wholly over its revolution. They call it the "Asia theory," in its simplest form the theory that Russia is an Asiatic nation in which even a "popular" revolution made in the great Western tradition of our other revolutions could not possibly end in the kind of Western democratic society we know in England, France, the United States. Granted that revolutions end in a return, not to the *status quo ante,* but to an equilibrium, a state of "normalcy" recognizably related to that of the old regime, then the end of the Russian Revolution should naturally be something a good deal more like the Russia of the Czars, of secret police, of civil violence, tyranny from above, even mass poverty and ignorance, than like the England of *habeas corpus,* the America of the Constitution of 1787, or the France of the *Charte* and the citizen-king Louis-Philippe. "New presbyter is but old priest writ large." "The more it changes, the more it's the same thing." These weary aphorisms from other revolutions mean that in Russia we really are back to normal in 1965—*normal for Russia.*

Now as a sole explanation this "Asia theory" will not do, but as one of the variables that go into a working explanation it should be acceptable even to liberals who are by temperament and training reluctant to accept it. Messrs. Beck and Godin—the names are pseudonyms for a German scientist and a Russian historian apprehended during the Yezhov period, and since fortunate enough to escape from Russia—clearly do not like the overtones of Western superiority the Asia theory carries, but they do not by any means wholly reject it. Basically, Russia was not in 1917 a society with a strong middle class trained in Western habits of political and other civil "rights," and it would indeed be extraordinary if a revolution guided by Lenin and Stalin had produced such a society in Russia.

Moreover, a simple obvious historical uniformity in our other revolutions needs here to be noted. The conceptual scheme of the fever is inadequate if it is taken to mean that the whole process ends in a simple "cure." Rather, in all our revolutions, there are clear *sequelae,* a series of lesser revolutions in which the forces present in the initial one are worked out. After 1640 in England there were the "glorious Revolution" of 1688, the long struggles of the eighteenth century, the reform bills of the nineteenth. After the American Revolution there were Shays' Rebellion, the Whiskey Rebellion, the legal but hardly quiet overturns that put Jefferson and Jackson in power, the long ordeal of our Civil War. After the French Revolution, as we know well, there were a series of nineteenth-century overturns in France and indeed in all Western and Central Europe so greatly influenced by French example. We have already noted that the time-sequence of the original Russian Revolution represents a kind of speeding up of the process of revolution as compared with the earlier ones. It seems likely that for the future historian the Russian troubles of the last thirty-five years will seem in fact a kind of *sequelae*, the working out of problems not wholly solved in the first bout of revolution, just as are the years 1820, 1830, 1848 for European history.

There still remains the problem of accounting for the specific form of the long Russian bout of revolutionary fever. Grant, as we have already granted, that the stable Russian society which should finally emerge will not be a society like our own, it still seems unlikely that such a stable society will really be subject to quite as much basic disturbance, quite as much overparticipation in politics for the common man, as Stalin's Russia. We are here edging into the quite unscientific field of prophecy. It may be that the Russia of Lysenkoism, of the Iron Curtain, the Russia that has frightened an Orwell or a Koestler even more than it has frightened good American conservatives—it may be that this Russia will go on indefinitely in a whole world in which the very words "stability," "equilibrium," "peace," "order" have lost their meaning. But here for the moment we must postulate a Russia, and a world, no longer in the midst of a perpetual nightmare.

The subject is enormous, and cannot be covered at all thoroughly in this very tentative study of four revolutions. But it may be suggested that the clues to the continuing crises in Russia are in part domestic, internal to Russia, and in part tied up with the whole international situation.

The internal reasons are very numerous. One may hazard the guess that one very important clue lies in the concrete promises of the Marxist religion. We have noted that in all our other revolutions an attempt was made to close the gap on this earth between the ideal and the real. Now the exact form of the ideal is important. In all our other revolutions, despite their apocalyptic fervor during the crisis period, despite their lunatic fringes demanding heaven on earth at once, the ordinary man was *not* specifically promised economic equality, the classless society, the Marxist formula of "from each according to his abilities, to each according to his needs." *The Russians were promised just that.* Marxism was much more specific in what it promised Ivan Ivanovich than was Puritanism in what it promised John Jones, or Jacobinism in what it promised Jacques Dupont.

All our revolutions indeed had to compromise with their ideals, had to turn the fine words into ritual. "Liberty, Equality, Fraternity" had eventually to end up as inscriptions on public buildings and—we need not be cynical—in the hearts of good French republicans; they could not be literally, concretely, carried out, say, in the working classrooms of the French schools on which they were inscribed, or the French schools would have been "permissive" bedlams beyond the wildest reality of the most progressive American private school. Americans have never quite taken the self-evident truth that all men are born equal in respect to their rights to mean that all men are—or should be—born with the ability to lead the league in home runs.

But the Russian Revolution did promise, not just political or spiritual equality, not just the career open to talents, but a society of economic equals. The Russians now have, as even fellow travelers know, a society in which the unevenness of distribution of consumer goods—of individual "income"—is conspicuously great. A major Russian politician, a Russian manager of industry, a popular Russian playwright or ballerina, a successful Russian scientist, enjoys a command over material wealth that makes Russian society essentially as much a society of economic inequality of actual income for use as any capitalist society today.

It is possible indeed for the rulers of Russia to tell their people that such inequalities represent merely a transitional stage, made necessary by the opposition of the wicked capitalist outside world. The dictatorship of the proletariat, essential prelude to the classless society, merely has had to be prolonged a bit. Someday, when the Communist revolution has conquered the world, the streetsweeper really will be the economic equal of the member of the Politburo. But not now. This is at bottom, however, a feeble argument, and there are signs that in Russia today an effort is being made to preach as an ideal something extraordinarily close to what the editors of *Fortune* regard as the actual American achievement: that is, a solid base line of material plenty shared by all, with special material rewards to those able leaders in all walks of life whose skills are constantly raising the level of that base line for all—or at least edifying the spirits of all.

Meanwhile, the actual base line in Russia, though building up fast since 1953, is low. The warmest Western sympathizers with what they take to be the basic aim of the Russian Revolution to improve the standard of living of the common man cannot maintain that that standard has yet reached those of most Western lands. That in hard actuality something like what the Marxist calls historical bourgeois "primitive accumulation" of capital—that is, produced means of further production obtained by abstention from immediate production for consumption—has had to be carried out under government direction in Russia; that in addition the war against Hitler, and preparation for a possible war against us, have further channeled Russian production into other than consumer goods—these facts may well explain in strictly economic terms why the more abundant life has not yet come for the Russian man in the street. But the fact remains that it has not come, and that it has been promised. One need not go all the way with bitter conservative enemies of the Russian experiment to admit that some of the whipped-up hatred of the West, some of the sustained tensions of a society still aware of being in revolution, can be explained as efforts to divert the attention of the common man from his lack of material abundance. Here again, under the present regime, such abundance seems on its way in the 1960's. But the existing gap between streetsweeper and ballerina would surely arouse the indignation of Marx—and perhaps, of Lenin.

Yet it may be possible for the present leaders of Russia to turn Marxist religious beliefs, properly seasoned with Russian nationalism, into a new kind of "opium of the people." It looks as if they were consciously trying to do just this. They may be able to keep the base line of material goods, the "standard of living" slowly increasing. What is perhaps of more importance in continuing Russian internal instability is the problem of those above the base line, the problem of the new Russian ruling class. That class is still essentially a managerial class, well rewarded in terms of income, social prestige, and political power, but hitherto without clear property rights, inheritance, and in general that complex of prescription that has so far in the West always enabled a new—or rather, partly new—ruling class to consolidate its position.

Especially since the Renaissance, there has been even without actual revolution a good deal of the career open to talents in the West. A rough equality of opportunity has held in our Western culture well before in the United States it became one of the great articles of social faith. But those who successfully rose in the world have succeeded quite rapidly in consolidating their position by securing property, founding a family, and becoming part of a ruling class accepted as such without too much opposition and hatred from among the classes which were obviously excluded from the very top of the social pyramid. This has been true even in the United States, where it is by no means the rule in fact that it is "three generations from shirt-sleeves to shirt-sleeves." The whole problem of the relation between individual social mobility and social stability in the group is indeed a knotty one, by no means well understood. It has not been solved in the West, but somehow or other we have come to terms with it, and not simply, as cynical observers of American life in particular have been tempted to say, by pretending that it doesn't exist, that ours, really, is the "classless society."

The ultimate test of how far the Russian revolution approximates achievement of a classless socialist society must lie in the relatively distant future. If the present privileged elite can somehow continue in the persons of most of its descendants to maintain its present position, the mere fact that there might still be no formally recognized "private property," "free enterprise," and "capitalism" would mean little. You would not have the socialism so many have thought, fought, and died for, but you would have a "socialist" state.

In contemporary Russia the position of the new ruling class seems still by no means that well consolidated. For one thing, many of its members must still be troubled in conscience by their new privileges, and by the gap between the facts of Russian life and the ideals of early Communism. More important, they are uncertain of holding on, aware of the great pressure from ambitious younger men below them. Indeed, at this distance the recrudescence of Terror in the Yezhov period begins to look less and less like the classical Terror of the true crisis period, the Terror when men are still fired with the ideal of the new perfect society, and more and more like the troubles of the original Thermidor in France, when the new leaders were still jockeying among themselves for high position, still plotting new *coups d'état*, still unable to settle rivalries without undue violence and irregularities. It is true that the purges of the late thirties in Russia were on a wholesale scale not found in our other revolutions at a comparable stage. But in part this is because everything in Russia was on a bigger scale of territory and population than ever before; in part because the threat from abroad, especially from Germany, increased rather than diminished as it had in the other revolutions we have studied; in part —we must keep to our method of multiple variables—because prerevolutionary Russia itself was not a country of freedom slowly broadening down from precedent to precedent.

Even those of us who believe that the chief blame for the present tension in world political relations is in fact Russian should grant that this tension itself is a part of the explanation of the long-continuing Thermidorean period in Russia. There are external as well as internal reasons for continuing Russian instability. In our summary of the reasons for the Terror in all our revolutions, we noted as a clear uniformity the existence of what it is now fashionable to call a war psychosis. The governments of the Terror are in part governments of national defense against war or the threat of war, against the menace of a foe. That the revolution may have been largely to blame for raising that foe may indeed be true, but that does not alter the fact of the pressure generated by the danger the foe presents. Now revolutionary England, America, and France all managed —France only after twenty-five years—to get themselves once more integrated as respectable, or almost respectable, members of the international state-system of their time.

They had to fear nothing worse than the usual dangers that face a state in balance-of-power politics. Not so Russia. Even in the early thirties, even in 1942-44 when she was allied with the Western powers, the Russians were never really in the club. Be it repeated: the fault may well be Russia's, or at least that of Stalin and his colleagues. But the fact remains that Communist Russia is outside the old Western system.

It is true enough that she is now the center of a new world-system. It is true that her foreign policy has had real successes. It may even be true that her appeal to Asians and Africans is "naturally" greater than ours. But she has also had failures—in Berlin, in the missile adventure in Cuba, and many others. She has had to witness the rise of a great rival, China, within her own Communist system. In short, however unwilling some Americans may be to admit the fact, Russians—important Russians at the top—find it at least as hard as we Americans do to feel that they are *really* winning the cold war. They still feel beleaguered, threatened.

Thermidor in Russia, then, still prevails to a degree in the mid-twentieth century. Its end depends on too many factors for any man to date it. But it is also true that the revolution in Russia has essentially run its course. The crisis, the Reign of Terror and Virtue, is over. The Marxist virus—and once more, remember that we are trying to use this term purely descriptively—has there lost its strength. Russia is indeed in part transformed by the fever, but so too is the virus. For the virus is at least enfeebled in that particular body. It is true that the virus may well be at work in societies like those of China, Southeast Asia, even the Near East and that there it has by no means run its course. But these revolutions are well beyond our central theme. They need the careful attention of our best experts. And they suggest a final word: The *ideas*, the *promises* of orthodox Marxism as now embodied in Russia may well prove in the next few years almost as embarrassing in Russian internal politics as useful in Russian external politics. The Marxist heaven on earth will do as a mere promise in Indonesia or Egypt, for a while; but in Moscow, it has got pretty soon to become in part visible—or the whole doctrine must undergo a still unpredictable transformation.

Yet unless we really are in Russia up against something wholly new, wholly unprecedented, something in short that would invalidate any kind of social science, the broad lines at least of that transformation are not *wholly* unpredictable. If the crisis period of the Russian Revolution is over, as we have here maintained it to be, if Russia is now in the midst of *sequelae* attendant on her main bout of fever, sooner or later she is bound to reach an equilibrium, a state of health or normality, not indeed like such a state for France or the United States, but something, say, nearer nineteenth-century Russia, the Russia of Turgenev as well as of Dostoyevski, of Pavlov and Yersin as well as Bakunin —in short, of a variety of men in full contact with the multanimous but somehow reasonably orderly West.

What keeps Russia still apart, still in the last throes of a revolution, is the incompleteness of Russian social and ritual reconciliation of word and flesh, ideal and real, the heaven of Marxist classless society with this harsh but not uninteresting earth. A merely expanding Russia, a Russia trying to grab more of the world, could be put up with by the rest of the world with no more trouble—great though such trouble is—than the rest of the world took with aggressors like the Spain, Austria, or France of early modern history. But a Russia expanding as the Arabs expanded, in the name of a fierce and intolerant faith, is a very different matter. Even here, however, there is no eternal fanaticism or, at any rate, there has not yet been an eternal fanaticism. Christian and Moslem have not come to understand one another, but they have come to abstain from holy wars against one another. The odds are that even with Lenin and Stalin as its prophets, Communism will prove a less intractable faith than Islam.

But we may well be mistaken. The Russians may have found a way, a way not found by Puritans or Jacobins, of keeping the ordinary man forever keyed to the intensities, the conformities, the perpetual participation in state ritual, the exhausting sacramental devotion, the holy-rolling unrelieved, the constant transcending of common weaknesses and common sense, the *madness* we have sought to analyze as the "Reigns of Terror and Virtue." Totalitarianism may in fact be as new on earth as some very able writers of our time believe it to be. Yet the historian must have his doubts, not merely about such Utopias à rebours as Orwell's *1984*, but even about such profound and persuasive analyses as Miss Hannah Arendt's *Origins of Totalitarianism*. At any rate the issue is clear: if the Russian Revolution in its later years follows the pattern of other great revolutions as clearly as it did in its beginnings and its earlier years, then most Russians will eventually be no madder than the rest of us, and we can communicate with them in our mutual misunderstandings—and flashes of insight; if there really is a new thing in Russia, a totalitarian element that really transforms human beings, we can look forward to more Yezhov periods, more Lysenkos, and more Stalins—"permanent revolution" indeed.

v. Summary

Thermidor is then not by any means something unique, limited to the French Revolution from which it takes its name. We have found in all three of our societies which underwent the full cycle of revolution a similar moral letdown, a similar process of concentration of power in the hands of a "tyrant" or "dictator," a similar seeping back of exiles, a similar revulsion against the men who had made the Terror, a similar return to old habits in daily life.

Even in the United States, which did not undergo quite the same sort of crisis as the other countries, which did not have a real Reign of Terror and Virtue, the decade of the 1780's displays in incomplete forms some of the marks of Thermidor. There were a relaxation of war discipline and war tension and a grand renewed scramble for wealth and pleasure. There were much financial speculation and much sheer suffering. Shays' Rebellion, a most ineffectual gesture, reminds one of the feeble attempts of suffering Frenchmen and Russians to protest against the newly rich of their Thermidors. There was even a moral letdown in this country. "Sober Americans of 1784," writes Jameson, "lamented the spirit of speculation which war and its attendant disturbances had generated, the restlessness of the young, disrespect for tradition and authority, increase of crime, the frivolity and extravagance of society." All this sounds very like the original Thermidor in France.

In some sense the phenomenon of reaction and restoration seems almost inevitably a part of the process of revolution. At any rate it seems hard for the most optimistic lover of revolution to deny that we have found such a phenomenon in all of the four societies we have chosen to study. The very, very faithful may still maintain that the great revolution in Russia has proved itself exempt from this reaction, that in Russia the noble aims of revolutionists in Western society have at last achieved, or are on the road to achieving, an unsullied reality. We ourselves cannot fit the facts of recent Russian history to any such interpretation. Yet the fact of Thermidor, even the fact of formal restoration as in 1660 or 1814, does not mean that revolution has changed nothing. We shall in the next chapter attempt to answer the very difficult question: Just what changes did these revolutions effect?

9

A SUMMARY OF THE WORK OF REVOLUTIONS

---

1. *Changes in Institutions and Ideas*

With that tendency to absolutism which common usage shares with more formal metaphysics, we are likely to think of the kind of revolution we have been studying as a cataclysmic break with the past. The revolution "marks a new era" or "ends forever the abuses of the old regime" or "digs a gulf between the old x and the new y." On the other hand, when disillusioned liberals come to turn against the revolutionary tradition, they conclude as sweepingly that in effect revolutions change nothing of importance—except perhaps for the worse—that revolutions are unpleasant and perhaps avoidable interludes in a nation's history. Now it should be clear that our present study of the English, American, French, and Russian revolutions can hardly permit any such absolute answers to the question: What did these revolutions really change? Some institutions, some laws, even some human habits, they clearly changed in very important ways; other institutions, laws, and habits they changed in the long run but slightly, if at all. It may be that what they changed is more—or less—significant for the sociologist than what they did not change. But we cannot begin to decide this last matter until we have got the actual changes straight. We are considering here, of course, those changes which are apparent at the end of the revolutionary fever, those changes which the history books are likely to catalogue as "permanent." With the changes promised but not achieved by the extremists, as with the many dramatic changes in the lives of the individual actors in the revolution, we are not here directly concerned at the moment.

It must be repeated that the social sciences, like the natural sciences, are quite content if they can establish working statistical uniformities. Individual experience may well go contrary to such a uniformity. It may well be more exciting, more dramatic than the uniformity. It will certainly be more real and telling to the individual than any statistics. Yet the statistics are there, and are inescapable. Thus any, even the most crude, method of contraception will, if widely practiced in a given *group*, cut down the birth rate of that group significantly. But for any given *individuals* practicing it, a crude method of contraception, indeed in careless hands a refined one, may easily prove a method of conception instead.

So in revolutions. To the Anglican clergyman "plundered" of his living in 1648, to the French *marquise* whose husband was guillotined as a traitor in 1794, to the American Loyalist squatting among frontier crudities in the woods of New Brunswick after the comforts of Boston or Cambridge, to the exiled White Russian aristocrat driving his taxi in Paris in 1919, it would have been an outrage to say that revolutions don't really change much. The authors of the Book of Job would have been very puzzled—and if they understood the question, outraged—to be asked whether they thought Job's experiences were statistically typical.

Fortunately or unfortunately our sense of morals and of drama is not based on scientific uniformities. Insofar as the memory of a revolution is actually incorporated in human emotions its real and abiding significance may well be the statistically false, or unreal, form it takes in such emotions, and in the moral stimulus—or solace—it provides. In one way or another, perhaps, all great revolutions end up in the custody of something like the Daughters of the American Revolution, or the *Légion d'Honneur*, or the *Istorik Marksist*. The legend is the fact, forever safe from the *naïvetés* of the debunker.

Politically the revolution ends the worst abuses, the worst inefficiencies of the old regime. It settles for a time at least the kind of internal conflict out of which the "dual sovereignty" arose. The machinery of government works more smoothly after than immediately before the revolution. France is here a typical case. The old overlapping jurisdictions, the confusions and the compromises inherited from the thousand-year struggle between the centripetal forces of the Crown and the centrifugal forces of the feudal nobility, the welter of accumulated precedents, were all replaced by the work of the French Revolution. An able bureaucracy operating within neatly subordinated administrative areas, a legal system efficiently codified, an excellent army well staffed and well provided for, enabled Napoleon to do much that his Bourbon predecessors could not possibly have done. Tocqueville long ago pointed out that the French Revolution came to complete the work of a long line of French monarchs, to make centralized power in France effective and complete.

Here is one detail among many. In the old France, weights and measures varied from region to region, indeed from town to town. A bushel at Toulouse might be much more than a bushel at neighboring Montauban. Worse yet, the very names of measures might be wholly different words. The coinage was, like the present English coinage, partly duodecimal, and very hard to handle by long division. What the revolution did about all this is familiar to every schoolboy. It substituted the uniform system of weights and measures known as the metric system, a system which has made its way without benefit of revolution through most of the world outside the British Commonwealth and the United States.

This achievement of governmental efficiency is really the most striking uniformity we can note in estimating the political changes effected by our revolutions. With suitable allowances for local differences, for accidents, and for the inevitable residue of the unique with which all history and sociology must deal, England, America, and Russia also emerged from their revolutions with more efficient and more centralized governments. The process is less clear in England, partly because it took place before the full maturing of economic and cultural forces tending to promote such forms of efficiency as the metric system or the *Code Napoléon*. But, for all its complexities, the English government after 1660 was much better geared to the needs of the nation of shopkeepers than was the England of 1620, with knights' fees, ship money, benevolences, Star Chamber, Court of High Commission, and the other appurtenances of the immature Stuart despotism. Parliament after 1660 was more completely master of England than the first two Stuarts had been.

Russia is in this respect as in so many still a subject for dispute. Soviet critics themselves sometimes almost go so far as to insist that the new bureaucrats are just as inefficient, pettily tyrannical, and stupid as they were said to have been under the Czars. Some of the sentiments involved in statements of this sort would seem to be more or less a constant of Russian life, and to a certain extent of life under any government. Gogol's admirable comedy, *The Inspector-General*, deals as certainly with uniformities as any scientist could. Yet all in all future historians will probably have to admit that as a piece of political machinery the Soviet system worked better than did that of the Czars, that the Soviet bureaucracy was on the whole a more capable one than that of the Czars. You may not like the Five Year Plans, but you must admit that beneath their parade of statistics lies a concrete economic achievement greater than anything the old regime could show for a similar period. The Communists have, in short, brought the Industrial Revolution to Russia. Perhaps it was coming under Stolypin; perhaps the Communists brought it harshly, cruelly. But bring it they did. After Sputnik, few Americans really doubted this.

These revolutions were all made in the name of freedom, were all directed against the tyranny of the few and toward the rule of the many. This whole phase of revolutions is peculiarly involved with the existence of certain sentiments in human beings which make it very hard to apply the methods of science to the study of men in society. Yet it would seem that the full importance of such matters as democracy, civil rights, written constitutions, and indeed the whole apparatus of popular government lies rather within that vague and important field the Marxists like to call ideology than in the field of concrete political agencies which we are now studying. Certainly one is struck by the fact that all our revolutions promoted the efficiency of the government rather than the "right" of the individual to a romantic freedom to be himself. Even the traditional apparatus of popular government can be analyzed as an instrument to get things done in a particular situation, however strange such an analysis might have seemed to conventionally minded contemporaries of Mussolini, Hitler, and Stalin—and still seems to some hostile critics of democracy. Bills of Rights, codes, and constitutions were in effect charters of the new ruling classes. Liberty as an ideal was one thing; liberty in politics, on the other hand, was another and less exalted matter.

These revolutions all saw much transfer of property by confiscation or forced sale. They saw the fall of one ruling class and its succession by another ruling class recruited in part, at least, from individuals who were before the revolution outside the ruling class. They were accompanied by a definite and concrete demand for the abolition of poverty, for the equal sharing of wealth; the men who guided the Russian Revolution continued long after its crisis period to insist that they were economic egalitarians, that Russia would not recognize private property in land and in capital goods. Marxist thought still separates our four revolutions into two different classes: the English, French, and American, all of which it considers to have been in their final results "bourgeois" revolutions, inevitable victories of business and industry over landed aristocracy; and the Russian Revolution, in its final phases a true "proletarian" revolution. We may nevertheless be more impressed with the fact that in all four revolutions economic power changed hands, and that a newly amalgamated "ruling class" in the new Russia as in the new France directed the economic as well as the political life of the society.

In more detail, the English Revolution took land from

the more devoted Cavaliers and ecclesiastical property from the more unyielding Episcopalians and Presbyterians and gave it to typical Puritans, businessmen and clergymen alike. The church livings came back at the Restoration of 1660 into Anglican hands, but save for the property of a few great lords very close to Charles II, confiscated Royalist lands remained in the possession of their new owners. Most of these owners made their peace with the Stuart government, and thus was laid the foundation for the ruling class under which England won an empire in the next two centuries, a ruling class in which landed wealth and industrial wealth were almost inextricably mixed, and which proved to be a very good ruling class.

The concrete economic changes in France follow a similar pattern. Lands confiscated from clergy and *émigré* nobles were acquired by revolutionists, and for the most part remained in the possession of the purchasers even after the Restoration of 1814. Much of this land no doubt finally ended up in the possession of small independent peasants, and helped to put the final touches on the establishment of that very French class, until yesterday the core of modern France. But much of this transaction also benefited the middle class, and certainly the French ruling class *after* the revolution represents as striking a mixture of old wealth and new, of land and trade, as did the English.

In Russia the differences are not so great as they ought to be according to Marxist theory. There has been a transfer of economic power from one group to another rather than an equal sharing of economic power, an equal distribution of consumer goods, an end of struggle over economic goods or power—but you may put the Marxist formula as you like. The new Russian bureaucracy is, as we have seen, a privileged class which enjoys wealth in the form of consumer goods without yet possessing it in the forms we conventionally call "property." It is a class as yet notably unstable, as yet not sure of itself. But already the sons of the privileged show signs of inheriting their father's status, and it is not inconceivable that inheritance of property will come shortly. What seems to have taken place is a development of the lines of movement of Russian economic history. Just as the French Revolution put the finishing touches on the position of the peasantry, but by no means "gave" them the land suddenly, so the present status of Russian agriculture and industry seems to be a development of slavophile and other elements favoring collective farming over the *kulaks*, and of almost world-wide tendencies favoring large-scale bureaucratically managed industry over small independent competitive concerns. Here as in other countries the revolution certainly does not draw institutions out of a hat—nor out of a book, not even out of so impressive a book as *Das Kapital*.

None of these revolutions quite substituted a brand-new ruling class for the old one, at least not unless one thinks of a "class" without bothering about the human beings who make up the class, which is a favorite procedure of the Marxists. What happens is that by the end of the convalescent period there is well begun a kind of amalgamation, in which the enterprising, adaptable, or lucky individuals of the old privileged classes are for most practical purposes tied up with those individuals of the old suppressed classes who, probably through the same gifts, were able to rise. Not even Djilas's "new class" is wholly new. This *amalgame* is especially noticeable in the army and the civil service, but it is almost as conspicuous in business and industry, and higher politics. This analysis would be confirmed by a detailed study of the social origins of Bonaparte's officers, or the officers in the present Red Army, or of the men who actually ran the government of England in 1670, France in 1810, Russia today, though in the Russian case less conspicuously so, for more time has passed. Moreover, the new men in the postrevolutionary ruling classes have made distinct compromises with the older ones, with that old world from which the crisis period of the revolution is so extreme a revulsion. Your Downings, Fouchés, and Khrushchevs have no longer the fine freedom a Trotsky could enjoy. They are no longer revolutionaries, but rulers, and as such they are in some respects bound to "learn" from their predecessors.

It is in the social arrangements that most intimately and immediately touch the average man that the actual changes effected by our revolutions seem slightest. The grand attempts at reform during the crisis period try to alter John Jones' relations with his wife, his children, try to give him a new religion, new personal habits. The Thermidoreans abandon most of this attempt, and in the end John Jones stands on certain matters about where he stood when the revolution began. Our study of revolutions should confirm something that sensible men have always known and that exasperated reformers have occasionally come to admit, at least to themselves—that in some very important ways the behavior of men changes with a slowness almost comparable to the kind of change the geologist studies.

We may take as an illustration of the foregoing uniformity the attempts of certain of our revolutionists to alter radically and quickly phases of the law of the family. Le Play has shown that the uniformities of the family are among the stablest and most persistent things in our Western civilization. The ardent Leftist revolutionist in the last few centuries has, therefore, naturally enough, tended to dislike this monogamous Christian family, to him a bulwark of individual selfishness, social snobbery, intellectual stuffiness, snarled up with testamentary red tape, dedicated to the myth of masculine superiority, hardened into rigidity by religious sanctions, a festering center which must be cleaned up before men and women can live as God, nature, or science intended them to live. The French Revolution saw no widespread attempt to destroy the family, and indeed its generally middle-class course is filled with pious praise of the family virtues. But the humanitarians did put through some far-reaching legislation in this field, such as generous laws of adoption and other measures tending to break down the rigid, almost Roman, family law of the old regime. Notably they attempted to make illegitimate children absolutely equal in every respect with legitimate children. As the law to put this into effect was passed, a glowing orator remarked: "There are no more bastards in France." We need hardly add that he was mistaken. In a monograph on *French Revolutionary Legislation on Illegitimacy*, the present author has tried to show how even the good bourgeois who passed this law were emotionally too entangled in the traditional family feelings to try to put it into effect. They *said* that bastards were free and equal to legitimate children; but they could not bring themselves to *act* as if they really believed or wanted it to be so. On the whole, the traditional family in its French form emerged unscathed from the revolution.

Russia has seen a much more determined attack on the monogamous Christian family, legislation making divorce even easier than in Nevada, legalizing abortion, encouraging collective household arrangements, establishing *crèches* and kindergartens, bringing children up as far as possible outside the home, and so on. Let there be no misunderstanding. Russian idealists who sought to do all of this were not nasty-minded folk seeking to make life easier for the sensualist. Quite the contrary, they had, as we have tried very hard to show, a strong streak of Puritanism. To this day, a young Russian Communist would be shocked to the fibers of his being at the sight of almost any American periodical rack with its display of nakedness and cheesecake. These idealists thought the bourgeois family corrupting, and agreed with Mr. Shaw that marriage combines the maximum of temptation with the maximum of opportunity. Their legislation was aimed at achieving the ideals behind Christian monogamy though destroying what they regarded as the corrupting family institutions within which it was hedged. The Chinese Communists in 1964 are busy decrying Western emphasis on an individual's love-life, urging the Chinese to put such bourgeois weaknesses behind them, and build Communism.

Here again we are not in the position of historians working with good sources, but through the conflicting reports coming to us from Russia we can make out that the reformers have failed, that the Christian monogamous family has survived the old Bolsheviks in Russia. Legislation has not only hedged legalized abortion so much as to limit it to cases of the strictest medical necessity, but has actually set up premiums for large families. Divorce has been made more difficult. Filial piety and indeed all the conventional bourgeois family virtues are now in high honor in press, movie, state, and school.

To take a very specific example, homosexuality was, for the old Bolsheviks, an abnormality, possibly open to medical treatment, but not of course a crime. It couldn't be a crime to them, just because it was a crime in the wicked, stupid world they were going to change from top to bottom. Naturally they had no narrow bourgeois disgust for the practice. But in March, 1934, homosexual practice was made a crime with a three- to eight-year prison penalty. We cannot refrain from adding that the Webbs explained this with their usual obligingness: "It is understood that this action followed the discovery of centers of demoralization of boys, due to the influence of certain foreigners, who were summarily expelled from Soviet territory." But even with the foreigners expelled, Russia retains the law. The fact is that Russian *sentiments* on the subject of homosexuality are nearly constant; only Russian *ideas* on the subject are variable, and in the long run the constant prevails.

The whole subject of change in the routines of the daily life of John Jones, in the more intimate of his relations with his fellows and his environment, is none too well explored. Here again common sense, with its decisive "human nature doesn't change," is much too absolute. But it does appear that our revolutions had but slight permanent effect on the important little things of life for John Jones. What is loosely called the "Industrial Revolution" had certainly a much greater effect, forced John into a more difficult series of adjustments than did our revolutions. And none of our societies, not even Russia, seems to have undergone changes as complete as those undergone by Turkish society since the wholesale, really revolutionary measures taken under Mustapha Kemal or by Japanese society during the Meiji Revolution—to say nothing of the MacArthur Revolution. It is tempting to record the apparent paradox that Western society is in some respects more slow to change than Eastern society. But the truth is much more complex than any such paradox. In Western Europe one can at least argue that the social and economic changes since 1945 ("Americanization," if you like) add up to a more significant set of changes than those of the Great Revolution of 1789-1815. Both the Turks and the Japanese seem to have preserved intact through social and economic change a series of national disciplines. In our Western societies, family, moral, and religious disciplines have in a similar way served as a balance to very important social and economic changes, of which the revolutions we have studied are only a part.

Modern Western society has indeed gone through in the last few centuries changes so continuous that, if we adopt the very plausible concept of social equilibrium, we must expect to find certain forces pulling in the opposite direction, in the direction of stability. These forces are not as a rule articulate. They do not seem to interest intellectuals as much as do forces making for change. They are perhaps a bit undignified, and certainly undramatic. Insofar as they do get themselves translated into language, they appear in a variety of logical disguises difficult to penetrate. But they are there, and as we have seen, they set a definite limit to what the reformer or revolutionist can do. Bastardy can hardly stand up against logic or biology; bastardy, however, exists by virtue neither of logic nor of biology, but of well-established, slow-changing human sentiments. Men may feel tearfully sorry for poor children stigmatized from birth for something clearly not their fault; but hitherto not even revolution has prevailed against those perhaps ignoble but certainly persistent sentiments behind the "man-made" and "artificial" distinction between children born after a certain rite has been performed and those born without benefit of such a rite. The rite seems fragile, changeable, unimportant—a mere matter of trival words and gestures. Actually it has proved effective against much grander words and more striking gestures, as well as against whole batteries of logic. For it is, to use Pareto's terminology, associated with the "persistent aggregates," patterns of sentiments and behavior very slow to change.

All this amounts to the statement that in our Western society men have continued to hold certain sentiments and to conform to certain set ways of doing things even after they have changed what they say about these sentiments and these acts. Our revolutions seem in many ways to have changed men's minds more completely than they changed men's habits. This is by no means to say that they changed nothing at all, that what men think is of no importance. Ideas are not quite magicians in this world, or Robespierre would not have fallen, and Trotsky (born 1879) might still be alive in Moscow, not dead in Mexico. But they are not to be dismissed as having no part in the social change. Indeed, what our Marxist friends would call the "ideological" changes effected by our revolutions deserve careful consideration.

One may distinguish two contrasting roles played by these ideas born of revolution. First, our revolutions in the end would seem to have taken the sting out of the radical ideas and slogans of their early days. They achieved the necessary miracle of reconciling aspiring men to the substantial failure of their aspirations toward heaven on earth. They turned what were originally verbal instruments of revolt, means of moving men to social action against the existing order, into something we shall have to be up-to-date about and call the myths, folklore, symbols, stereotypes, rituals, of their respective societies. "Liberty, Equality, Fraternity," which once was the trumpet call to the storming of heaven on earth, is now in the latest French Republic no more than a bit of national liturgy, a comforting reminder that Frenchmen are the privileged heirs of an heroic past. There are signs that in Russia the hope of a withering away of the state can be reconciled with the existence of a strong centralized police-state. After all, as too-logical radicals have pointed out, the Bible itself is full of good revolutionary doctrines; what organized Christianity has done with the Bible organized Communism ought to be able to do with the writings of Marx and Engels.

A second role is a more positive one. Even in their use as ritual, these ideas are not purely passive, mere bits of mumbo-jumbo. We have seen that the idea of the classless society weighs heavily on Russia's new ruling class. We cannot here go into the important and involved question of the role of these myths and symbols in a society. We certainly must avoid the stupid question as to whether such symbols "cause" any kind of social change. Here as almost everywhere in the social sciences the cart-and-horse formula of causation is useless, and indeed misleading. Sufficient for us that in all our societies we find that the memory of the great revolution is enshrined in practices that seem to be an essential part of the national state as a going concern. Insofar as men are today in England,

France, America, and Russia heartened by awareness of membership in a nation, guided perhaps, and certainly consoled, by the nobler and more abstract beliefs, made conscious of some kind of security, of a status, by all sorts of ritualistic acts associated with the State or with the Church as a department of the State, fortified by the prospects still held out in the grand words of a Milton, a Jefferson, a Danton, a Lenin—insofar as men are so moved, the revolutions we have studied have given largely to the content of their emotions. In England, in America, in France, the memory of their great overturns has become a factor in the stability of existing society: in Russia, unless all signs fail, a similar state of affairs must sooner or later be reached.

Yet our revolutions have also left behind a tradition of successful revolt. What is to established, contented, conforming, conventional men merely a ritualistic satisfaction, remains for discontented men a spur to activate their discontent. Our modern Western revolutionary tradition is to a certain extent cumulative, and the Russians have carried their awareness of revolutionary history almost to an obsession. Trotsky, for instance, though he naturally never uses the conceptual scheme of the fever as we have employed it, seems in his writings to be watching the course of the Russian Revolution almost clinically, constantly looking for events to take courses observed before in France, in England, or wherever men have revolted in the name of the many against the few.

Again this tradition of revolt is an imponderable, but it seems to have gone into the making of the Western democracies. From these democracies, and from Russia too, this tradition of revolt has now spread around the world. To state the existence of this revolutionary tradition is not necessarily to make a judgment of value. We bring it forth as an observable fact, one not to be effectively denied by partisans of any stripe.

The mid-twentieth-century search for social justice, though its slogans and its methods no longer seem much like the "principles of 1776 and 1789," is in Asia, Africa, and Latin America in some sense a result of, and affiliated with, the revolutions we are here studying. This relation is not one of cause-and-effect in any sense that phrase may have for the physical sciences. It is such, inescapably, in a human sense. In China, in Ghana, in Cuba, they want what they think we in the West wanted when we began our revolutions, something still best summarized by the French *Liberté, Egalité, Fraternité,* and certainly not wholly summarized by any simple nationalistic economic formula. Or perhaps we can content ourselves with calling these movements revolutions of rising expectations.

II. *Some Tentative Uniformities*

When all necessary concessions are made to those who insist that events in history are unique, it remains true that the four revolutions we have studied do display some striking uniformities. Our conceptual scheme of the fever can be worked out so as to bring these uniformities clearly to mind. We shall find it worth while, in attempting to summarize the work of these revolutions, to recapitulate briefly the main points of comparison on which our uniformities are based.

We must be very tentative about the prodromal symptoms of revolution. Even retrospectively, diagnosis of the four societies we studied was very difficult, and there is little ground for belief that anyone today has enough knowledge and skill to apply formal methods of diagnosis to a contemporary society and say, in this case revolution will or will not occur shortly. But some uniformities do emerge from a study of the old regimes in England, America, France, and Russia.

First, these were all societies on the whole on the upgrade economically before the revolution came, and the revolutionary movements seem to originate in the discontents of not unprosperous people who feel restraint, cramp, annoyance, rather than downright crushing oppression. Certainly these revolutions are not started by down-and-outers, by starving, miserable people. These revolutionists are not worms turning, not children of despair. These revolutions are born of hope, and their philosophies are formally optimistic.

Second, we find in our prerevolutionary society definite

and indeed very bitter class antagonisms, though these antagonisms seem rather more complicated than the cruder Marxists will allow. It is not a case of feudal nobility against bourgeoisie in 1640, 1776, and 1789, or of bourgeoisie against proletariat in 1917. The strongest feelings seem generated in the bosoms of men—and women—who have made money, or at least who have enough to live on, and who contemplate bitterly the imperfections of a socially privileged aristocracy. Strong feelings, too, as James C. Davies suggests, are roused in those who find an intolerable gap between what they have come to want—their "needs"—and what they actually get. Revolutions seem more likely when social classes are fairly close together than when they are far apart. "Untouchables" very rarely revolt against a God-given aristocracy, and Haiti gives one of the few examples of successful slave revolutions. But rich merchants whose daughters can marry aristocrats are likely to feel that God is at least as interested in merchants as in aristocrats. It is difficult to say why the bitterness of feeling between classes *almost* equal socially seems so much stronger in some societies than others—why, for instance, a Marie Antoinette should be so much more hated in eighteenth-century France than a rich, idle, much publicized heiress in contemporary America; but at any rate the existence of such bitterness can be observed in our prerevolutionary societies, which is, clinically speaking, enough for the moment.

Third, there is what we have called the transfer of allegiance of the intellectuals. This is in some respects the most reliable of the symptoms we are likely to meet. Here again we need not try to explain all the hows and whys, need not try to tie up this transfer of allegiance with a grand and complete sociology of revolutions. We need state simply that it can be observed in all four of our societies.

Fourth, the governmental machinery is clearly inefficient, partly through neglect, through a failure to make changes in old institutions, partly because new conditions —in the societies we have studied, pretty specifically conditions attendant on economic expansion and the growth of new monied classes, new ways of transportation, new business methods—these new conditions laid an intolerable strain on governmental machinery adapted to simpler, more primitive, conditions.

Fifth, the old ruling class—or rather, many individuals of the old ruling class—come to distrust themselves, or lose faith in the traditions and habits of their class, grow intellectual, humanitarian, or go over to the attacking groups. Perhaps a larger number of them than usual lead lives we shall have to call immoral, dissolute, though one cannot by any means be as sure about this as a symptom as about the loss of habits and traditions of command effective among a ruling class. At any rate, the ruling class becomes politically inept.

The dramatic events that start things moving, that bring on the fever of revolution, are in three of our four revolutions intimately connected with the financial administration of the state. In the fourth, Russia, the breakdown of administration under the burdens of an unsuccessful war is only in part financial. But in all our societies the inefficiency and inadequacy of the governmental structure of the society come out clearly in the very first stages of the revolution. There is a time—the first few weeks or months—when it looks as if a determined use of force on the part of the government might prevent the mounting excitement from culminating in an overthrow of the government. These governments attempted such a use of force in all four instances, and in all four their attempt was a failure. This failure indeed proved a turning point during the first stages, and set up the revolutionists in power.

Yet one is impressed in all four instances more with the ineptitude of the governments' use of force than with the skill of their opponents' use of force. We are here speaking of the situation wholly from a military and police point of view. It may be that the majority of the people are discontented, loathe the existing government, wish it overthrown. Nobody knows. They don't commonly take plebiscites just *before* revolutions. In the actual clash—even Bastille Day, Concord, or the February Days in Petrograd—only a minority of the people is actively engaged. But the government hold over its own troops is poor, its troops fight half-heartedly or desert, its commanders are stupid, its enemies acquire a nucleus of the deserting troops or of a previous militia, and the old gives place to the new. Yet, such is the conservative and routine-loving nature of the bulk of human beings, so strong are habits of obedience in most of them, that it is almost safe to say that no government is likely to be overthrown from within its territory until it loses the ability to make adequate use of its military and police powers. That loss of ability may show itself in the actual desertion of soldiers and police to the revolutionists, or in the stupidity with which the government manages its soldiers and police, or in both ways.

The events we have grouped under the names of first stages do not of course unroll themselves in exactly the same order in time, or with exactly the same content, in all four of our revolutions. But we have listed the major elements—and they fall into a pattern of uniformities—financial breakdown, organization of the discontented to remedy this breakdown (or threatened breakdown), revolutionary demands on the part of these organized discontented, demands which if granted would mean the virtual abdication of those governing, attempted use of force by the government, its failure, and the attainment of power by the revolutionists. These revolutionists have hitherto been acting as an organized and nearly unanimous group, but with the attainment of power it is clear that they are not united. The group which dominates these first stages we call the moderates, though to emotional supporters of the old regime they look most immoderate. They are not always in a numerical majority in this stage—indeed it is pretty clear that if you limit the moderates to the Kadets they were not in a majority in Russia in February, 1917. But they seem the natural heirs of the old government, and they have their chance. In three of our revolutions they are sooner or later driven from office to death or exile. Certainly there is to be seen in England, France, and Russia a process in which a series of crises—some involving violence, street fighting, and the like—deposes one set of men and puts in power another and more radical set. In these revolutions power passes by violent or at least extralegal methods from Right to Left, until at the crisis period the extreme radicals, the complete revolutionists, are in power. There are, as a matter of fact, usually a few even wilder and more lunatic fringes of the triumphant extremists—but these are not numerous or strong and are usually suppressed or otherwise made harmless by the dominant radicals. It is therefore approximately true to say that power passes on from Right to Left until it reaches a limit usually short of the most extreme or lunatic Left.

The rule of the extremists we have called the crisis period. This period was not reached in the American Revolution, though in the treatment of Loyalists, in the pressure to support the army, in some of the phases of social life, you can discern in America many of the phenomena of the Terror as it is seen in our three other societies. We cannot here attempt to go into the complicated question as to why the American Revolution stopped short of a true crisis period, why the moderates were never ousted in this country, or at least ousted only in 1800. We must repeat that we are simply trying to establish certain uniformities of description, and are not attempting a complete sociology of revolutions.

The extremists are helped to power no doubt by the existence of a powerful pressure toward centralized strong government, something which in general the moderates are not capable of providing, while the extremists, with their discipline, their contempt for half measures, their willingness to make firm decisions, their freedom from libertarian qualms, are quite able and willing to centralize. Especially in France and Russia, where powerful foreign enemies threatened the very existence of the nation, the machinery of government during the crisis period was in part constructed to serve as a government of national defense. Yet though modern wars, as we know in this country, demand a centralization of authority, war alone does not seem to account for all that happened in the crisis period in those countries.

What does happen may be a bit oversimply summarized as follows: emergency centralization of power in an administration, usually a council or commission, and more or less dominated by a "strong man"—Cromwell, Robespierre, Lenin; government without any effective protection for the normal civil rights of the individual—or if this sounds unrealistic, especially for Russia, let us say the normal private life of the individual; setting up of extraordinary courts and a special revolutionary police to carry out the decrees of the government and to suppress all dissenting individuals or groups; all this machinery ultimately built up from a relatively small group—Independents, Jacobins, Bolsheviks—which has a monopoly on all governmental action. Finally, governmental action becomes a much greater part of all human action than in these societies in their normal condition: this apparatus of government is set to work indifferently on the mountains and molehills of human life —it is used to pry into and poke about corners normally reserved for priest or physician, or friend, and it is used to regulate, control, and plan the production and distribution of economic wealth on a national scale.

This pervasiveness of the Reign of Terror in the crisis period is partly explicable in terms of the pressure of war necessities and of economic struggles as well as of other variables: but it must probably also be explained as in part the manifestation of an effort to achieve intensely moral and religious ends here on earth. The little band of violent revolutionists who form the nucleus of all action during the Terror behave as men have been observed to behave before when under the influence of active religious faith. Independents, Jacobins, Bolsheviks, all sought to make all human activity here on earth conform to an ideal pattern, which, like all such patterns, seems deeply rooted in their sentiments. A striking uniformity in all these patterns is their asceticism, or if you prefer, their condemnation of what we may call the minor as well as the major vices. Essentially, however, these patterns are a good deal alike, and all resemble closely what we may call conventional Christian ethics. Independents, Jacobins, and Bolsheviks, at least during the crisis period, really make an effort to enforce behavior in literal conformity with these codes or patterns. Such an effort means stern repression of much that many men have been used to regarding as normal; it means a kind of universal tension in which the ordinary individual can never feel protected by the humble routines to which he has been formed: it means that the intricate prerevolutionary network of customary interactions among individuals—a network which is still to the few men devoted to its intelligent study almost a complete mystery—this network is temporarily all torn apart. John Jones, the man in the street, the ordinary man, is left floundering.

We are almost at the point of being carried away into the belief that our conceptual scheme is something more than a mere convenience, that it does somehow describe "reality." At the crisis, the collective patient does seem helpless, thrashing his way through a delirium. But we must try to avoid the emotional, metaphorical appeal, and concentrate on making clear what seems to be the really important point here. Most of us are familiar with the favorite old Tory metaphor: the violent revolutionist tears down the noble edifice society lives in, or burns it down, and then fails to build up another, and poor human beings are left naked to the skies. That is not a good metaphor, save perhaps for purposes of Tory propaganda. Even at the height of a revolutionary crisis period, more of the old building is left standing than is destroyed. But the whole metaphor of the building is bad. We may take instead an analogy from the human nervous system, or think of an immensely complicated gridwork of electrical communications. Society then appears as a kind of network of interactions among individuals, interactions for the most part fixed by habit, hardened and perhaps adorned as ritual, dignified into meaning and beauty by the elaborately interwoven strands of interaction we know as law, theology, metaphysics, and similar noble beliefs. Now sometimes many of these interwoven strands of noble beliefs, some even of those of habit and tradition, can be cut out, and others inserted. During the crisis period of our revolutions some such process seems to have taken place; but the whole network itself seems so far never to have been altered suddenly and radically, and even the noble beliefs tend to fit into the network in the same places. If you kill off *all* the people who live within the network, you don't so much change the network of course as destroy it. This type of destruction is as yet rare in human history. Certainly in none of our revolutions was there even a very close approach to it.

What did happen, under the pressure of class struggle,

war, religious idealism, and a lot more, was that the hidden and obscure courses which many of the interactions in the network follow were suddenly exposed, and passage along them made difficult in the unusual publicity and, so to speak, self-consciousness. The courses of other interactions were blocked, and the interactions went on with the greatest of difficulties by all sorts of detours. The courses of still other interactions were confused, short-circuited, paired off in strange ways. Finally, the pretensions of the fanatical leaders of the revolution involved the attempted creation of a vast number of new interactions. Now though for the most part these new interactions affected chiefly those strands we have called the noble beliefs—law, theology, metaphysics, mythology, folklore, high-power abstractions in general—still some of them did penetrate at an experimental level into the obscurer and less dignified part of the network of interactions among human beings and put a further strain on it. Surely it is no wonder that under these conditions men and women in the crisis period should behave as they would not normally behave, that in the crisis period nothing should seem as it used to seem, that, indeed, a famous passage from Thucydides, written two thousand years before our revolutions, should seem like a clinical report:

> When troubles had once begun in the cities, those who followed carried the revolutionary spirit further and further, and determined to outdo the report of all who had preceded them by the ingenuity of the enterprises and the atrocity of their revenges. The meaning of words had no longer the same relation to things, but was changed by them as they thought proper. Reckless daring was held to be loyal courage; prudent delay was the excuse of a coward; moderation was the disguise of unmanly weakness; to know everything was to do nothing. Frantic energy was the true quality of a man. A conspirator who wanted to be safe was a recreant in disguise. The lover of violence was always trusted, and his opponent suspected. He who succeeded in a plot was deemed knowing, but a still greater master in craft was he who detected one. On the other hand, he who plotted

from the first to have nothing to do with plots was a breaker up of parties and a poltroon who was afraid of the enemy. In a word, he who could outstrip another in a bad action was applauded, and so was he who encouraged to evil one who had no idea of it. . . . The tie of party was stronger than the tie of blood, because a partisan was more ready to dare without asking why.

With this we may put a quotation from a much humbler source, an obscure Siberian co-operative leader protesting against Red and White Terror alike. Mr. Chamberlin quotes:

And we ask and appeal to society, to the contending political groups and parties: When will our much-suffering Russia outlive the nightmare that is throttling it, when will deaths by violence cease? Doesn't horror seize you at the sight of the uninterrupted flow of human blood? Doesn't horror seize you at the consciousness that the deepest, most elementary bases of the existence of human society are perishing: the feeling of humanity, the consciousness of the value of life, of human personality, the feeling and consciousness of the necessity of legal order in the state? . . . Hear our cry and despair: we return to prehistoric times of the existence of the human race; we are on the verge of the death of civilization and culture; we destroy the great cause of human progress, for which many generations of our worthier ancestors labored.

Certainly, however, none of our revolutions quite ended in the death of civilization and culture. The network was stronger than the forces trying to destroy or alter it, and in all of our societies the crisis period was followed by a convalescence, by a return to most of the simpler and more fundamental courses taken by interactions in the old network. More especially, the religious lust for perfection, the crusade for the Republic of Virtue, died out, save among a tiny minority whose actions could no longer take place directly in politics. An active, proselyting, intolerant, ascetic, chiliastic faith became fairly rapidly an inactive, conformist, worldly ritualistic faith.

The equilibrium has been restored and the revolution is over. But this does not mean that nothing has been changed. Some new and useful tracks or courses in the network of interactions that makes society have been established, some old and inconvenient ones—you may call them unjust if you like—have been eliminated. There is something heartless in saying that it took the French Revolution to produce the metric system and to destroy *lods et ventes* and similar feudal inconveniences, or the Russian Revolution to bring Russia to use the modern calendar and to eliminate a few useless letters in the Russian alphabet. These tangible and useful results look rather petty as measured by the brotherhood of man and the achievement of justice on this earth. The blood of the martyrs seems hardly necessary to establish decimal coinage.

Yet those who feel that revolution is heroic need not despair. The revolutionary tradition is an heroic one, and the noble beliefs which seem necessary to all societies are in our Western democracies in part a product of the revolutions we have been studying. They were initiated, even in Russia, by Peter Gay's "party of humanity." Our revolutions made tremendous and valuable additions to those strands in the network of human interactions which can be isolated as law, theology, metaphysics and, in the abstract sense, ethics. Had these revolutions never occurred, you and I might still beat our wives or cheat at cards or avoid walking under ladders, but we might not be able to rejoice in our possession of certain inalienable rights to life, liberty, and the pursuit of happiness, or in the comforting assurance that one more push will bring the classless society.

When one compares the whole course of these revolutions, certain tentative uniformities suggest themselves. If the Russian Revolution at the end of our series is compared with the English at its beginning, there seems to be a development of conscious revolutionary technique. This is of course especially clear since Marx made the history of revolutionary movements of the past a necessary preparation for revolutionists of the present. Lenin and his collaborators had a training in the technique of insurrection which Independents and Jacobins lacked. Robespierre seems almost a political innocent when his revolutionary training is compared with that of any good Bolshevik leader. Sam Adams, it must be admitted, seems a good deal less innocent. All in all, it is probable that this difference in the explicitness of self-conscious preparation for revolution, this growth of a copious literature of revolution, this increasing familiarity of revolutionary ideas, is not one of the very important uniformities we have to record. It is a conspicuous uniformity, but not an important one. Revolutions are still not a form of logical action. The Bolsheviks do not seem to have guided their actions by the "scientific" study of revolutions to an appreciably greater degree than the Independents or the Jacobins. They simply adapted an old technique to the days of the telegraph and railroad trains.

This last suggests another conspicuous but not very important tendency in our four revolutions. They took place in societies increasingly influenced by the "Industrial Revolution," increasingly subject to those changes in scale which our modern conquests of time and space have brought to societies. Thus the Russian Revolution directly affected more people and more square miles of territory than any previous revolution; its sequence of events compresses into a few months what in England in the seventeenth century had taken years to achieve; in its use of the printing press, telegraph, radio, airplanes and the rest it seems, as compared with our other revolutions, definitely a streamlined affair. But again we may well doubt whether such changes of scale are in themselves really important factors. Men's desires are the same, whether they ride toward their achievement in airplanes or on horseback. Revolutions may be bigger nowadays, but surely not better. Our prophets of doom to the contrary notwithstanding, the loudspeaker does not change the words.

Finally, at the risk of being tedious, we must come back to some of the problems of methods in the social sciences which were suggested in our first chapter. We must admit that the theorems, the uniformities, which we have been able to put forward in terms of our conceptual scheme, are

vague and undramatic. They are by no means as interesting or as alarming as the ideas of revolution held by the
late George Orwell, who really believed that totalitarian
revolutionary leaders have learned how to change human
beings into something wholly different from their immediate predecessors. On the contrary, even Communist Russians begin to look more and more like—Russians. Our
uniformities cannot be stated in quantitative terms, cannot
be used for purposes of prediction or control. But at the
very outset we warned the reader not to expect too much.
Even such vague theorems as that of the transfer of allegiance of the intellectuals, that of the role of force in the
first stages of revolution, that of the part played by "religious" enthusiasm in the period of crisis, that of the pursuit of pleasure during Thermidor, are, one hopes, not
without value for the study of men in society. In themselves they amount to little, but they suggest certain possibilities in further work.

In the first place, by their very inadequacies they point
to the necessity for a more rigorous treatment of the problems involved, challenging those who find them incomplete
and unsatisfactory to do a better job. In the second place,
they will serve the purpose of all first approximations in
scientific work—they will suggest further study of the
facts, especially in those fields where the attempt to make
first approximations has uncovered an insufficient supply of
the necessary facts. Notably here the facts for a study of
class antagonisms are woefully inadequate. So, too, are the
facts for a study of the circulation of the elite in prerevolutionary societies. But there are a hundred such holes, some
of which can surely be filled. Our first approximations will
then lead the way to another's second approximations. No
scientist should ask more, even though the public does.

III. *A Paradox of Revolution*

Wider uniformities will, to judge by the past of
science, someday emerge from more complete studies of
the sociology of revolutions. Here we dare not hazard
much that we have not already brought out in the course
of our analysis of four specific revolutions. After all, these

are but four revolutions of what seems to be the same type, revolutions in what may be not too uncritically called the democratic tradition. So precious a word is "revolution" to many in that tradition, and especially to Marxists, that they indignantly refuse to apply it to such movements as the relatively bloodless but certainly violent and illegal assumption of power by Mussolini or Hitler. These movements, we are told, were not revolutions because they did not take power from one class and give it to another. Obviously with a word in some ways as imprecise as "revolution" you can play all sorts of tricks like this. But for the scientific study of social change it seems wise to apply the word revolution to the overthrow of an established and legal parliamentary government by Fascists. If this is so, then our four revolutions are but one kind of revolution, and we must not attempt to make them bear the strain of generalizations meant to apply to all revolutions.

We need not, however, end on a note of blank skepticism. It would seem that there are, from the study of these revolutions, three major conclusions to be drawn: first, that, in spite of their undeniable and dramatic differences, they do present certain simple uniformities of the kind we have tried to bring together under our conceptual scheme of the fever; second, that they point sharply to the necessity of studying men's deeds and men's words without assuming that there is always a simple and logical connection between the two, since throughout their courses, and especially at their crises, they frequently exhibit men saying one thing and doing another; third, that they indicate that in general many things men do, many human habits, sentiments, dispositions, cannot be changed at all rapidly, that the attempt made by the extremists to change them by law, terror, and exhortation fails, that the convalescence brings them back not greatly altered.

Yet one hesitant major generalization binding all four of these revolutions together may here be made from many anticipations earlier in this book. These four revolutions exhibit an increasing scale of promises to the "common man"—promises as vague as that of complete "happiness" and as concrete as that of full satisfaction of all material wants, with all sorts of pleasant revenges on the way.

Communism is but the present limit of this increasing set of promises. It is not for us here to rail or protest, but simply to record. So far, these promises in their extreme form have been fulfilled nowhere. That they are made at all offends the traditional Christian, the humanist, perhaps even the man of common sense. But they are made, more vigorously perhaps today in China, in Southeast Asia, in the Near East, wherever Communism is still a young, fresh, and active faith. It is not enough for us Americans to repeat that the promises are impossible of fulfillment, and ought not to be made. It would be folly for us to tell the world that we Americans can fill these promises, especially since we have not filled them at home. Revolution is not a fever that will yield to such innocent and deceptive remedies. For a time, at least, we must accept it as being as incurable as cancer.

As to what the experience of a great revolution does to the society that experiences it, we cannot conclude here too widely without trespassing on wider fields of history and sociology. Yet it does seem that the patient emerges stronger in some respects from the conquered fever, immunized in this way and that from attacks that might be more serious. It is an observable fact that in all our societies there was a flourishing, a peak of varied cultural achievements, after the revolutions. Certainly we may not moralize too much about the stupidities and cruelties of revolutions, may not lift up our hands in horror. It is quite possible that wider study would show that feeble and decadent societies do not undergo revolutions, that revolutions are, perversely, a sign of strength and youth in societies.

One quiet person emerges from his study, not indeed untouched by a good deal of horror and disgust, but moved also with admiration for a deep and unfathomable strength in men which, because of the softer connotations of the word, he is reluctant to call spiritual. Montaigne saw and felt it long ago:

> I see not one action, or three, or a hundred, but a commonly accepted state of morality so unnatural, especially as regards inhumanity and treachery, which are to me the worst of all sins, that I have not the

heart to think of them without horror; and they excite my wonder almost as much as my detestation. *The practice of these egregious villainies has as much the mark of strength and vigor of soul as of error and disorder.*

Berkman the anarchist, who loathed the Russian Revolution, tells a story which may represent merely his own bias, but which may nonetheless serve as a brief symbolical conclusion to this study. Berkman says he asked a good Bolshevik acquaintance during the period of attempted complete communization under Lenin why the famous Moscow cabmen, the *izvoschiks*, who continued in diminished numbers to flit about Moscow and to get enormous sums in paper roubles for their services, were not nationalized like practically everything else. The Bolshevik replied, "We found that if you don't feed human beings they continue to live somehow. But if you don't feed the horses, the stupid beasts die. That's why we don't nationalize the cabmen." That is not an altogether cheerful story, and in some ways one may regret the human capacity to live without eating. But clearly if we were as stupid—or as sensible—as horses we should have no revolutions.

EPILOGUE: 1964

The thirty years since this book first took shape as Lowell lectures have not diminished the importance of its subject. We are even further away than in the 1930's from the hopes embodied in the Victorian "evolution, not revolution." Phrases like "world-wide revolution" are nowadays simple realism, not mere stereotypes of journalism. More than half of the hundred-odd member states of the United Nations Organization are either directly the creation of some kind of revolutionary action, or came into being because their rulers saw fit to yield to demands inspired by successful revolutions elsewhere. Statistically this number is swollen by the granting of independence without violent revolution to many former colonial possessions of Western powers. Clearly, however, violence in India, the Near East, Algeria, Kenya, Indonesia, and elsewhere triggered these actions of emancipation. True socio-economic revolution, by no means the old-fashioned "Latin American revolution," which used to be so close to the "palace" or "harem" revolution, has come to our neighbors, Mexico and Cuba. Indeed, all Latin American revolutions now begin to look serious.

The United States is at present one of the oldest of settled governments, its successful revolution nearly two centuries past, its great abortive revolution more than a century past. That abortive revolution has, we now know, left unsolved a very great problem indeed. Yet though the American Negro "revolution" of the 1960's is in some senses deserving of the name, though it displays some of the uniformities we have discerned in our four revolutions, it is not a movement aimed at overthrowing our government—our "old regime"—and putting another in its place. The United States, in spite of the violence of our controversies, in spite of conservative fears about Communist conspiracies, in spite of the worries of our intellectuals, looks like a stable society in which a real revolution is highly unlikely. Even in the 1930's, with sixteen million unemployed, the closest we came to actual violence was some milk-spilling in the Middle West and the pathetic march of unemployed veterans to the makeshift camp on Anacostia Island in Washington.

We have already noted as an obvious uniformity of our revolutions that once the revolution has succeeded, once the new regime has got well established, the emotional overtones of the word "revolution" change for that society. The original revolution becomes part of history—"oratorical history," as Croce called it—respectable and dead; but current or threatening revolutions become menaces, disreputable, objects of condemnation. This is clearly true for the American and French revolutions, and seems about to become true in Russia for the Russian Revolution. So very stable and law abiding did England become in the nineteenth century that the English Revolution of the 1640's wasn't even gilded with respectability as, for instance, the Daughters of the American Revolution have gilded ours; good Victorian Englishmen were so ashamed of having cut off a king's head that they tried, not altogether unsuccessfully, to forget the whole business.

This is written, one may hope, without bitterness and in fact without ironic intent. It would seem to be true that conventional—that is, most—Americans today find the feelings aroused by the concept "revolution" unpleasant; for them the word is dyslogistic, not eulogistic. The matter is not quite so simple, and ordinary, average Americans are pretty ambivalent about the present world-wide revolution.

They are against the old "imperialist" powers and for the colonial peoples who rebelled against their masters. By and large, they side with the underdogs, unless the underdogs begin to snap at them. Americans really "believe in" democracy, naturally enough defining democracy in their own way, and would like to see the rest of the world do so as well.

But let us see how the matter appears to an outsider. Arnold Toynbee has recently published a series of lectures called *America and the World Revolution*, the separate titles of which pretty well explain his thesis: "The Shot Heard Round the World," "The Handicap of Affluence," "Can America Rejoin Her Own Revolution?" We Americans, according to Toynbee, began at Lexington and Concord a democratic revolution to achieve social justice for all men; as a rich and successful society we have now lost touch with those vast numbers of men in the rest of the world who are still moved by the echoes of that famous shot, by "the principles of 1776 and 1789"; we must get back in touch with them, or we shall lose the sympathies of mankind, and miss the wave of the future. In a characteristic—and surely somewhat misleading—figure of speech Toynbee says we Americans must now choose between playing the role of a Metternich and playing that of a Mazzini.

Of course Toynbee oversimplifies. His position, however, is close to that of "liberal" opinion in the West, and not nearly as extreme as that of our thoroughgoing enemies, Communist and neutralist, in whose opinion we have already chosen the role of defender of the possessing classes, the old regimes, throughout the world. Even more in international than in interpersonal relations, Burns's wish that we might see ourselves as others see us is nowhere near realization. Most Americans think our role in recent international politics has been one of supporting the underprivileged, the victims of imperialism, those who want to achieve the good democratic way of life. And we *have* come closer to playing that role than the Toynbees, the Bertrand Russells, the Sartres, will admit. But the fact remains that we are in the outside world tagged as hostile to revolutions, not only to Communist or Fascist, but to any kind of revolution.

It is not our purpose here to preach a sermon like Toynbee's. The United States is a stable, affluent nation, heir to the never very secure position of top of the international pecking order held in the nineteenth century by

Great Britain. What we can do is at least limited, if not "determined" in any sense—Marxist, Calvinist, positivist or neo-positivist—by that position. We cannot be a collective Mazzini. But we can surely avoid being a collective Metternich. We can try to understand as well as possible the world-revolution—or world-revolutions—of our time.

Both singular and plural are valid here. For the historian willing to see uniformities as well as differences, the last four or five centuries have been one long revolution. In an interesting study of Communist tactics in the current struggle for power, *Communism and Revolution: The Strategic Uses of Political Violence*, Professor Cyril Black writes of a master revolution beginning in the late Middle Ages in Western and Southern Europe, and now world-wide. He and his colleagues in this collaborative study are willing to settle for a most noncommittal name for this revolution, "modernization," although they note that it is "variously known as Europeanization, Westernization, social change, the revolution of rising expectations." They might have added others, such as "Americanization" (a name significantly enough usually given by those, as for instance French intellectuals, who dislike most of the concrete changes brought by this revolution) or "scientific and technological revolution" or "quest for social justice," or even "revolt of the masses."

Most of these phrases add something to our knowledge of this complex—and in the perspective of human history and prehistory, rapid and universal—revolution. It is unprofitable for us here to attempt to achieve more rigorous definition. In terms of intellectual analysis, no simple definition is possible. As a brief verbal symbol, no one has done much better than "*Liberté, Egalité, Fraternité*"; or for a longer one, Jefferson's preamble to our Declaration of Independence. Over the long years, and especially right now when both sides appeal to it, just "democracy" has done very well.

This last should remind us that within this great master revolution there are very different constituent revolutions. The Russian Revolution, though it appealed to "democracy," though even more obviously it was a "revolution of rising expectations," is quite different from the Gandhian revolution in India, and indeed from the American and French "democratic revolutions. Though both were socioeconomic revolutions appealing to collectivist or socialist principles, the Mexican and the Cuban revolutions were very different. Two revolutions rarely compared, the Irish and the Algerian, still have very much, and that most enlightening, in common; but it would be absurd to deny that there is much in each not found in the other. All sorts of variables do indeed vary—time, place, personalities, the state of international politics, and much else, even the weather. There are still a few French Jacobins who hold that if there had not been a terrific downpour on the night of July 27, 1794, the Parisian *sans culottes* would have risen and saved Robespierre. And, since even the Cuban Revolution is in part already history, there is for all revolutions the horrid variable of historical uncertainty. Some historians maintain that there was no serious rain in Paris on the night of July 27, 1794. Finally, there is always, until we attain omniscience, what we must call accident, and in particular the accident that puts one man instead of another in high place. If Ben Bella had died in a French prison, instead of improving his education by reading the classics of revolution, the Algerian Revolution would surely not have taken exactly the course it has taken.

Yet with all these due allowances, there does, it seems to this writer, remain a residue of uniformities, some of which we have sought to discern from what we know of our four revolutions, and which can have some application to the world of the 1960's. One such uniformity needs special emphasis, for a very strong current in American opinion tends to reject it, or at any rate, not to give it the importance it deserves. For reasons the historian and the sociologist of knowledge in collaboration could certainly help explain, most Americans believe revolutions are initiated and carried through by underdogs against upperdogs. This in itself is basically true, if platitudinous. But they think of the underdogs as poverty-stricken, deprived of relatively simple material satisfactions, oppressed, enslaved, without education (which has been denied them by their masters), strong only in their numbers. The above is exaggerated, of course. We may perhaps put the matter more fairly if we say that the American, heir of eighteenth-century optimistic rationalism, tends to emphasize the rational and individualistic economic motive and to minimize such motives as pride, envy, the "pooled self-esteem" of nationalism (and racism), to say nothing of religious and moral idealism, romantic longings, the team spirit, the whole bottomless reservoir of capabilities of the damned human race. The result is the grave oversimplification, to which our columnists call frequent attention, that if we can give enough economic aid to nations in need of it we can make them revolution-proof, grateful, peaceful—at least toward us— and stable.

For the long, long run it is probably true that large groups of men adequately fed, clothed, housed, and entertained are unlikely to indulge in revolution. Witness ourselves at this moment of time. But as the world now stands, we have to consider the short run, and in the short run there will be large groups of men not as well off as they feel—think, if you are a good rationalist—they ought to be and can be. It might be possible, in spite of the population explosion, to feed adequately the billion or two we are told are not yet so fed. We may hope that the men of good will working toward that end will make real progress. But, to revert to the anecdote from Alexander Berkman with which we originally closed this book (see above, p. 264), though full feeding makes most beasts quiet, this is not so of *homo sapiens*. He needs much more than a full belly if he is to behave himself as a peaceful, law-abiding, productive citizen. In fact—and this is the uniformity Americans really must master if we are to adjust ourselves to a world we cannot wholly remake—if he has a full or tolerably full belly and a grievance, a sense of being treated underservedly, unjustly, if something inspires in him that feeling it would seem no other animal can have, that of *moral indignation*, he will revolt; or rather, he will make a revolution, not a mere revolt.

Now moral indignation, unlike mere physical appetite, is very hard indeed to allay. Marie Antoinette alive and dead has to bear the stigma of that "let them eat cake," though she may well have never uttered the phrase. We Americans, though no American may have had a part in the business, though indeed the sign may never have existed, will for a long time share the blame for that sign in a Shanghai park, "Dogs and Chinese not allowed." Deservedly or undeservedly we share all over the globe—and again, in spite of our frequent good intentions and even our good achievements—blame for the indignities the white European has, often quite unintentionally, inflicted on those over whom he once held dominion.

To sum up very briefly: We cannot possibly stop this series of "revolutions of rising expectations." We cannot even do a great deal to hasten them over their crisis periods, to allay their violence, to guide their course toward true democracy. But we—our leaders, supported by a public opinion educated to a certain amount of patience—can do something better than we have done with, for example, the Chinese and the Cuban revolutions. We cannot intervene to crush a revolution we do not like, as the Russians did in Hungary; but we can avoid mistakes like the Bay of Pigs. We cannot, as a Toynbee would like us to, put ourselves at the head of such revolutions. But we can avoid our present policy of belling with the hounds of the awakened multitudes, and especially the awakened intellectuals, of Asia and Africa and running with the hares of the old *effendi* or possessing classes. For one thing, the odds are overwhelming that these particular hares will be caught— and then we shall be in a very bad position.

Since this is after all a historian's book, and since we have already made much of Toynbee's metaphor, we may conclude in a similar vein. There really isn't much chance we shall play the role of either Metternich or Mazzini. There is some chance we shall be caught in a role like that of Napoleon III, who always did try to satisfy everybody —and failed sadly. Perhaps we can do as well as Canning, Castlereagh, and Talleyrand? These gentlemen, confronted with the aftermath of the French Revolution and Napoleon, did nothing very noble or elevating, but they did lay the foundations for a century of comparative peace—at any rate, a century more nearly peaceful than ours has yet proved to be. They were not extremists, and Canning and Talleyrand were not very high-minded or principled. They even got on with revolutions they did not like.

BIBLIOGRAPHICAL APPENDIX

The following bibliography is intended solely as a guide to individuals or groups who may wish to attempt the difficult but rewarding study of revolutions. As such, it is merely suggestive, but it is complete enough so that anyone using all the leads these books and *their* bibliographies offer would soon find himself very completely immersed in the subject.

1. *Historical Writing on the Four Revolutions*

The first part of this bibliography aims to introduce the reader to some of the best-known historical writing about the four revolutions with which we are here concerned. Some of the later and not yet tested writing on these periods will also be included. But here least of all could anything like completeness be attempted. A full bibliography of French history alone from 1750 to 1815 would list books enough to fill a library; at a guess, including pamphlets and articles in periodicals, there would be well over three hundred thousand titles. Writings on the Russian Revolution are already almost as numerous, and even more varied. The reader will, however, find in these books an opportunity to check the supply of facts from which we have attempted to discover uniformities in the course of our revolutions.

A. *England*

W. C. Abbott, *The Writings and Speeches of Oliver Cromwell.* 3 vols. Cambridge, Mass., 1937-45.
A splendid scholarly job.

J. W. Allen, *English Political Thought, 1603-1660.* London, 1938.
History in the traditional manner of histories of formal political thought—i.e., a bit too exclusively interested in how ideas breed further ideas, but very full. Unfortunately only Vol. I, to 1644, has appeared.

M. P. Ashley, *England in the Seventeenth Century.* Harmondsworth, 1952.
Part of the excellent introductory Pelican history of England.

Eduard Bernstein, *Cromwell and Communism.* London, 1930.
A belated but useful translation of the famous revisionist's *Sozialismus und Demokratie in der grossen englischen Revolution* which appeared in German before the war. This is a necessary correction to the purely political and conventional interests of Gardiner, and even of Firth.

Louise F. Brown, *The Political Activities of the Baptists and Fifth Monarchy Men in England during the Interregnum.* Washington, 1912.

Godfrey Davies, *The Early Stuarts, 1603-1660.* Oxford, 1937.
A volume in the standard scholarly *Oxford History of England.* An excellent book, with a most useful bibliography.

C. H. Firth, *Oliver Cromwell and the Rule of the Puritans in England.* 3rd edition. London, 1924.
The great work of our generation on Cromwell.

S. R. Gardiner, *A History of England. 1603-1642; A History of the Great Civil War, 1642-1649; A History of the Commonwealth and Protectorate, 1649-1656.*
Various editions and volumes. The whole work is usually in some 17 volumes. This is the "classic" history of the period, written in the last half of the nineteenth century. It is a sound but rather dull political history, but it does not touch at all on much that would interest us in the fields of economic, social, and intellectual history.

G. P. Gooch, *English Democratic Ideas in the Seventeenth Cen-*

tury. 2nd edition with notes and appendices by H. J. Laski. Cambridge, England, 1927. Also Torchbook paperback.
Indispensable.

H. J. C. Grierson, *Cross Currents in English Literature of the Seventeenth Century.* London, 1929.
Excellent intellectual history.

J. H. Hexter, *The Reign of King Pym.* Cambridge, Mass., 1941.
A first-rate study of party politics.

Margaret James, *Social Problems and Policy During the Puritan Revolution.* London, 1930.
Maintains that the social and economic consequences of the Puritan Revolution were, unlike the political ones, really revolutionary.

David Mathew, *The Social Structure in Caroline England.* Oxford, 1948.
Suggestive lectures packed with concrete information.

J. E. Morpurgo, ed., *Life under the Stuarts.* London, 1950.
Collaborative survey at an elementary level with much interesting material and a good simple "Further Reading List."

Wallace Notestein, *The English People on the Eve of Colonization 1603-1630.* New York, 1954.
A good survey including social history.

T. C. Pease, *The Leveller Movement.* Washington, 1916.
A very useful monograph, especially as a corrective to Bernstein's socialistic view of Lilburne and the Levellers.

Leopold von Ranke, *A History of England Principally in the Seventeenth Century.* English translation. 6 vols. Oxford, 1875.
Another classic of narrative history.

G. M. Trevelyan, *England under the Stuarts.* 15th edition. New York, 1930.
Perhaps the best of our modern manuals, though distinctly in the traditions of pleasant British liberalism, which are always a bit shocked by the facts of revolution. This book has a convenient bibliography.

H. R. Trevor-Roper, "The Gentry, 1540-1640," *Economic History Review, Supplement,* 1953.
An important study of class lines. Should be read with R. H. Tawney, "Rise of the Gentry, 1558-1640," *Economic History Review,* Vol. XI (1941).

Basil Willey, *The Seventeenth Century Background*. London, 1934.

Indispensable for intellectual history.

B. *America*

R. G. Adams, *Political Ideas of the American Revolution*. Durham, N. C., 1922.

A useful survey.

C. W. Alvord, *The Mississippi Valley in British Politics*. 2 vols. Cleveland, 1917.

An important monograph opening up an important field neglected in earlier studies of the American Revolution.

C. M. Andrews, *The Colonial Background of the American Revolution*. New Haven, 1924.

Bernard Bailyn, *Pamphlets of the American Revolution, 1750-1776*. 4 vols. Cambridge, Mass., 1965—

The first volume of this important work now in course of publication contains a long introduction surveying the whole field of these pamphlets. See also the forthcoming *The Popular Sources of Political Authority* by Oscar and Mary Handlin, documents from Massachusetts town meetings dealing with the proposed constitution for the new state (1780). Bailyn and the Handlins represent a moderate revisionist attitude toward the American Revolution, which for Bailyn "was above all else an ideological-constitutional struggle and not primarily a controversy between social groups undertaken to force changes in the organization of society" (p. viii).

C. A. Barker, *The Background of the Revolution in Maryland*. New Haven, 1940.

A careful regional study.

C. L. Becker, *The Eve of the Revolution* (Vol. XI of the *Chronicles of America*). New Haven, 1918. *The Declaration of Independence*. New York, 1922.

Both these books bring to the study of political change a rare and thorough knowledge of how men think and feel.

G. L. Beer, *British Colonial Policy, 1754-1765*. New York, 1907.

The last volume of a thorough monographic treatment of the old British Empire, especially with respect to matters of trade and taxation.

Catherine D. Bowen, *John Adams and the American Revolution*. Boston, 1950.

Lively and careful. Its form, touching that of *biographie romancée*, need not worry the student.

Carl and Jessica Bridenbaugh, *Rebels and Gentlemen*. New York, 1942.

A socio-intellectual study of Philadelphia in the "Age of Franklin," and hence of the intellectual background of the American Revolution, not unlike that of D. Mornet for France. More such works are needed.

W. A. Brown, *Empire or Independence*. University, La., 1941.

A very careful study of the efforts to keep the colonies and Britain together, which throws light on the role of moderates and extremists.

E. C. Burnett, *The Continental Congress*. New York, 1941.

Philip Davidson, *Propaganda and the American Revolution, 1763-1783*. Chapel Hill, N. C., 1941.

Bernard Fay, *The Third Revolutionary Spirit in France and America, 1763-1783*. Chapel Hill, N. C., 1941.

L. H. Gipson, *The Coming of the Revolution 1763-1775*. New York, 1954, and J. R. Alden, *The American Revolution, 1775-1783*. New York, 1954.

These two volumes in the new American Nation series are the latest products of American scholarship; they have critical bibliographies.

L. R. Gottschalk, *The Place of the American Revolution in the Causal Pattern of the French Revolution*. Easton, Pa., 1948.

An interesting study of interconnections.

E. B. Greene, *The Revolutionary Generation, 1763-1790* (Vol. IV of *A History of American Life*). New York, 1943.

The appropriate volume in a standard series of social history. Useful bibliography.

J. F. Jameson, *The American Revolution Considered as a Social Movement*. Princeton, 1926. Also a Beacon paperback.

Suggestive, and in many ways a pioneer essay. But a long and thorough monograph with the same title would be useful.

Bernhard Knollenberg, *Washington and the Revolution*. New York, 1940.

A most balanced and scholarly treatment.

M. Krause, *Intercolonial Aspects of American Culture on the Eve of the Revolution*. New York, 1928.

J. C. Miller, *Sam Adams: Pioneer in Propaganda.* Boston, 1936. *Origins of the American Revolution.* Boston, 1943. *Triumph of Freedom, 1775-1783.* Boston, 1948.

These three are a most important revision of scholarly history of the subject.

C. L. Rossiter, *Seedtime of the Republic,* New York, 1953.

From an intellectual conservative's point of view.

Max Savelle, *Seeds of Liberty; the Genesis of the American Mind.* New York, 1948.

For the background of the Enlightenment in the American colonies. Readers can further consult the well-known general intellectual histories of the United States by Parrington, Gabriel, and Curti.

A. M. Schlesinger, *The Colonial Merchants and the American Revolution.* New York, 1918.

This monograph brought the realistic study of the American Revolution a tremendous leap forward.

G. M. Trevelyan, *The American Revolution. George III and Charles James Fox,* the concluding part of *The American Revolution.* Bound with the above in a uniform edition of 6 vols. New York, 1920-22.

This is a "classic" with the overtones of being dated which the word often carries. Written by a distinguished Whig historian, it is more favorable to American "rights" in the War of Independence than most of the foregoing American books. It seems to our generation to omit very important economic and social considerations.

M. C. Tyler, *The Literary History of the American Revolution.* 2 vols. New York, 1897.

A "classic" but not by any means dated.

C. H. Van Tyne, *The Causes of the War of Independence* and *The War of Independence,* being vols. I and II of *The Founding of the American Republic.* Boston, 1922, 1929. *The Loyalists in the American Revolution.* New York, 1929.

Both standard works of professional historical scholarship.

W. M. Wallace, *Appeal to Arms: A Military History of the American Revolution.* New York, 1951.

Not directly germane to the study of revolutions, but has interesting material on British generals and their attitudes toward the revolutionists, important for the study of the British ruling class and the revolution.

c. France

Willy Andreas, *Das Zeitalter Napoleons und die Erhebung der Völker*. Heidelberg, 1955.

An admirable summary of modern study of the period.

A. Aulard, *The French Revolution: A Political History*. English translation. 4 vols. New York, 1910.

The best example of official Republican history of the great revolution, by one who was in some ways a spiritual descendant of the Girondins. Leftist and anticlerical bias.

C. L. Becker, *The Heavenly City of the Eighteenth Century Philosophers*. New Haven, 1932.

A thought-provoking thesis as to the role of ideas in the eighteenth century; severely criticized of recent years—see especially Peter Gay, *The Party of Humanity*, New York, 1964.

Crane Brinton, *The Jacobins*. New York, 1930. Reprint edition, New York, 1961.

With special emphasis on the provincial network of clubs.

W. F. Church, *The Influence of the Enlightenment on the French Revolution: Creative, Disastrous, or Non-existent?* Boston, 1964.

This little book, meant for classroom use, has a most useful bibliography for a case study of the role of "ideas" in preparing a society for revolution.

Augustin Cochin, *Les sociétés de pensée et la démocratie*. Paris, 1921.

Essential to the study of the work of pressure groups in the preparation of the revolution. Conservative bias.

Pierre Gaxotte, *The French Revolution*. English translation. New York, 1932.

Perhaps the most sensible of modern works written avowedly from a point of view far to the Right—Royalist, in fact. But since almost all Americans get their knowledge of the French Revolution from conventional anticlerical Republican professors of the Third Republic, Gaxotte's work is recommended as an antidote.

Leo Gershoy, *The French Revolution and Napoleon*. New York, 1964.

New edition of a book originally published in 1933. It has the best and latest critical bibliography of the French Revolution.

J. Godechot, *La Grande Nation: L'expansion révolutionnaire de la France dans le monde de 1789 à 1799.* 2 vols. Paris, 1956.
The great work on the subject. Good bibliographies.

Martin Göhring, *Geschichte der grossen Revolution.* 2 vols. Tübingen, 1950-51.
One of the important historical syntheses of our time. A third volume, with *bibliographie raisonnée,* is promised.

A. Goodwin, *The French Revolution.* New York, 1962. A Torchbook paperback.
A first-rate brief account.

Donald Greer, *The Incidence of the Terror during the French Revolution.* Cambridge, Mass., 1935. *The Incidence of the Emigration during the French Revolution.* Cambridge, Mass., 1951.
Two important statistical studies, with many leads for further study in other revolutions.

Daniel Guérin, *La lutte de classes, sous la première république: bourgeois et "bras nus."* Paris, 1946.
A Marxist interpretation, well beyond Mathiez. The *bras nus* are the *real* proletariat at last.

N. Hampson, *A Social History of the French Revolution.* Toronto, 1963.
A very good general "social" history in the broadest sense.

Paul Hazard, *La crise de la conscience européenne.* 3 vols. Paris, 1935. *La pensée européenne au XVIII siècle.* 3 vols. Paris, 1946.
The most complete survey of the whole intellectual scene.

C. E. Labrousse, *Esquisse du mouvement des prix et des revenus en France au XVIII siècle.* 2 vols. Paris, 1933. *La crise de l'économie française à la fin de l'ancien régime et au début de la révolution.* Paris, 1944.
These two put the developed French Republican thesis of the "causes" of the revolution very clearly. Another volume of the *Crise de l'économie* is promised.

W. L. Langer, ed., *The Rise of Modern Europe.*
Three volumes in this series are pertinent: Leo Gershoy, *From Despotism to Revolution, 1763-1789,* New York, 1944; Crane Brinton, *A Decade of Revolution, 1789-1799,* New York, 1934; Geoffrey Bruun, *Europe and the French Imperium, 1799-1814,* New York, 1938.

G. Lefebvre. *La révolution française (Peuples et Civilisations,*

XIII). Paris, new edition 1957. English translation, *The French Revolution*, 2 vols. New York, 1962-64.

This is an admirably well-balanced work, generally considered in the historical profession to be the best short history of the French Revolution.

Gaston Martin, *Le franc-maçonnerie et la préparation de la révolution*. Paris, 1926.

Standard work, a fair balance to Cochin.

Albert Mathiez, *The French Revolution*. English translation, New York, 1928, new edition (Universal Library paperback) 1964. *La vie chère et le mouvement social sous la Terreur.* Paris, 1927.

Mathiez was the heir of the Mountain as Aulard was of the Gironde. He was a reliable investigator of facts, and he was interested in the kind of facts we are now interested in. His generalizations are ruled by an extremely innocent version of the doctrine of economic interpretation of history. Although he indignantly denied he was partisan, he clearly belongs rather far to the Left.

Daniel Mornet, *Les origines intellectuelles de la révolution française*. Paris, 1933.

Most of the necessary material implied in the title, conveniently assembled. Mornet has conventional French Republican notions about the role of the *philosophes* in the preparation of the revolution. Excellent bibliography.

R. R. Palmer, *The Age of the Democratic Revolutions*. 2 vols. Princeton, 1959-64.

A major work dealing with American, French, and other eighteenth-century revolutions.

Félix Rocquain, *The Revolutionary Spirit Preceding the French Revolution*. English translation, abridged. London, 1894.

An attempt to lessen attention on the writings of the *philosophes* and turn it to concrete quarrels and grievances in the last years of the old regime.

G. Rudé, *The Crowd in the French Revolution*. Oxford, 1959. Excellent social analysis.

Preserved Smith. *A History of Modern Culture*. Vol. II, *The Enlightenment*. New York, 1934.

Essential manual of intellectual history.

A. Soboul, *Précis d'histoire de la révolution française*. Paris, 1962.

An excellent summary of the latest Marxist position on the French Revolution.

H. A. Taine, *The Origins of Contemporary France*. English translation. 6 vols. New York, 1876-94.

The classic attack on the revolution and all its works, written by a disappointed liberal and French patriot after the War of 1870. Still a mine of information, though its particular bias is no longer shared by many in the modern world.

J. M. Thompson, *The French Revolution*. New York, 1945.

An admirable survey, especially good on local Parisian politics.

Gérard Walter, *Histoire des Jacobins*. Paris, 1946.

A reconstruction of the history of the Paris club only.

D. *Russia*

The total output of books on Russia since 1917 is enormous, and little of it measures up to the more rigorous standards academic historians like to impose. It is suggested that an intelligent reader of the following would not, however, be hopelessly misinformed about the movement, and could attempt to integrate his knowledge of what has been going on in Russia with what has gone on in other modern revolutions.

G. A. Almond, *et al., The Appeals of Communism*. Princeton, 1954.

A good study of the dissemination of Communist ideas.

F. Beck and W. Godin, *Russian Purge and the Extraction of Confession*. New York, 1951.

The authors are a German scientist and a Russian historian escaped to the West and protected by pseudonyms. Their Chapter VIII, "The Theories," is a most interesting attempt to explain the revival of Terror in 1936-39.

F. Borkeman, *World Communism*. New York, 1939 and *European Communism*. New York, 1953.

Studies of party organizations and methods.

E. H. Carr, *The Soviet Impact on the Western World*. London, 1946.

A brief but crowded book. Mr. Carr, like most English intellectuals, exaggerates the role of ideas in human relations. But he writes admirably, and brings out a thesis which basically contradicts that of this book. Mr. Carr believes Russia really is *revolutionized*.

E. H. Carr, *A History of Soviet Russia*. 6 vols. London, 1950-60.

A thorough scholarly treatment, basically friendly to the Revolution.

W. H. Chamberlin, *The Russian Revolution.* 2 vols. New York, 1935.

A careful piece of work, written by an American with a command of Russian sources. Chamberlin is not a Communist, but save to more rigid Marxists, his work will appear reasonably detached. Good bibliography.

Isaac Deutscher, *Stalin. A Political Biography.* New York, 1949.

Hostile, almost inevitably, or at least unsympathetic, but an admirable job of scholarship.

Isaac Deutscher, *Trotsky.* 3 vols. New York, 1954-63; *The Prophet Armed, 1879-1921; The Prophet Unarmed, 1921-1929; The Prophet Outcast, 1929-1940.*

The authoritative study—friendly.

M. H. Dobb, *Soviet Economic Development since 1917.* London, 1948.

By one of the most scholarly of British Marxists.

M. Fainsod, *How Russia Is Ruled.* Revised and enlarged edition. Cambridge, Mass., 1963.

Indispensable.

Harvard University. Russian Research Center.

This center is attempting to focus our knowledge of the social sciences objectively on the U.S.S.R. Its publications should be watched by all interested in understanding contemporary Russia. This important series, begun in 1950, now (1964) numbers 48 volumes. They are listed in the catalogues of the Harvard University Press.

H. J. Berman, *Justice in Russia. An Interpretation of Soviet Law.* Cambridge, Mass., 1950.

Alex Inkeles, *Public Opinion in Soviet Russia.* Cambridge, 1950.

Barrington Moore, Jr., *Soviet Politics. The Dilemma of Power.* Cambridge, 1950.

History of the Communist Party of the Soviet Union. Short Course. New York, 1939 (International Publishers).

This is an "official" translation of an "official" history.

T. H. Von Laue, *"Die Revolution von aussen als erste Phase der russischen Revolution 1917," Jahrbücher für Geschichte Osteuropas,* IV, 2 (Munich, 1956).

Valuable emphasis on (1) the fact that the Russia of 1917, unlike the England of 1639 and the France of 1789, was a *backward* country; (2) the fact that much of what made that Revolution was imported from outside Russia.

Eugene Lyons, *Assignment in Utopia*. New York, 1937.

Lyons is an American radical whose long residence as a newspaper correspondent in Russia turned him against Stalin's rule. When allowance is made for this bias, the book remains one of the best accounts in English of "Thermidor in Russia"—though see under Trotsky below.

P. E. Mosley, ed., *The Soviet Union since World War II*. American Academy of Political and Social Science, *Annals*, CCLXIII (May, 1949).

A miscellany, but with many good leads for further study.

Bernard Pares, *A History of Russia*. 5th edition. New York, 1947.

This is a good introductory survey for the general reader who needs the Russian background filled in.

R. E. Pipes, *The Formation of the Soviet Union: Communism and Nationalism, 1917-1923*. Cambridge, Mass., 1954.

A thorough historical study.

M. N. Pokrovsky, *Brief History of Russia*. Translated by D. S. Mirsky. New York, 1933.

Vol. II deals with the preparation, the background, of the October Revolution in a thorough Marxist style.

Faith A. Popkin, "Advertising in Russia," *Nieman Reports*, December, 1963.

An interesting brief report on a subject often neglected in studies of Soviet Russia.

O. H. Radkey, *The Election to the Russian Constituent Assembly of 1917*. Cambridge, Mass, 1950.

A thorough monographic study with much bearing on the contest between extremists and moderates.

David Shub, *Lenin*. New York, 1948.

Hostile but careful, scholarly, detailed.

N. N. Sukhanov, *The Russian Revolution, 1917*. 2 vols. New York, 1955.

Also in 2 volumes in Torchbook paperbacks. Abridgement of memoirs of an eyewitness.

N. S. Timasheff, "The Russian Revolution: Twenty-Five Years After," *Review of Politics*, V (1943), pp. 415-440.

Reprinted in W. Gurian, ed., *Soviet Union: Background,*

Ideology, Reality, Notre Dame, Ind., 1951, a useful collaborative survey of Russia today.

Leon Trotsky, *The History of the Russian Revolution*. English translation. 3 vols. New York, 1936 (also a single-volume edition).

This will probably be Trotsky's masterpiece. A vivid narrative, heightened by excursions into Marxist interpretation, mostly very keen and even sensible. Chamberlin and Trotsky, read together, make the best introduction possible to the study of the Russian Revolution. Trotsky's *The Revolution Betrayed*, New York, 1937, is a bitter and interesting attack on the then regime in Russia, which he himself christened "Thermidorean." Finally, there is an interesting "Supplement" on the Thermidorean Reaction in Trotsky's *Stalin*, translated by Charles Malamuth, New York, 1941, pp. 384-410. Of course this last major work of Trotsky's is throughout interesting, though highly prejudiced.

D. W. Treadgold, *Twentieth Century Russia*, Chicago, 1959. An excellent handbook.

Robert C. Tucker and Stephen F. Cohen, eds., *The Great Purge Trial*. New York, 1965.

Fascinating source material in verbatim report.

O. Utis, "Generalissimo Stalin and the Art of Government." *Foreign Affairs*, XXX (January, 1952).

The pseudonymous author (*outis* is Greek for "nobody") is clearly familiar with contemporary Russia, and here presents some interesting ideas on the problem of how far the Russian Revolution has run its course.

A. B. Ulam, *The New Face of Soviet Totalitarianism*. Cambridge, Mass., 1963.

Sidney and Beatrice Webb, *Soviet Communism: A New Civilization?* 2 vols. New York, 1936.

For American readers, this remains probably the best and most persuasive defense of the present regime in Russia, and may be recommended as an antidote to the writings of disenchanted liberals and angry Trotskyites. But it is a very soft and academic book, and the Webbs are surely at least as much doctrinaries as others who have written on Russia. And, of course, it was written so long ago!

Alexander Weissberg, *The Accused*. New York, 1951.

An admirable detailed account of the experiences of a person accused of high political crime during the Yezhov period, and a useful supplement to Beck and Godin's book above listed.

B. D. Wolfe, *Three Who Made a Revolution. A Biographical History*. New York, 1948.

Lenin, Trotsky, Stalin. Mr. Wolfe has been more sympathetic than he is now with Stalin and the U.S.S.R. But he is very fair-minded, by no means the "disillusioned" radical.

II. *The Wisdom of the Ages*

The formal study of revolutions as a part of the science of sociology is a very recent thing. But revolutions are not new, nor is serious thinking on revolutions new. From Plato and Aristotle on one can collect a very valuable set of remarks on different phases of revolution, mostly from books not primarily concerned with revolutions. We have not here attempted to do more than give a random sample of what might be done with this sort of thing. Most of the men we have chosen to cite here were not purely intellectuals in anything like the modern sense, and it would seem that, unsystematic though this section of our bibliography is, it contains more wisdom about revolutions than our fourth section, in which we list a few contemporary works formally concerned with the sociology of revolutions. Most contemporary writers on matters sociological are of course intellectuals.

Plato, *The Republic*, especially Books VIII and IX.

Aristotle, *Politics*. Book V is the famous discussion of revolutions, but the whole work, and especially Book II, is almost as pertinent.

Polybius, *History*. Book VI contains the well-known account of the reasons for Roman political stability, which by contrast throws a good deal of light on our subject, political instability.

Thucydides, *History*. Book III, 82.2, begins one of the best clinical reports ever written on what we have called the crisis of revolutions.

Machiavelli, *Discourses on the First Decade of Titus Livius*. Almost every chapter contains something of use for the student of revolution. Book I, chapters xxv and xxvi, are especially recommended for the light they throw on differences between revolutions like those of England and France and those of contemporary Turkey or Italy.

Sainte-Beuve, "Le Cardinal de Retz," in *Causeries du Lundi*, vol. V, especially the passage beginning "ces pages de ses

Mémoires qu'on pourrait intituler: Comment les révolutions commencent." The interested reader may well wish to follow this up by reading De Retz's own memoirs, which are easily available in numerous editions in French. There is an English version in Everyman's Library.

Burke, *Reflections on the Revolution in France*. This by no means dispassionate work nonetheless contains a good deal that no student of revolutions can neglect. Better, his political writing as a whole can be well studied in R. J. S. Hoffman and Paul Levack, eds., *Burke's Politics; Selected Writings and Speeches on Reform, Revolution, and War*, New York, 1949.

Bagehot, *Physics and Politics*. This book, together with Maine's *Ancient Law*, sets forth a point of view about social change which denies the possibility of achieving large-scale reforms by revolution. Like the work of Burke, which they supplement and clarify, they must be met and understood before the objective study of revolutions can be carried very far.

Pareto, *The Mind and Society*. This is a study of general sociology, almost all parts of which are germane to our purposes in this book. Chapters ix and x deal especially with the problem of social stability and instability, but are hard to understand without reference to the rest of the work. A careful study of L. J. Henderson, *Pareto's General Sociology: A Physiologist's Interpretation*, Cambridge, Mass., 1935, will help get around this difficulty. Pareto is cited here as in a sense summing up, clarifying, and codifying views about revolution contained in this section of our bibliography. All such views—neither "anti-intellectualist" nor "conservative" adequately describes them—are anathema to most Marxists and "liberals" in present-day America. But they have been held so long and so firmly by men who were not altogether fools or villains that the least the liberal can do is examine them.

Le Play, *L'organisation de la famille;* also the volumes of *Les ouvriers européens*. Le Play and his school merit our attention for much the same reason as does Polybius. Le Play studied the family with great care, and came to certain conclusions about the persistence of certain sentiments and actions among men which no student of attempted social change can afford to neglect.

William Graham Sumner, *Folkways*. There is an edition with an introduction by W. L. Phelps, Boston, 1940. Sumner, who coined the phrase, is in some intellectual circles today a "forgotten man." This great study of the way people actually behave in groups is one of the pioneer works of modern anti-intellectualism.

F. S. Oliver, *The Endless Adventure.* Oliver was a conservatively minded Englishman who in this volume wrote about one of the least revolutionary of statesmen, Robert Walpole. Again it is useful to us because if we do not understand social stability we cannot hope to understand social instability. Walpole himself is as perfect an example of the man fitted to preserve an old society as Lenin is of the man fitted to guide a new society.

E. H. Erikson, *Young Man Luther.* New York, 1958.

E. Fromm, *Escape from Freedom.* New York, 1941.

D. Riesman, *The Lonely Crowd.* New Haven, 1950.

Most of the above writers doubt the magic power of the word and of man's reason; they are in a sense anti-intellectuals. Revolutions are made, at least at first, by intellectuals. The reader who wants to follow this lead further can see the influence of this anti-intellectualism (which does not necessarily end in totalitarianism) in such recent books as Bertrand de Jouvenel, *On Power,* New York, 1948; A. H. Leighton, *The Governing of Men,* Princeton, 1945; Clyde Kluckhohn, *Mirror for Man,* New York, 1949; and Richard Humphrey, *Georges Sorel,* Cambridge, Mass., 1951. See also Crane Brinton, *Ideas and Men,* 2nd ed., New York, 1963, chapters 13 and 14, and bibliography, pp. 440-441.

III. *The Marxists*

There is no doubt that Marx and his followers have made great contributions to our understanding of revolutions—contributions almost as great as those they have made to the making of revolutions. We cannot, however, regard even the best Marxist writing as an altogether satisfactory approach to the scientific study of revolutions. Marxist thought is a mixture of useful and genuinely objective observations properly framed as uniformities, and of prophecies, moral exhortations, theological and philosophical speculation, and other elements we may loosely call propaganda. The concept of the class struggle, for instance, belongs to the first sort; in itself, it is a fruitful notion, and one which has enriched sociology, in spite of the exaggerations and simplicities with which it has been applied by many Marxists. The notion of the dictatorship of the proletariat belongs in a sense to both sorts; it is, especially

in the form Lenin gave it, a useful lead in the study of past—
and current—revolutions, but it is also in Marxist hands an
ideal, a goal, a prophecy. Finally, the notions of the classless
society and the withering away of the state are almost wholly
theology or, more specifically, eschatology.

In any given work by a Marxist, the disentanglement of
what we may call the *scientific* elements from what we may
call, with an equal desire to use good rather than bad words,
the *moralistic* elements is almost as difficult as a similar operation on the work of the classical economists. In each case it
has to be made separately. We need here only caution against
certain of the more specific forms in which Marxist moral
fervor and good intentions may be found distorting their work
as scientists.

First there is pure fervor, writing obviously intended for
the faithful, writing which from its very form is clearly a
kind of rhapsody. Then there is writing definitely aimed at
achieving a specific revolutionary end, writing closely aimed at
action, writing not even meant by the writer to be detached
and objective. There is the much-too-simple application of
formulas and clichés to specific situations. Much of this writing
is sincere and earnest, and the writers really believe that they
are applying scientific methods to sociological problems. The
narrow application of the economic interpretation of history is a
very frequent example of this kind of thing. All human action
is by the more innocent Marxists interpreted as the rational, if
perhaps not always conscious, and certainly never free, application of economic interests to a concrete situation. It must be
said in fairness to Marx, Engels, and their greater followers
that they are not themselves usually guilty of such unrealistic
simplification.

Finally, current Marxist writing is confused by the number of
sects that have developed within the movement, each one
claiming to be orthodox. Of the sect which in a *de facto*
way can most clearly claim orthodoxy, that established in
power in Russia today, one may say that it represents a
kind of hardening of doctrine, a fixation of theory into dogma
which may in the long run permit a good deal more actual
open-mindedness and experiment than is now possible. In the
meantime official Marxism has become in Soviet Russia and her
allies and sympathizers a conservative and established belief.

The literature is enormous, and we do not intend to do more
than list below a few general elementary discussions of
Marxism, and a few of the more important works of the
great men in the tradition. We have deliberately chosen,
wherever possible, works in which the concrete discussion of
actual revolutions is more important than pure theory.

I. Berlin, *Karl Marx: His Life and Environment.* 2nd ed. Oxford, 1948.
Excellent for both life and ideas.

M. M. Bober, *Karl Marx's Interpretation of History.* Revised edition. Cambridge, Mass., 1948.

M. H. Dobb, *Studies in the Development of Capitalism.* London, 1946.
A typical advanced and subtle Marxist analysis of early modern economic history.

Max Eastman, *Marx and Lenin: The Science of Revolution.* New York, 1927.

Karl Federn, *The Materialist Conception of History.* London, 1939.

Sidney Hook, *Towards the Understanding of Karl Marx.* New York, 1933.

H. J. Laski, *Communism.* New York, 1927.

A. D. Lindsay, *Karl Marx's Capital: An Introductory Essay.* New edition. Oxford, 1937.

Vilfredo Pareto, *Les systèmes socialistes.* 2 vols. Paris, 1902-03.

J. A. Schumpeter, *Capitalism, Socialism, and Democracy.* 3rd edition. New York, 1950.
This book really belongs under "The Wisdom of the Ages." Schumpeter was one of the few economists bred in the "classical" tradition who could study Marxism at all steadily and sensibly.

P. M. Sweezy, *The Theory of Capitalist Development: Principles of Marxian Political Economy.* New York, 1942.
An admirably balanced analysis by a very able American Marxist.

E. Wilson, *To the Finland Station.* New York, 1953. An Anchor paperback.
A sympathetic account of Marxist and other socialisms since 1790.

[E. Burns], *A Handbook of Marxism.* New York, 1935.
This is still one of the most useful of the various collections of bits of the writings of the great Marxists. It includes some of the most important work of Marx, Engels, Lenin, and Stalin. It can be profitably supplemented by L. S. Feuer, ed., Marx and Engels, *Basic Writings and Politics and Philosophy.* New York, 1959. An Anchor paperback.

Karl Marx and Friedrich Engels, *The Communist Manifesto*. Edited by D. Ryazanoff. London, 1930.

The rich notes in this full-sized volume expand the brief original Manifesto into a critical commentary on Marxism.

Of Marx the following is a suggested beginning, neglecting entirely the ponderous *Capital: The Eighteenth Brumaire of Louis Bonaparte; Revolution and Counter-Revolution, or Germany in 1848; Civil War in France* (sometimes called the *Paris Commune*); and *The Poverty of Philosophy*.

Of Engels: *The Condition of the Working Class in England in 1844; Landmarks of Scientific Socialism* (Anti-Dühring).

Of Lenin: *Imperialism; The State and Revolution*. Both of these are in a handy single volume issued by the Vanguard Press, New York, 1926.

Of Stalin: Joseph Stalin, *Leninism*. London, 1940.

Actually a collection of Stalin's writings, including the famous brief outline, *The Foundations of Leninism*. An adequate sampling.

IV. *The Sociology of Revolutions*

The following section contains a selected list of modern books on revolutions in general. Such writing is necessarily very varied indeed. Some of the books listed below are careful studies by trained sociologists; some are the work of cranks with a variety of cutting tools to grind; some, directly in the Marxist tradition, seem to belong here rather than in the preceding section because of their direct preoccupation with the sociology of revolutions. We have been obliged to be fairly narrow in our interpretation of the subject. In a sense almost everything that appears nowadays on social and political problems might be catalogued as dealing at some point with the sociology of revolutions. To take a wide and somewhat random choice of well-known figures, most of the important work of writers like Spengler, H. G. Wells, Ortega y Gasset, Max Weber, Tawney, Mannheim, A. J. Toynbee, and Hannah Arendt touches upon the question of revolutions and social change. But a bibliography as inclusive as this would be pointless or endless. We have, therefore, simply made a choice of general books on the specific subject of the comparative study of revolution. The reader who wishes a preliminary guide in the vaster field of social change in history will find an admirable "Selective Reading List" by Ronald Thompson in *Bulletin 54* of the Social Science Research Council, *Theory and Practice in Historical Study*, New York 1946. In Part III of L. Gottschalk, ed., *Generalization in the Writing of History*. Chicago, 1963, the aforesaid list has been brought up to date by Martin Klein.

Brooks Adams, *The Theory of Social Revolutions*. New York, 1913.

One of the earliest predictions of the decline of the West. Should be read with Mr. George Soule's book below.

H. Arendt, *On Revolution*. New York, 1963.

Based on the American and the French Revolutions. Emotional, intellectual, full of existentialist despair, poles apart from the approach attempted in this book, *The Anatomy of Revolution*. If Miss Arendt and Mr. Rosenstock-Hüssy make sense, this book is nonsense; the converse, one hopes, may also be true.

Arthur Bauer, *Essai sur les révolutions*. Paris, 1908.

Approaches the problem from the psychology of the individual and his activity in crowds. Has an interesting conceptual scheme of revolutions as a general phenomenon.

C. E. Black and T. P. Thornton, eds., *Communism and Revolution: the Strategic Uses of Political Violence*. Princeton, 1964.

Interesting comparative studies of Communist techniques, preceded by a brief introductory essay on our current revolutions of "modernization" or "of rising expectations."

Wulf Bley, ed., *Revolutionen der Weltgeschichte; Zwei Jahrtausende Revolutionen und Burgerkriege*. Munich, 1933.

A collaborative work aimed at the old-fashioned German book trade, but worth the student's while for its illustrations (nearly 1000) drawn from contemporaneous sources. On the whole, emphasizes the horror of revolutions.

Jean de Boissoudy, *Le phénomène révolution*. Paris, 1940.

Carl Brinkman, *Soziologische Theorie der Revolution*. Göttingen, 1948.

A temperate, brief essay by a cultured German sociologist, essentially in the Western tradition.

C. D. Burns, *The Principles of Revolution*. London, 1920.

D. W. Brogan, *The Price of Revolution*. London, 1951.

A stimulating essay, especially for Jeffersonians.

E. H. Carr, *Studies in Revolution*. London, 1950.

All of Mr. Carr's great expository virtues, but pretty intellectualist.

R. Dahrendorf, *Class and Class Conflict in Industrial Societies*. Stanford, 1961.

Translated and expanded by the author from a German original. A most important study of "conflict," which after all is the basic fact of revolutions.

J. C. Davies, "Towards a Theory of Revolution," *American Sociological Review*. Vol. 27 (1962) pp. 5-19. Reprinted in H. L. Ross, *Perspectives on the Social Order*. New York, 1963, pp. 437-450.
An important contribution.

Lawrence Dennis, *The Dynamics of War and Revolution*. New York, 1940.

This privately printed book is a highly colored American Fascist blast at the universe. But an interesting piece of the mind of one of the lunatic fringe.

Harry Eckstein, "On the Etiology of Internal Wars," *History and Theory*, IV, 2 (1965), pp. 133-63.
A stimulating and important essay.

Editors of Fortune, *USA: The Permanent Revolution*. New York, 1951.

This book does not quite belong here. It is not a sociology of revolution. But the editors' use of the word is interesting and important if we are to understand the very subtle connotations of the word "revolution" in America today.

L. P. Edwards, *The Natural History of Revolution*. Chicago, 1927.

Unpretentious, suggestive, tentative. One of the best introductions to the subject available in English. Mr. Edwards does not pretend to do more than sketch the essential problems and indicate possible further work. Admirably free from special pleading.

Elizabeth Eisenstein, *First Professional Revolutionist: Filippo Michele Buonarroti*. Cambridge, Mass., 1959.

A very good study of a professional European revolutionary of the late eighteenth and early nineteenth centuries.

Charles A. Ellwood, "A Psychological Theory of Revolutions," *American Journal of Sociology*, XI (July, 1905). This interesting psychological interpretation has been restated in Professor Ellwood's numerous general books on sociology, as for instance *The Psychology of Human Society* (New York, 1925) and *Sociology: Principles and Problems* (New York and Cincinnati, 1943).

Guglielmo Ferrero, *The Principles of Power*. New York, 1942.
The trilogy of which this is the final volume—the others on Napoleon and on Talleyrand round out a study of the

French revolutionary era—aims at major generalizations about men in society. It suffers from Ferrero's reluctance to admit that anyone else ever approached the study of revolution as he does, but it is an interesting work.

Theodor Geiger, *Die Masse und ihre Aktion: Ein Beitrag zur Soziologie der Revolutionen*. Stuttgart, 1926.

A psychological study, with a Marxist tinge. To a non-German, a bit in the clouds.

Karl Griewank, *Der neuzeitliche Revolutionsbegriff*. Weimar, 1955.

A suggestive study of the widening of the concept of revolution since the fifteenth century.

Robert Hunter, Revolution: *Why, How, When?* New York, 1940.

A modest but often suggestive essay by an experienced social worker.

Eric Hoffer, *The True Believer: Thoughts on the Nature of Mass Movements*. New York, 1951. A Mentor paperback.

An unpretentious little book with much more sense in it than many a heavy sociological study. Basically skeptical, realistic, even Machiavellian.

H. M. Hyndman, *The Evolution of Revolution*. London, 1920.

By one of the pioneers of Marxist Socialism in England. Not very illuminating nowadays.

Gustave Le Bon, *The Psychology of Revolution*. English translation. New York, 1913.

Le Bon's reputation as a social psychologist has sunk considerably. This is the work of a frightened anti-intellectualist.

Arthur Liebert, *Vom Geist der Revolutionen*. Berlin, 1919.

A brief discussion of the rational and emotional origins of revolution, and an analysis of the crisis period.

J. J. Maguire, *The Philosophy of Modern Revolution*. Washington, 1943.

A clear statement from the point of view of a trained Catholic scholar.

Curzio Malaparte, *Coup d'état, the Technique of Revolution*. English translation. New York, 1932.

An annoyingly bright young Italian Fascist intellectual writes on *the only* way to make a revolution. As narrow and, in a perverted sense, idealistic as any Marxist writing.

E. D. Martin, *Farewell to Revolution*. New York, 1935.

A very able and sensible writer on political and social problems has here allowed his fears to lead him into writing a bad book. Mr. Martin, as his choice of title indicates, is writing a book *against* revolutions of all sorts. Hastily assembled from inadequate materials. Stands up badly in comparison with L. P. Edwards' book above.

Alfred Mensel, "Revolution and Counter-revolution," *Encyclopedia of the Social Sciences*, XIII, pp. 367-376. New York, 1934.

Very brief, but with good selective bibliography.

Barrington Moore, Jr., *Agrarian Origins of Dictatorship and Democracy: Lord and Peasant in Reform and Revolution.*

This forthcoming study in comparative history (or sociology) is an important corrective to conventional modern over-emphasis on the role of industrialism in modern social change.

Max Nomad, *Dreamers, Dynamiters, and Demagogues.* New York, 1964.

The latest in a long series of books about revolutions and revolution by a wise and experienced rebel.

W. M. F. Petrie, *The Revolutions of Civilization.* 3rd edition. New York, 1922.

By the distinguished Egyptologist. Does not really belong in this list, but is included to remind the reader of the great range of meaning—even within history—of "revolution."

G. S. Pettee, *The Process of Revolution.* New York, 1938.

A careful comparative study of major modern revolutions, never tempted into the great big philosophical generalizations.

Léon de Poncins, *Les Forces secretes de la révolution.* Paris, 1929.

A good example of the kind of writing which attributes modern revolutions to wicked conspirators—in this case Jews and freemasons. See also Mrs. Nesta H. Webster.

R. W. Postgate, *How to Make a Revolution.* New York, 1934.

An English Leftist, formerly a Communist and now apparently just Labour, writes rather wistfully about the possibilities of a decent, respectable revolution in Western countries. A good deal of useful discussion of the techniques of modern revolutionary parties to the Left, with touches of very English humor.

R. W. Postgate, *Revolution from 1789 to 1906.* London, 1920.

Mr. Postgate has here made a handy collection of constitutions, bills of rights, manifestoes, and similar documents touching the important revolutionary movements of the period.

S. A. Reeve, *The Natural Laws of Social Convulsion*. New York, 1933.

A most ambitious attempt to apply the methods of the physical sciences to the subject. Mr. Reeve is not skeptical enough to be a scientist. He emerges with forty-five "natural" or "cosmic" laws, of which Law XLV is a not unfair example: "Man would rather Die, even in Prolonged Agony, than to Think." The work of a doctrinaire person on the edge of the lunatic fringe, and much influenced by the position of men like Herbert Spencer, it has nonetheless a good deal of useful material.

Eugen Rosenstock-Hüssy, *Out of Revolution: Autobiography of Western Man*. New York, 1938.

Written in what to an American seems the German cloud-cuckoo-land of beautiful and inexact ideas, choosing convenient and rejecting inconvenient facts, something in the tradition of Spengler, but with the kindly hopes of a man of good will. Full of interesting suggestions and flashes of insight, poetic to a prosaic nature.

S. D. Schmalhausen, ed., *Recovery through Revolution*. New York, 1933.

Chapters contributed by Louis Fischer, Harold Laski, Carleton Beals, Robert Briffault, Gaetano Salvemini, and others. Rapid narrative accounts of the principal fields of revolutionary activity since the war—Germany, Russia, China, South America, Italy, and Spain.

H. E. See, *Evolution et Révolutions*. Paris, 1929.

A somewhat pedestrian examination of the English, French, and American revolutions, those of the nineteenth century, and the Russian Revolution. Excellent brief bibliographies for the revolutions discussed.

A. M. Sievers, *Revolution, Evolution and the Economic Order*. Englewood Cliffs, N. J., 1962. A Spectrum paperback.

The author examines the current economic revolution in the U.S. (compare p. 292, above, the Editors of Fortune, *USA: The Permanent Revolution*) in the perspective of the writings of Keynes, Schumpeter, Galbraith, Hansen, and Clark, and concludes it is unfinished.

P. A. Sorokin, *Social and Cultural Dynamics*. Vol. III, *Fluctuation of Social Relationships, War, and Revolution*. New York, 1937.

Mr. Sorokin's general position is an emotional dislike for the contemporary world, which is, he thinks, about to undergo a worse series of wars and revolutions than any the human race has yet had to put up with. This Volume III has a most imposing set of statistics to show that revolutions have been more or less endemic in Western civilization. Some such conclusion might have been made safely without all these statistics, which in detail are not altogether reliable. They tend to exaggerate the amount of violence and bloodshed since 1900. But see Tilly and Rule below.

George Soule, *The Coming American Revolution*. New York, 1934.

Charles Tilly and James Rule, *Measuring Political Upheaval*. Princeton, Center of International Studies, forthcoming.

A major study with a valuable up-to-date bibliography.

Charles Tilly, "Reflections on the Revolutions of Paris," *Social Problems*, XII (1964).

A review-essay on recent work.

Arnold J. Toynbee, *America and the World Revolution, and Other Lectures*. Oxford, 1962.

A tract urging the United States to take an active part in the "revolution for social justice" throughout the world.

ᐱ Wallace, "Revitalization Movements," *American Anthropologist*, Vol. 58, April, 1956.

A thoughtful, temperate work written by one of the more temperate of American "liberals." The work deals much more widely with the general subject of revolutions than its title would indicate.

Nesta H. Webster, *Secret Societies and Subversive Movements*. London, 1924.

A necessary specimen for the collection. Mrs. Webster is an extreme devotee of the "plot" theory of revolution.

Colin Wilson, *The Outsider*. Boston, 1956.

Important for the study of the alienation of intellectuals in the modern West; in a sense a symptom of such alienation.

Harry Eckstein, *Internal War*. New York, 1964.

By various hands, wide-ranging.

D. H. Pinkney, "The Crowd in the French Revolution of 1830," *American Historical Review*, LXX, pp. 1-17 (1964).

New evidence on a neglected revolution.

INDEX

CRANE BRINTON was born in Winsted, Connecticut, in 1898. He received his B.A. from Harvard in 1919 and was a Rhodes Scholar at Oxford from 1920 to 1923, when he received his doctorate. Since then he has been in the History Department at Harvard University, becoming a full professor in 1942 and also Chairman of the Society of Fellows. From 1942 to 1945 he was a Special Assistant to the Office of Strategic Services in the European Theater of Operations. He is the author of *The United States and Britain* (1945); *From Many One* (1948); *Ideas and Men* (1950); *The Temper of Western Europe* (1953); and *The Shaping of the Modern Mind* (1953).

VINTAGE WOMEN'S STUDIES